INVENTORY SYSTEMS AND CONTROLS HANDBOOK

Stanley E. Larson

Prentice-Hall, Inc., Englewood Cliffs, N.J.

Prentice-Hall International, Inc., *London*
Prentice-Hall of Australia, Pty. Ltd., *Sydney*
Prentice-Hall of Canada, Ltd., *Toronto*
Prentice-Hall of India Private Ltd., *New Delhi*
Prentice-Hall of Japan, Inc., *Tokyo*

© 1976 by
Prentice-Hall, Inc.
Englewood Cliffs, N.J.

Library of Congress Cataloging in Publication Data

Larson, Stanley E
    Inventory systems and controls handbook

    Includes bibliographical references.
    1. Inventory control.   I.   Title.
HD55.L37   658.7'87   75-25813
ISBN 0-13-502351-3

Printed in the United States of America

ABOUT THE AUTHOR

Stanley E. Larson is Manager of Spare Parts and Logistics with Mitsubushi Aircraft International, Inc., San Angelo, Texas. Previously, he was associated with the Cessna Aircraft Company in Witchita, Kansas, for 18 years, gaining a broad background in replacement parts procurement, sales and inventory management, involving both manual and automated systems.

At Cessna, Mr Larson held such posts as Data Processing Coordinator for the Citation Jet Division's inventory function and manager of Support Systems. Many of the ideas and solutions recommended in this book have grown out of this experience. Among the author's credits are the development of cost saving methods and systems, from automated assembly scheduling programs to the establishment of a new service parts center to the creation of a computerized system for spare parts administration.

Mr. Larson serves as consultant and manager in the industries with which he is associated.

How This Book Will Help You Manage Inventory More Profitably

Companies that will thrive in the decade that lies ahead must provide exceptionally fine customer service. Their methods and procedures should offer ample flexibility to meet unusual and often unreasonable demands upon their resources—human, physical, and operational. At the same time top product quality, as well as low cost, must be maintained in order to be competitive.

Companies must keep a careful checkrein on their physical inventories; economic necessity alone compels them to do so. Inventory losses are considered to be one of the primary direct causes of business failures and have been widely present in most cyclical business declines and depressions. It is not without cause that inventories are frequently referred to as "the great graveyard of business."

It follows, then, that to meet these objectives careful control becomes mandatory. Production planning and control systems must provide for the effective employment of all plant facilities, materials and manpower skills.

This book presents an almost inexhaustible array of ideas and solutions to those problems, occurring in most plants, which are urgently in need of attention. A virtual flood of novel approaches for attacking excessive operations costs is provided. Who is better qualified and prepared to effectively cope with these problems than the manager who is skilled and knowledgeable in modern management techniques and disciplines? Here you will discover the latest techniques, systems, procedures, modern practices, ideas, concepts, controls, goals and inspiring thoughts expressed and explained in great detail, and done so thoroughly that there is little chance of misunderstanding. Helpful examples, practical cases in point, graphs, charts and checklists are included, all having been carefully selected from the author's wide experience in this field.

Chapter One contains several control devices for reducing overall equipment costs, increasing warehouse efficiency and raising productivity.

Proper development of, or change-over to, the part number control system described in Chapter Two can provide better inventory control and will assist in cutting total company operating costs.

Other cost cutting benefits can result from using a simple inventory management technique described in Chapter Three—that of "management by emphasis."

Three methods are provided in Chapter Four to permit accurate monitoring of inventory availability, reaction response to customer demand, and customer attitudes—to let you get the edge on competition.

Tighter dollar value control is obtainable, without any loss of customer service, by identifying demand trends on inventory items and using ordering strategy compatible with those patterns. Chapter Four describes these demand patterns and suggests associated workable ordering strategies.

Learn to appraise inventory dollar investment by its *working value* to prevent obsolescence build-up. Chapter Five offers this simple formula—and others that will bring about maximum investment return and control.

Chapter Six presents comprehensive detailed data needs for improving current applications of inventory management, customer order processing and invoicing in manual systems; or for conversion of these applications to EDP systems control when the time arrives. The solutions given for common processing problems, experienced by most companies in converting to EDP, can save many headaches and long months of lost time in problem analysis and solving.

Several valuable productivity improvement devices are suggested, in Chapter Seven, for use in processing customer (and other) order demands. These devices will permit efficient job assignment, order control and performance evaluation within the "picking" function.

Big dollar returns, with minimum investment need, can be achieved in the shipping function by using the many obvious cost reduction ideas found in Chapter Eight.

The "when" and "what to order" subjects receive more than adequate coverage in Chapter Nine. Two handy methods are detailed for improving "when to order," while several adaptable guidelines are presented for controlling "what to order." A unique ordering method (that saved one company many thousands of dollars per year) is fully described for controlling order requirements after the "when" and "what" results have been decided.

Chapter Ten provides four workable methods for "squeezing" the most from your vendors: the control over freight charges by monitoring prepaid concessions obtained; keeping material costs down by using a formal vendor rating system; using special purchase orders to improve service support while reducing inventory costs; and improving operating profits through the "value analysis" technique.

Chapter Eleven outlines developmental steps for originating warranty and other return goods policy, provides methods for limiting and controlling inventory expenses resulting from such returns, and introduces the "decision table" as a quick method for arriving at policy answers on return programs.

Various control techniques are described, in Chapter Twelve, for seeing that you get what you pay for—when you want it. Methods are given for reducing the costs of material receiving, handling and stocking. One of these methods—inspection through "sampling"—can be used to increase the capability of a single inspector by up to fifty times, while automatic vendor quality/quantity ratings result.

Control over merchandise storage, and rearrangement, are objectively discussed in Chapter Thirteen. This chapter offers benefits in the form of small ideas that can generate big dividends. One such idea concerns the use of empty storage containers in signalling the need for expeditious action, inventory reduction review, or potential location reassignment capability. (A case where a merchandise stock-out condition can be turned into something good.)

Chapter Fourteen discusses a step-by-step program for controlling surplus and obsolete material: how to identify, classify, write off and dispose of such material. Cost reduction benefits are obtained by development of a preventive program, arrived at by verifying the causes of surplus and obsolescence conditions.

All facets of a physical inventory and audit are covered in minute detail in Chapter Fifteen. Nothing is left to chance. A special comprehensive outline is presented as a checklist to guarantee a successful physical inventory result.

Chapter Sixteen expounds the need for document filing, and storage, policy and procedures. Three particularly important questions are answered: What to file? How to file it? How long to file it? Specific guidelines are given to assure good forms design, and to support the need for company control over such forms design.

The benefits of low prices, consistent quality, time savings and availability in procurement of EDP and special forms, and other inventory supply items for office, warehouse or shipping use, give mounting support to Systems Contracting—a new innovation that can really pay off. Chapter Seventeen discusses how you can use Systems Contracting in your company's operation.

Chapter Eighteen contains a workable (and proven) seven-point program for developing a sound company security system. The emphasis is *prevention;* the results are reduced inventory costs and increased profits.

An earnings improvement program is presented, in Chapter Nineteen, to maximize profits and minimize expenses. Several "sample" earnings-improvement suggestions are offered, in various expense areas, to serve as a springboard for still further creative ideas and earnings improvements.

An employee's job enrichment program is suggested for addition to a company's training program. The 11 basic factors outlined in Chapter Twenty will provide a successful company training program, and the job enrichment program adds a creative touch. The use of two management tools, associated with the job enrichment program, can result in reduced employee turnover: these tools are the employees' skills inventory and the promotion chart.

Stanley E. Larson

Table of Contents

The primary objective . . . Planning aids . . . Architectural drawings . . .
Three-dimensional models . . . Computer utilization . . . Security safeguards . . . Facility guidelines . . . Pinpointing material handling problems . . . In-out work flow . . . New facility flow checklist . . . Long
range space planning . . . Cube use . . . A growth plan-of-action . . . Marketing research . . . Receipts and shipping trends . . . Material handling
equipment use . . . Equipment inventory . . . Communications . . . Inventory storage growth . . . Compatible storage equipment . . . Inventory
location system . . . Storage assignment by classification . . . Part number
sequence . . . Row-section-shelf assignment . . . Offices and support needs
for variable expenses.

The part number and the computer . . . Why assign a part number? . . .
Guidelines for developing a part number system . . . Keep the part
number field short . . . Allow for adequate growth . . . Use numeric
numbers . . . Provide adequate part number identification . . . Proprie-
tary/non-proprietary status . . . Basic part number . . . Product model . . .
Major product component . . . Product sub-assembly or detail . . . Limit
alphabetic and special character use . . . Change status . . . The dash
number . . . Part number "fielding" . . . Using a part number guide . . .
Changing to a controlled part number system . . . One-time costs to
consider . . . Trade-off benefits . . . EDP consideration.

Relating "when to order" to expected demand during the procurement lead time . . . The order point system . . . Controlling order points in a manual system . . . Computer smoothing . . . Selecting a demand period . . . Demand averaging . . . Varying forecast strategy . . . Forecast restrictions . . . Fixed order point forecasting . . . Low order point forecast . . . Item forecast variables . . . Order point symbols . . . Order point calculation . . . Order point reviewed . . . "Available" quantity guide . . . Automated requirements-estimating systems . . . The suggested order guide . . . Manual systems bypass the suggested order guide . . . Manual order release . . . Relating "what to order" to expected demand, and the procurement and storage activity costs . . . Replacement order variables . . . EOQ order strategy . . . Order strategy restrictions . . . The EOQ formula . . . Acquisition costs . . . Maintenance costs . . . Controlling order quantity (EOQ) in a manual system . . . Controlling orders after "what" and "when" to order have been decided . . . Order release pick tags . . . The pick tag concept . . . Pick tag results . . . Matching system sophistication to people capability.

Selecting the right vendor . . . Vendor rating . . . Developing multi-vendor sources . . . Vendor file prepared . . . Vendor contact made . . . Periodically review vendor files . . . Controlling purchases with a purchase order request . . . Request for cost quotation . . . Documenting the purchase authorization . . . Adding contractual information to the purchase order . . . Prepaid freight can be costly . . . Multi-part number reference . . . Contractual data requirements . . . Classifying purchase orders for company use . . . Single shipment orders . . . Standard purchase orders . . . Time limitation orders for specific material . . . Time limitation orders with material open . . . Special purchase orders . . . One form with many functions . . . Controlling product specifications . . . Anticipating vendor lead time problems . . . Increasing the inventory service support . . . Pipeline stocking . . . Vendor drop-shipments . . . Pre-packaging for improved profits . . . Rating vendors to keep costs constant . . . Reducing costs through value analysis . . . Using shared advertising . . . Obtaining vendor warranty and return agreements.

Allow for liberal but positive interpretation . . . Separate warranty from merchandise return policy . . . Warranty policy formulation . . . Determine the warranty period . . . Keep warranty wording simple, short and understandable . . . Use the warranty policy as a sales tool and not as a sales approach . . . Warn the customer of himself . . . Keep warranty records . . . Keep tabs on warranty costs . . . Protect the customer against poor warranty support . . . Warranty effect on inventory planning and control . . . Development and organization of merchandise return policy . . . Shipment errors . . . Customer buying errors . . . Unclaimed C.O.D. shipments . . . Periodic surplus or obsolescence return . . . Termination of distribution contract . . . Effect of non-warranty returns on inventory planning and control . . . Effect of non-warranty returns on inventory expense . . . Pricing guideline for termination returns . . . A selective return policy is needed . . . Returned goods management is a policy-making position . . . Support a written company policy on adjustments . . . An operating manual . . . Offer an adjustments training program . . . Good will—a most valuable possession . . . How do you give the customer the benefit of any doubt?

Plan for parts receiving . . . Don't pay for damaged merchandise . . . Verify the packing sheet-receiver before signing . . . Verify open order status and date due . . . Early shipments can be costly . . . Note lead time discrepancies . . . Inspect merchandise received . . . Sampling shortcuts inspection . . . Sampling guidelines . . . Count merchandise quantity received . . . Record shortages and/or rejections . . . Sign packing sheet-receiver, as corrected, for payment . . . Identify customer backorder items . . . Direct allocate backorder items . . . Identify merchandise before stocking . . . Find and assign storage locations . . . Pre-package multi-quantity "pack" items . . . Stocking sheets help move receipts . . . Process receiving paperwork . . . A new receipts idea saved time and money.

Assigning item locations . . . Random location assignment . . . Preparing receipts for stock . . . Deciding the stocking method . . . "Open" stocking . . . Sorting eliminates extra walking . . . Importance of location assignment . . . "Zone" stocking . . . Assigning a new storage location . . . Manual systems . . . Batch processing computer systems . . . "On-line" computer systems . . . Preventing discrepancies from location reassignment . . . Location assignment card is cross-reference . . . Purging cross-reference cards . . . Using receivers for assigning locations . . . Rearranging space for better use . . . Make use of empty containers . . . Empty container listing . . . Discrepancy prevention . . . Inventory stocking guidelines.

Pinpointing causes of obsolescence . . . Establishing a remedial action plan . . . Promote "common" parts usage . . . Review questions . . . Report findings . . . Obtain corporate guidelines . . . A positive approach . . . Classify—then appraise inventory regularly . . . A high value inventory listing . . . An open order summary sheet . . . A high value receipts listing . . . An order review listing . . . A dust check . . . An inventory write-off and disposal program . . . Write-off reserve . . . Selecting write-off items . . . Write-off approval . . . Write-off removal from active inventory . . . Write-off disposal.

Physical inventory action steps . . . Frequency of inventory . . . Perpetual inventory . . . Annual (or periodical) inventory . . . Physical inventory planning . . . Setting the inventory date . . . Cut-off requirements . . . Choosing an inventory method . . . Pre-printed inventory tags . . . Inventory tag flow sequence . . . Record cards . . . Flow sequence for record card use . . . Handwritten tags . . . Flow sequence for handwritten tags . . . Handwritten lists . . . Flow sequence for handwritten lists . . . Recording devices . . . Flow sequence for recording devices . . . Pre-printed forms . . . Inventory supervision assignment . . . Inventory procedures . . . Training of inventory personnel . . . Training schedule . . . Supervision training . . . Subordinate training . . . Handout instructions . . . Inventory "do and don't" items . . . Equipment and supplemental needs . . . Pricing the inventory . . . Inventory reconciliation . . . Inventory audit needs . . . Control audits . . . Discrepancy audits . . . Discrepancy audit findings.

Providing a convenience factor . . . Undergoing a shock treatment . . . Performing work simplification . . . Providing orientation and training . . . Developing "action" procedures . . . Monitoring performance . . . Controlling new forms additions . . . The control logbook . . . Document numbering system . . . An index is recommended . . . Tie form information together . . . Form number change-over . . . Guidelines to good forms design . . . Implementing filing and storage policy and procedures . . . What to file? . . . How to file it? . . . How long to file it? . . . Introducing recycled paper . . . The advantages of paperless systems.

Categorizing inventory supplies . . . Contract guarantees . . . Contract benefits . . . Controlling the EDP and special forms inventory . . . A five-step approach . . . Contract results . . . The inventory status report . . . Benefits . . . Extending the systems contract to other inventory supplies . . . Contract differences . . . A single vendor is big advantage . . . Paperwork system is key to benefits . . . Delivery cycles established . . . Results are beneficial.

1

New Techniques in Physical Storage: Keystone to High-Level Customer Service

Storage would be unnecessary to support sales if merchandise could be scheduled to arrive exactly when a need occurs. But, since it can't be predicted precisely when something will be asked for, it's necessary to buy some things early if immediate availability is to be offered. Then the worry becomes one of dollar investment, and how the movement or non-movement of this investment can be controlled. This is where physical parts storage enters the picture.

Ten facility guidelines are listed in this chapter which, if followed, will insure that maximum benefits will be obtained from the physical storage area used (or planned). Additionally, a checklist is offered for obtaining a successful systems flow through the storage area. Planning methods are given for forecasting physical growth potential, justifying equipment needs, controlling and assigning item storage locations and projecting future personnel requirements. The result of it all is high level customer service.

THE PRIMARY OBJECTIVE

Nobody wants inventory but everyone wants service. The primary objective of a storage facility should be to provide customer service, whether the customer is the company itself (for support of its own manufacturing or maintenance use), another manufacturing concern, another sales distribution level or an end user.

True, storage facilities give the manufacturer, the wholesaler and the retailer a method to offset potential market shortages; to be flexible for sudden sales increases; and to procure merchandise at the lowest possible cost through industry price breaks. But, as we get closer to the end user, customer service appears to be the only justifiable answer to the use of storage for inventory purposes.

PLANNING AIDS

Planning aids are helpful in developing a storage concept. Errors in planning, found while using planning aids, are the least costly to correct.

Architectural Drawings

Architectural drawings can be good planning aids. Outside views illustrate the influence the building will have on the environment. The internal floor plans show a scale model drawing of the finished facility. Accuracy of drawings must, however, be determined before use. (If the storage facility is a minor part of a building complex, obtain floor plans for the area assigned as storage, or prepare a layout to accurate dimensions. All critical points should be measured to verify dimensions. Don't guess!) Draw in the areas for the basic storage functions and activities—or use overlays. Include all proposed entrances and exits; all telephone, electrical, heater and air outlets or connections; plumbing locations; posts or pillars; drains; floor slopes. Lay out a work flow through each activity area. Show aisle space. Get a view of what is going to happen—and how. Make sure there is ample working room and proper entrances and exits for all areas before installing any equipment.

Three-Dimensional Models

Added depth can be obtained by using three-dimensional models for visual representation. Greater perspective is obtained. Potential problems will be more noticeable than with the simpler scale layouts. Growth proposals, either "up" or "out," can be better illustrated to top management personnel. Three-dimensional models don't need to be expensively made solid likenesses. Common construction paper can provide interesting color coded models with less cost.

Computer Utilization

Computer assistance, as a planning aid, is offered by several consultant firms to determine warehouse or storage space needs, feasibility of automated systems use, location of merchandise in functional flow areas, and even to offer arrangement of people units for office layouts.

SECURITY SAFEGUARDS

Security has become a necessary cost in business today, and must be considered in all inventory growth aspects. An expenditure equal to over 20% of the cost of reported business is estimated to be spent annually by American businesses to stop or control theft. This expenditure must necessarily increase the product cost. "Security in Materials Control: A Seven-Point Program That Works," Chapter 18, offers a seven-point program for achieving a sound security program. The important factor to be covered here is that security should be designed into any new building plans—or into facility expansion.

The overall physical arrangement of inventory facilities can do much to reduce theft losses and security manpower costs. The design and organization of the inventory areas should establish the strategy and concern for security.

FACILITY GUIDELINES

The location of storage, physical characteristics, equipment allocation, and environment all have a direct influence on the success of an inventory management system.

1. Plan the storage facility to allow for future growth potential.
2. Design the building's physical appearance to create good will and to invite business.
3. Arrange storage for fast and easy customer order processing.
4. Use compatible storage or display equipment to create good interior appearances.
5. Ensure accurate location and identification of all merchandise in storage.
6. Install good lighting to prevent theft, parts damage and errors in stocking and picking.
7. Plan storage for easy shelf-life rotation to permit "first in-first out" control.
8. Segregate rebuilt, remanufactured, used and new merchandise.
9. Include safety as a part of the storage facility plan.
10. Maintain a periodic housekeeping and rearrangement plan.

PINPOINTING MATERIAL HANDLING PROBLEMS

Existing operating problems must be recognized before new facility planning is started. The five most common material handling problems today appear to fall under terms such as "lack of space," "disorganization," "people," "peak load requirements" and "poor shipping capability." Each is very real—but in the final analysis, all of these can be combined into one general problem: lack of proper long range planning.

Lack of space, an associative symptom of the other problems listed, has to do with growth planning. Initial disregard to growth trends, unplanned company diversification of products, and other general market trends create the need for space, and lack of it causes a material handling problem.

Disorganization generally results from too fast a growth without proper planning. One manufacturing concern outgrew the capacity of a building complex originally purchased. Additional building space is no longer available close to the present location. The present operating flow, although as efficient as the facility will allow, is more costly than necessary. The only real answers for this situation are either to move or to decentralize operations.

Another manufacturer, growing faster than it anticipated, grew both "out" and then "up." The many floor levels now required for normal operation create disrupted communications and poor work coordination because no real plan was followed. Vertical and horizontal conveyors are seen as possible measures to alleviate this problem.

Case in point: One company, finding itself handling its department store distribution from a couple of multi-floor buildings located on both sides of a street, considered a move to a new single floor building. However, after extensive review and analysis of distribution flexibility and costs and site selection and location, a decision was made to modernize the existing buildings to achieve a single floor storage effect with the proper use of handling equipment. The two buildings were connected by an enclosed conveyor, high above the street. Material handling methods introduced in the succeeding modernization included a grid system for storage aisles (and redirecting material to other stores); color coded tags to easily establish shipping date identity; accumulation lanes for gathering material for pallet loads; an automated sorting technique at conveyor intersections; and an interrelated system of inclined belt, roller and pallet conveyors and freight elevators. Their older buildings were transformed into an efficient multi-floor high-rise storage and retrieval system, a distribution center which the company nows feels has competitive operating costs—without moving.

People object when close working conditions exist. They also object to extra walking created because aisles are too small to move merchandise mechanically.

Peak loads in receiving create a stocking bottleneck when storage bins are inadequate in size, and material must be collected and relocated in storage.

Lack of shipping capability creates a package pile-up into the shipping areas and slows performance.

Define any of these existing problems and seek answers that will fit into long range plans. Start with a review of the in-out work flow.

IN-OUT WORK FLOW

When lack of space is a problem, a drop in work flow performance during sales peaks is signalled by the telltale signs of line-up trucks, receipts piled up unprocessed, growing inventory discrepancies, clogged aisles, increased shipping mistakes and other related items.

Review and constantly monitor the in-out work flow to spot telltale signs early. Confirm that a good efficient work flow exists—or improve it—before crying wolf. More space may be the only answer, but the following checks might buy time and productivity increase until a new storage facility or expansion becomes a reality. And, if setting up a new facility flow, incorporate these items into it for a more successful system:

New Facility Flow Checklist

— Docks, if used, should be built level to truck or rail car heights, or dock levelers should be used to speed up the material handling function.

— Storage entry and exit doors used by material handling equipment should, wherever possible, be rigged to open and close while the operators are on the equipment.

— Receiving and shipping areas must afford sufficient room for incoming or outgoing material, material handling equipment, personnel and working space.

— Inventory scheduling factors should be reviewed to correct abnormal bunching of incoming receipts—if regular peaks are occurring.

— Material handling equipment and use should be reviewed to determine adequacy and reliability.

— Storage aisles should be wide enough for efficient use by currently designed material handling equipment, and, if possible, with main aisles wide enough to permit two-way traffic.

— Obstructions hanging from the ceilings, such as lines and light fixtures, should be discouraged or eliminated where equipment must travel.

— Inventory material should be located in stock bins or on storage equipment so there is no overhang into aisles to slow travel or cause accidents.

— Customer order processing should be reviewed to correct for any large volumes of individual shipments to a single destination.

The in-out work flow should be the quickest, most direct flow through the storage facility, with easy access to faster moving merchandise—with minimum steps taken.

LONG RANGE SPACE PLANNING

Long range planning is a must when building, expanding or leasing new storage facilities. Adequate space is necessary to obtain an efficient materials control system, and determining space needed for growth is an integral part of long range planning.

Plan for a minimum of five years' future growth. Make sure the growth factor used is a minimum of 25%. If it isn't, recheck the growth projections carefully. They could be wrong. The biggest oversight in the planning function is not allowing enough for full growth potential. Even companies employing the use of consultants either disregard or underestimate future growth factors, as they too are growing into space problems.

Cube Use

More and more companies are thinking cube instead of square foot requirements, due to high (and climbing higher) space costs. New material handling equipment, designed for "high rise" storage, allows inventory concentration without expanding the width or length of existing buildings.

A furniture distributor in the Midwest estimated about 15% savings by going "up" instead of "out." A manufacturer in California estimated almost 20% in savings, and felt that the inventory control functions were strengthened by growing "up." Even better results were achieved by a manufacturer in Michigan who claims inventory security was doubled against theft, damage was reduced by 75% and storage handling costs were down 50% through using a "high rise" rack storage concept.

A Growth Plan-of-Action

The long range marketing plan is the best guide for growth considerations. Marketing sales estimates, coupled with corporate operating policies and materials management objectives, will picture future space needs and aid in building a plan of action.

The plan of action should be based on marketing research information, future trends in the receiving and shipping work areas, future anticipated use of material handling equipment, inventory storage growth, and office and people support needs.

Growth potential should not, however, be limited just to the physical inventory needs. An expansion "out" from present building walls, if desirable or necessary, will overflow into areas presently assigned or needed for future expansion of landscaping, parking facilities and building access. Ample space for these needs must also be a part of the plan of action.

Marketing Research. Most larger companies, realizing the need for direction on consumer trends, have their own marketing research departments. Other companies must place reliance on industry trends found in publications such as the Conference Board Reports, or they must contract research on a consultant basis. Data from marketing research can be valuable in the identification of changing consumer trends—an important variable in defining the design and/or location of building needs. Documentation might already exist on the comparisons between a company depot or branch storage concept, leasing of public warehousing, or expansion of present facilities. A talk with research people, associated with companies which are now doing what you want to do, can help. A savings in budget expenditures might be found, with an added benefit of improved customer service. Marketing research information is essential in planning long range growth.

Receipts and Shipping Trends. The receiving and shipping functions are two good indicators for sounding out growth trends. A review of receiving and shipping records will identify such trends. New space requirements can be projected by adding suggested trend requirements to the space now allocated for the present activity level. If activity records aren't available, or present space requirements are not accurately known, consider at least 12% to 15% of total space needs to be for receiving and shipping functions. Manufacturing industries will use the majority of this space (60% to 80% of it) in the shipping area—largely because compact raw material comes in and bulkier finished products go out. Wholesalers and retailers will normally place more than half of this space in the receiving function, because of the delay in preparing receipts documentation, the extent of receiving inspection accomplished, and pre-packaging of receipts prior to stocking.

Dock sizes should be designed to handle future trend volume without causing a continual waiting line of trucks to occur, wherever the use of receiving and shipping docks is demanded. Review the dock area flow efficiency and volume of movements to determine if expansion is becoming necessary in these areas.

Material Handling Equipment Use. Properly selected material handling equipment will provide the tool for the safest and most efficient method of handling material. Material handling equipment should be selected before internal storage layout dimensions are finalized. Smaller equipment (and a larger increasing variety) is offered today. However, initial costs, maintenance requirements, weight-lifting capacities and turning radius of such equipment should be known before aisle widths, types and kinds of storage and building width and heights are decided on. Will new storage characteristics relate well to the operating equipment needed for reaching higher levels of storage, if future growth requires a move "up" in inventory? If a move "out" is made, will side loading equipment be necessary where row lengths are extended? Will presently planned aisles allow the use of side loading equipment? If guided vehicles will be used in the future, will aisles allow width for installation of rails?

Equipment Inventory. An equipment inventory should be taken on present material handling equipment. Check new equipment innovations and future needs. Add new purchases to the inventory list as acquisitions are made. Establish records for recording types of equipment, costs, hours in use, accidents sustained, and downtime of equipment. A periodic comparison of recorded costs and performance should be made with similiar equipment used by other company departments or other companies, to determine acceptable equipment performance and worth.

Exhibit 1-1 shows a typical equipment record card. Maintenance tickets for refueling/recharging equipment, downtime reports, repair tickets, and accident reports are to be filed with each equipment record card. This card contains all pertinent data reflecting the equipment's performance and provides a trade-in "alert" signalled by lowered performance and/or increasing downtime. These cards are filed by equipment number.

Communications. Two-way communication should be used with equipment operators and materials control personnel when a limited amount of handling equipment is available for use. A system of lights and buzzers can be used, interconnected with all significant areas of the storage facility, to alert a given control point when and where material handling equipment is needed. A public address system would substitute for the two-way lights and buzzers, if all operating areas have access to the PA system. However, conflicting needs for equipment at the same time requires priority judgment—which might best be left to the materials control area.

EQUIPMENT NUMBER_____

EQUIPMENT NAME:_____OPERATOR_____

SERIAL NUMBER_____ DATE PURCHASED_____ ORIGINAL COST $_____ CARD
DATE_____

FUNCTION: _____
_____
_____
_____

OPERATING DATA:	JAN	FEB	MAR	APR	MAY	JUN	JUL	AUG	SEP	OCT	NOV	DEC	TOTAL
# ACCIDENTS													
HOURS DOWNTIME													
TOTAL HOURS USED													
FUEL COSTS													
PARTS COSTS													
LABOR COSTS													

SPECIAL NOTES:

EXHIBIT 1-1:   Equipment Record Card

Inventory Storage Growth. Select inventory storage equipment that will grow with the business. In this respect, deal with reputable distributors for a manufacturer who will be in business long enough to supply any future long range needs. Sometimes it's even necessary to question the manufacturer directly when deciding on storage needs. One Midwest company has an office filing system which is made up of several types of uprights, with incompatible colors and shelves. These were all procured from the same source, but the manufacturer changed the product line without providing any allowance for support of the older styles.

Buy material strong enough to double-deck or multi-stack if growth trends indicate the need; or, buy material which will withstand a second working level of catwalks for bulk storage capacity.

Arrange storage equipment, initially, so that new units may be added on for increased storage capacity. Design storage so that additional units, when added either to the length or to the height of original units, will not invalidate the storage location system used.

Storage equipment is prolific in sizes, shapes, function and flexibility. Some of the most popularly used storage equipment includes pegboard (or hanging) storage, display racks or cases, shelves, open storage, bins, cantilever racks, open steel racks, stack racks, pallets, drums, tanks, and vaults. Many types of other special storage equipment are available.

Compatible Storage Equipment. Don't be tempted to mix types of storage equipment together in a given area, just because all types of equipment are available. Choose storage equipment assortments which are compatible to each other. Layouts of storage areas will be easier and neater. So will housekeeping. Overhead lighting can be more uniform and useful. Aisles will be square and the same throughout a given area. Assembly and maintenance of storage units will be easier. Manual systems of locating parts will be simpler to follow. Material which requires special handling equipment to move it, can all be located together to better utilize equipment.

Growth is simpler and easier with the use of compatible storage. Double-decking or multi-stacking is possible; and growth expansion can be done on a piecemeal basis as budgets allow, without looking out of place. Adjustment to growth can be gradual.

Compatibility and neatness breed accuracy. If odd sizes and shapes of storage equipment are carelessly butted together, merchandise may be stocked the same way. Customers view the storage areas often, and relate the storage facility condition to the type of service offered. Give the customer the feeling of good service and care.

Inventory Location System. Merchandise must have a specific location in inventory storage to permit such activities as adding stock, picking orders, taking physical inventory audits. Manufacturers and wholesalers normally use a storage system which allows an exact location to be assigned to each item. Storage assignments can then be made on the basis of an inventory classification system. Retailers differ by using a classification method for the storage location system, because it is a simple and "general" method for storing and locating inventory items.

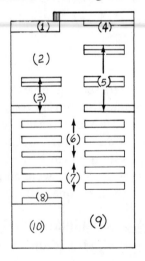

LEGEND:

(1) Receiving inspection test equipment
(2) Receiving and inspection area
(3) Bulk liquids and raw material/supplies
(4) Hazardous material storage
(5) Bulk (or secondary) storage areas—Class "C"
(6) Slower moving inventory items—Class "B"
(7) Faster moving inventory items—Class "A"
(8) Locked cabinets for high-value items
(9) Shipping preparation, staging and control areas
(10) Offices area

EXHIBIT 1-2:   A Sample Finished Goods Inventory Layout

Exhibit 1-2 presents a sample finished goods inventory layout, using "ABC" classification with row-section-shelf assignment, showing logical placement of various inventory items and control areas. Important points to remember are these:

1. A straight-line storage layout should be planned, whenever possible, for controlling activities from receiving—to stocking—through shipping.
2. Receiving and shipping areas should be physically separated.
3. Consideration should be given to work-in-process volume prior to layout, if production/shop

facilities are supported from the finished goods inventory, especially when using "ABC" method for inventory classification and arrangement.

4. Hazardous material requires special storage, and should be located on the fringe of the storage area—preferably close to the inspection area, as frequent checks are necessary on such material.
5. Aisle space, though not "productive" looking, should provide easy flow and be ample for future growth needs:
   a. main and secondary aisles from 10' to 12'.
   b. storage bin aisles from 3' to 5'.
6. All storage bin and secondary storage aisles should "flow" into the main aisle.

Storage Assignment by Classification. There are many ways to classify inventory. The most popularly used classifications will be discussed in deatil in "Classifying Inventories for Control," Chapter 3. A general description is given here on some classification methods for illustrative purposes, because most retail businesses seldom use a formal storage location assignment method. They improvise. They locate inventory either by numerical part number or item number sequence, product line, item function, color and size. Of these, product line, item function, color and size lend themselves to easy location of merchandise.

Product line classification has material sequenced in storage by type of product. A department store has housewares in one department, drugs in another, automotive items in another, etc. Item function is similar to product line, except that it is more specific in nature. An automotive parts dealer, using the item function for parts location, would have all sparkplugs together in one area, all gasket sets together in another, all the wheel bearings together in another, etc. A job shop printer uses the color or size classifications on paper, ink, print type, etc., to locate his inventory items.

The use of classifications by retail establishments works well in locating inventory where customers do the looking and selecting of material. In the manufacturing and wholesale trade industries, however, a time problem exists where many thousands of items are moved many times a day or week by many different people—few if any being customers. In this situation, a fast and accurate method of locating merchandise is necessary.

Part Number Sequence. Most parts distributors use a part's number to develop storage of merchandise by part number sequence. The part number—and the part number only—must be known to find a part in storage. The storage locations do not have to be posted anywhere to be remembered. However, two major disadvantages often occur and should be considered before classifying an inventory by part number sequence:

1. Addition of new products usually requires mass movement of parts within storage to "fit" them in sequence with the other parts.
2. Added stocking volume will also require mass movement, or will create a "double" stocking location situation.

Row-Section-Shelf Assignment. A variation of the row-section-shelf method is a commonly used method for storage location assignments:

1. Bins are placed together in rows. (Other kinds of storage equipment can also be used where compatible shelves of some type exist.)
2. Each row is assigned a letter (or number) identification.

3. The bin (or storage) sections in a row are then numbered from one end of the row to the other end, in alternating fashion.

4. The shelves in each bin (or storage unit) are numbered in sequence from the bottom shelf up. (The shelf direction must remain the same throughout the storage areas, but the number of shelves per bin can vary.)

Exhibit 1-3 illustrates the bin location numbering system and direction flow. Storage locations are assigned by the row-section-shelf method. Each row is assigned a letter or number. The bins in each row are assigned an ascending number from one end of the row to the other. Direction sequence is normally associated with picking direction flow. Shelves are numbered from the bottom shelf (floor level) up in all cases, and the number of shelves in a bin can vary from one bin to another.

Materials can still be stocked on a shelf by a supplemental classification method if desired (i.e., part number), but don't need to be, when using the row-section-shelf identification system. Any new inventory item can be stocked in any open area without rearrangement of other stock. A storage location assignment system identifies exactly where material is located; allows anybody to handle inventory with little training (a handy thought during peak sales periods or vacations); reduces the volume of lost parts; and permits a better means for processing inventory discrepancies. These advantages multiply as the number of stocked items increases.

Offices and Support Needs for Variable Expenses. The growth in variable expenses is another important part of the physical storage plan of action. Inventory growth must have people support to sustain and keep activities running smoothly. People support is perhaps the largest single expense most companies have. When payroll increases, other items such as taxes, insurance, utilities, supplies, training, capital equipment, offices and recreational needs increase.

Variable expenses should be reflected in the plan of action as projected space needs for offices and related support. Offices and related support will include all space requirements for offices, office equipment and supplies, restrooms, training areas, lounges, lunchrooms, and air conditioning/heating/plumbing needs.

A simple graph can be prepared to help speed calculation of planning data for offices and related support space needs. To prepare this graph:

1. Review and obtain the recorded gross sales dollars for each of the last five years, and the estimated gross sales dollars for each of the next five years of operation:

Year	Actual Gross Sales Dollars	Estimated Gross Sales Dollars
-4	$ 3,750,000	
-3	4,800,000	
-2	5,100,000	
-1	5,300,000	
Current	6,500,000	
+1		$ 7,600,000
+2		8,800,000
+3		10,000,000
+4		11,700,000
+5		12,800,000

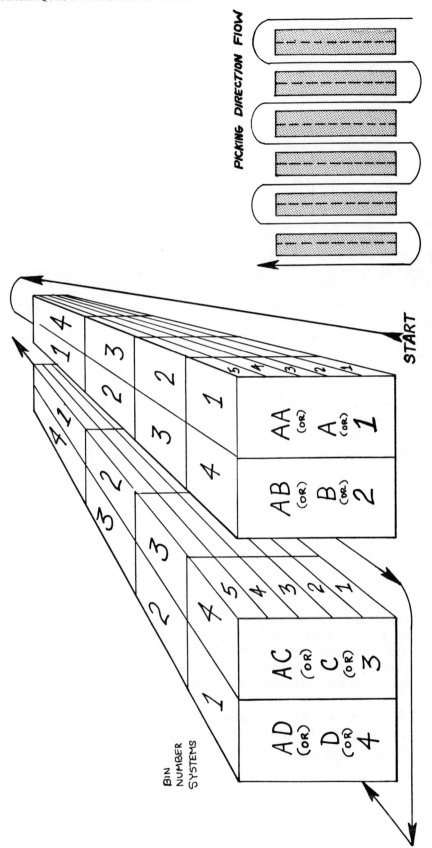

EXHIBIT 1-3:   Bin Location Numbering System and Direction Flow

2. Determine the exact number of employees working during each of the last five years:

Year	Number of Employees
-4	25
-3	29
-2	32
-1	30
Current	38

3. Prepare a graph outline with the vertical line representing the number of employees; the horizontal line representing gross sales dollars; with the intercept point of the two lines zero for both figures. (Refer to Exhibit 1-4. Recorded gross sales dollars and total employees available during a company's last 5-year operating period are used to plot this graph. A trend line is extended out to the right hand side of the graph. Gross sales estimates for the next 5-year plan, by year, are plotted on this trend line. Corresponding estimated employee requirements are found, and divided by the current year's employee total, to obtain a multiplier for projecting future space requirements, by year, for offices and related support.)

4. Make sure the horizontal line is extended long enough for fitting on the projected (or estimated) long range gross sales dollars.

5. Plot a point for each of the last five years which corresponds to the sales dollars and matching number of employees.

6. Draw a line which best fits these five points and extend this trend line out to the right of the graph.

7. Plot the gross sales dollar estimate onto the extended line, for each of the next five years of the long range plan.

8. Draw a line parallel to the horizontal line of the graph, from the plotted dollar estimates, left to the graph's vertical lines, and record the estimated number of employees for each of the next five years:

Year	Number of Employees
+1	42
+2	48
+3	53
+4	59
+5	65

9. Divide each of the employee estimates by the current employee figure. These results (percentages) are to be used in projecting increasing requirements for offices and related support. (These percentages are shown on Exhibit 1-4.)

10. Find the total square footage space now used for offices and related support requirements, and multiply by the graph factors to obtain anticipated total growth needs.

Measured manhours can be used in place of total employees, if the labor force is small and dollar sales are highly volatile. Otherwise, use that period of time which will most accurately reflect the change in past employee growth.

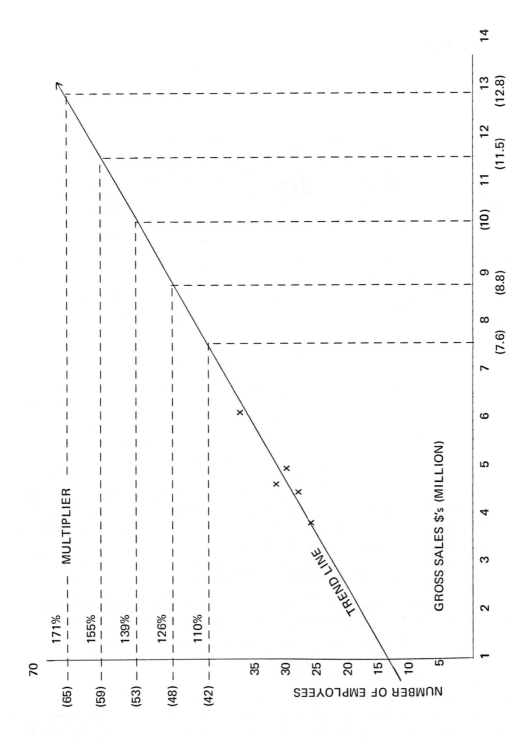

EXHIBIT 1-4: A Graph to Determine Space Needs for Offices and Related Support

2

A Simple Part Number
Gives Big Control

The critical importance of the part number is usually underrated. This chapter advances the need for a well-thought-out part numbering system, and presents guidelines for designing such a system. Properly organized, the part number becomes an invaluable tool in inventory management, especially in administration of the record keeping function.

THE PART NUMBER AND THE COMPUTER

When an item's identity must be made by computer, input time and machine processing time is wasted if the description is too long, and errors are more probable in transposition or missing digits. Sorting and matching of related information is keyed to the number of digits in the field being tested. Control and identity become less accurate, if descriptions must be abbreviated to correspond to a limited number of assigned digits. Computer storage space becomes very expensive where the "maximum" description space must be assigned the same length for each item in computer storage. The part number makes identity and control of an item logical, easy to process in a computer, faster in processing time, more economical in storage use, and supplies a uniform "description" that can't be misinterpreted.

WHY ASSIGN A PART NUMBER?

The part number system is a method used in compacting descriptions, applications, and peculiar item characteristics of a product, for permitting:

1. Classification of an item, such as for model, function or stock-handling characteristics.
2. Quick and uniform identification of an item.
3. A standard, "minimized," field length for all items.
4. Faster item processing and control for all inventory management activities.

The part number does not eliminate the item's description, although the description is restricted to small abbreviated (almost useless) field length; but for purposes of control, the part number obviates the name. The part number offers a general description of an item, and permits a cross-reference to documentation records which can offer a complete detailed description which might cover several pages, including control specifications.

GUIDELINES FOR DEVELOPING A PART NUMBER SYSTEM

A part number format should be designed carefully. Its use will extend over the life of the company. Where current "no-part-number-system" part numbers are assigned, it might pay to develop a uniform system now, if long range company operating plans are indicated. The need for assignment of part numbers is usually most predominant among manufacturers. However, "company crafted" items (items manufactured for a company, with the company's name or identification on them) require some form of a part (or item, model, etc.) number. Guidelines for developing a part number system include:

1. The part number "field" length should be limited to 15 digits, and kept shorter if possible.
2. Adequate growth potential should be allowed.
3. Numeric digits should be used predominantly.
4. Adequate part number identification should be provided.
5. Company identity should be considered and/or included.
6. The use of alphabetic and special characters should be limited to beneficial purposes, and provide a function not permitted by numeric digits.
7. A part number "configuration change" should be identified without a loss of original part number identity.
8. "Dash numbers" should be used sparingly.
9. A simple part number "fielding" should be agreed to.

Keep the Part Number Field Short

Fewer digits result in less writing, less thinking and less chance for error. Computer storage is expensive, and costs are less where fewer digits are involved. Government procedures limit part number length to 15 digits. Those planning to do contract work with the government should keep this in mind.

Allow for Adequate Growth

Adequate growth should be permitted so that the original design concept can continue without dual systems being started. Dual systems add confusion, especially where the new system's numbers are not similar to the original. The growth potential should be considered in the basic number portion of the part number.

Use Numeric Numbers

Computers can process, store and identify numeric digits more economically than they can alphabetic or special characters. This is because the alphabetic or special characters are made up of a numeric and a zone "identifier" combination. More numeric digits can be stored in the same space (than alphabetic or special character digits) because of this. Sorting alphabetic and special character information requires a check on both the numeric and the zone portions of the digit. Numeric digits appear easier to remember and "speak" than alphabetic and special characters, and seem to be preferred by most parts people.

Provide Adequate Part Number Identification

The part number format concept is a subjective decision. No set number of digits is uniformly used to denote typical segments of the part number. However, the basic segments should be distinguishable. Four basic segments are usually found in a part number format, although not necessarily in the same sequence. These are:

1. Proprietary/non-proprietary status.
2. Basic part number.
3. Change status.
4. Dash number.

```
AAA        BBCCDDD       E        FFF
 '            '          '         '
 '            '          '         '
 '            '          '          '  Dash number
 '            '          '
 '            '           '  Change status
 '            '
 '             '  Basic part number
 '
  '  Proprietary/non-proprietary status
```

Proprietary/Non-proprietary Status. Segment "AAA" of the part number is usually represented by alphabetic digits. These digits are for company identity, but are not normally part of the computer stored part number. One of the digits, if used, is for division responsibility. The basic number segment can purposely include divisional responsibility (in the model portion) and prevent using an extra digit here. Up to three digits should be used in front of all vendor part numbers (non-proprietary), to prevent duplicate part numbers among the various vendors' part numbers being stocked. (These digits would remain as part of the computer stored part number.)

Basic Part Number. The basic part number segment is the most important, and descriptive, portion of the part number. It is grouped into three separate variables:

```
BB       CC       DDD
 '        '        '
 '        '         '
 '        '          '  Product sub-assembly or detail
 '        '
 '         '  Major product component
 '
  '  Product model
```

1. *Product model.* A two-digit numeric model variable will allow up to 99 model separations. If more model coverage is needed, another numeric digit is recommended in place of alphabetic substitution. Model coding can provide divisional responsibility. If this is desired, an assigned group of sequential numbers should be decided in the beginning, to keep all of a division's models (now and in the future) together. Model code is usually assigned to the highest level product offered. In the case of an automobile, a Ford Pinto or a Ford Maverick would each be considered a separate model.

2. *Major product component.* A two-digit numeric product component allows up to 99 such separations for each model offered. In the case of an automobile, the engine would be considered a major product component, the frame another, etc.

3. *Product sub-assembly or detail.* A three-digit numeric variable will allow up to 999 sub-assemblies or detail items for each separate major component. A connecting rod assembly *(sub-assembly)* for an engine *(major product component)* for a Ford Pinto *(model)* would be described by a product sub-assembly or detail part number segment. A further breakdown of "end-item" details would be provided by the part number's dash number.

Limit Alphabetic and Special Character Use

The desire to use alphabetic or special characters in designing a part number should be conditioned by benefits obtained, such as a functional use capability not obtainable with numeric digits—except through sacrifice on growth potential. Two specific functions should consider alphabetic and/or special character use: company identification and modification of product.

The alphabetic prefix for company identity is not punched or stored within the company's computer file or on manual records. The prefix can be a "constant," if needed, and added to the part number whenever output printing or outside correspondence occurs. However, non-proprietary part numbers should be computer stored with vendor prefixes to prevent the occurrence of duplication among a company and vendor, or between two vendors' part numbers.

Modification of an existing part can be achieved by an alphabetic suffix following the basic part number segment and before the dash number. This alphabetic code is usually assigned only to vendor product changes when a vendor fails to reassign a new part number, but can also be used on proprietary parts where frequent change is necessary—for instance, with kits (a group of items placed together "loose" in a bag or box).

Change Status. The "E" segment (of the part number) provides identification of a change in an item's configuration. An alphabetic digit should be used here for positive identification of a product change made—without changing the item number itself. Where engineering, or a designer, determines that the configuration change in an item is significant enough to warrant the assigning of a new part number, then a dash number change might be made. This would eliminate the need for a change status code. All vendor parts which undergo a configuration change without a part number change will require a change status digit. Multi-changes can occur on the same part number without a new dash number being given. When this happens, the alphabetic code is simply changed to the next letter, i.e., from A to B to C, etc.

The Dash Number. The dash number can be several digits in length (up to five numeric digits is common), and extends the capability of the sub-assembly or detail coverage. The dash number will permit a further breakdown of sub-assemblies, with a possibility of 99999 different details definable for a given sub-assembly (where a five-digit dash number is used). In the case of details already defined without a dash number needed, a dash number is not used. Sometimes an additional "second" dash number is used. Specific examples for a second dash number would be the defining of color coding, sizes, or voltages, etc.

Part Number "Fielding." The need for accuracy and speed in creating part number "input" data, for a computer system, is self-evident. The key to success is in the part number "fielding." In other words: "How is a part number to be keypunched for computer 'input' use?" Since the computer is normally programmed to match the "input" part number with a part number already on an "internal" computer file, both numbers must be exactly the same—or a non-match situation will exist, and processing will not be completed. Manual systems permit greater latitude than this, in most cases of part number matching, because of visual sight capability.

Part number fielding procedures furnish uniform rules for everyone to follow and use. Some rules to consider are:

1. The part number should always start in the first column of the part number "field" (high order left position) and be punched straight across (from left to right).

2. A space should be left between a base number and a dash number, or between two dash numbers, where the separated digits are *both* either numeric or alphabetic. Where the separated digits are different—one numeric and the other alphabetic—no space will be left. A space will not be left where a change configuration code (alphabetic) is inserted between the base number and a dash number.

3. Dash numbers should be spaced to the back of the dash number "field" (low order right position), where normal "collator" sequence is used for sort priority. This sequence is, by order of priority: special characters first, blanks second, alphabetic characters next and numeric characters last. This sequence will permit a logical ascending sequence of dash numbers, i.e., 1 before 11; 11 before 111; etc. (This rule can not always be followed on vendor dash numbers, as the dash number length is not always known.)

4. Special characters which cannot be printed with available computer equipment, should be left blank. (Such omitted characters should be listed for guidance.)

5. Vendor identity coding should be a part of each non-company part number. Exceptions to this, found when keypunching, should be listed and given to supervision for possible correction.

RULE NUMBER	NUMBER OF PART, MODEL, ITEM	1	2	3	4	5	6	7	8	9	10	11	12	13	14	15
		DIGIT REPRESENTATION (left to right):														
(1)	SSS1234567	S	S	S	1	2	3	4	5	6	7					
	*XXX1234567	1	2	3	4	5	6	7								
(2)	EK-9AV-GE	E	K	9	A	V		G	E							
	624-HB-72W-120V	6	2	4	H	B	7	2	W	1	2	0	V			
	*XXX1234567-A-11	1	2	3	4	5	6	7	A		1	1				
	NAS-42DD-4-4	N	A	S	4	2	D	D	4		4					
(3)	SSS1234567-1	S	S	S	1	2	3	4	5	6	7		1			
	*XXX1234567-1	1	2	3	4	5	6	7				1				
	*XXX1234567-11	1	2	3	4	5	6	7			1	1				
	*XXX1234567-111	1	2	3	4	5	6	7		1	1	1				
(4)	#180	1	8	0												
	#180	W	W	W	1	8	0									

EXHIBIT 2-1. An Example Table of Part Number "Fielding" Rules

In Exhibit 2-1, which illustrates part number "fielding," three things should be noted: (1) Proprietary part numbers are not stored with company identity. The "*" denotes this fact. Proprietary numbers used here have a three-digit dash number. (2) A vendor's dash number must be "fielded" as written, as the lengths of vendor dash numbers are not always known. (3) Every attempt should be made to add the vendor's identity to a stored part number, as the chance for duplication with another vendor's number is great, and procurement information would otherwise be missing.

USING A PART NUMBER GUIDE

Set up a part number guide "control book," by vendor name sequence, showing a typical part number and its format. Identify the basic parts of the formatted number to show vendor code, basic part number, change status and dash numbers. Break the basic number portion into product model, major product component and sub-assembly or detail segments—where applicable. This information can provide an invaluable aid to inventory management in order taking, receiving or storage control. A vendor's number, usually marked on (or attached to) the product itself, can be easily associated to the merchandise number ordered and stocked, by this cross-reference "part number guide" method.

CHANGING TO A CONTROLLED PART NUMBER SYSTEM

Time, effort and costs should be critically reviewed and analyzed before face-lifting a company's part number system. The company's future (in the market place), and its anticipated product diversification, will play a big part in the final decision made. The expectation that company product lines will become more numerous and complex (in the future) will help justify bringing order, now, to "no-part-number-system" part numbers.

One-Time Costs to Consider

1. *Preparing a master part number control system.* A product outline is required in order to construct the new part number control system. Time estimates can be applied to the guidelines presented in this chapter.
2. *Time Phasing.* Cut-off times should be established for deleting old part numbers; providing new part number identification; updating inventory records; controlling open purchase orders and customer backorders; and notifying vendors and customers of new changes.
3. *Lost Sales Prevention.* Tooling, nameplate, or printing changes must be developed and obtained prior to conversion of new control system, or lost sales might result due to production halts or slowdowns.
4. *Paperwork Changes.* Information contained on engineering, production and other support paperwork must be corrected. Such paperwork should include product specifications, bills of material, assembly parts lists, routings or operation sheets, production schedules, "where used" lists and quality control data.
5. *Sales Data Changes.* Published product information must be revised for new product identification. Included would be brochures, price lists, labels, containers, parts catalogs, maintenance manuals and warranty data.

Trade-Off Benefits

1. Costs for change-over (and maintenance) from a manual operation to a computer system should be much less, and permit more economical program applications.
2. Part numbers can be more accurately associated with a product's name by employees and distribution personnel—a timesaver in training new employees.
3. A natural classification of inventory items, by product line, can be more easily developed and with less cost.

4. Improved company management can result through availability of "finite" answers on inventory levels, receipts, sales, expenses, profits and warranty transactions—for each product line. Weak products can be more quickly determined and controlled.

5. Part number control results. Similar or duplicated numbers for different products should not occur.

EDP Consideration

A new part number control program could generate significant operating costs in changing drawing control and manufacturing records data, where EDP resources are not now being used, if a large volume of products exists. Increasing awkwardness in following the present part number system should be weighed against the anticipated increase in products to be controlled in the future. Above a certain operating level EDP utilization becomes a necessary evil, and its requirements must be appraised in the change-over study.

3

Classifying Inventories for Control

The inventory classification methods given in this chapter provide the solutions to the broadest ranges of inventory control desired. The ABC principle is highlighted as the most effective means for developing an inventory classification—by providing "management by emphasis." Control priorities are easily established under the ABC methods shown. Management emphasis is placed on the few items that bring about the most results. Detailed methods are illustrated for developing these various control priorities, whether it be on inventory dollar investment, for storage location assignment or over obsolescence. These priorities can be placed in immediate use, with immediate results obtained in increased operating efficiency.

CONTROLLING INVENTORY INVESTMENT BY THE ABC'S

A limited number of inventory items (say up to 1000 items) would be relatively easy to control. But as the number of different stockable items grows in number (to perhaps over 100,000 items), control becomes exceedingly more difficult—even with computer assistance—without some form of classification for the items being stocked. A method of classification should be developed to assign "time priorities" over replenishment ordering, before customer service deteriorates and inventory investment gets too far out of hand—which can often result due to an unmanageable number of items requiring action.

The Principle of ABC

The ABC inventory classification creates a three-segmented inventory based on the accumulation of total annual sales dollars for each individual item. The underlying principle is that a few percent of the items (A) will contribute a large percent of the sales dollars, and, conversely, a large percent of the items (C) will contribute only a small percent to sales dollars. The group in between (B) is arbitrarily considered the third (or normal) group of items.

The Standard ABC Relationship

The standard relationship normally cited in ABC analysis is that 20% of the items handled will contribute 80% of the annual sales dollars, because of its general application to wholesale distribution activities. However, when the ABC analysis is applied to retail institutions, we find the same 20% of the items would be contributing less, or about 60% of the overall dollar sales. And on the other end, in the industrial situation (and especially the rapidly changing industry using large percentages of common items), the same 20% would be controlling from 85% to as much as 99% of the annual sales dollars. The ABC relationship is not restricted to dollar sales alone. It can be applied to any activity. (Later in this chapter, it is applied to quantity sales and annual bin trips.)

Preparing an ABC Analysis

The ABC analysis provides a simple method for controlling inventory investment. Computer assistance should be obtained in preparing an ABC analysis, if large numbers of items are handled, as many calculations will be required. However, the ABC analysis can be done manually, and should not be overlooked because of the manual effort involved. Manual steps for creating an ABC analysis are as follows:

1. Obtain annual sales quantity and unit cost data for all inventory items.
2. Calculate and record annual sales dollars for each item. It is recommended that separate 3" x 5" cards be used for each item. Each card should have item number, annual units used or sold, unit cost, and the extended annual unit cost recorded. (Exhibit 3-1 illustrates how a 3" x 5" card may be used.)
3. Arrange the 3" x 5" cards in a descending dollar sequence of extended annual unit cost (F). The item bringing in the most dollar revenue would be on top, and the item bringing in the least dollar revenue at the bottom.
4. Assign an item count (B) to each 3" x 5" card after all cards have been placed in correct descending dollar sequence. The top card would be marked item 1, the next card item 2, etc. If 1500 items were making up the ABC analysis, the bottom card would be marked item 1500.
5. Compute the "% of Items" (C) for each item. This is obtained by dividing each card's item number by the total items in the ABC analysis—the item number on the bottom card.
6. Accumulate the extended annual unit costs. Add the extended annual unit cost from item card one to that of item card two and record in an assigned place on item card two (G). Add the newly accumulated extended annual unit cost of item card two to the extended annual unit cost of item card three, etc., with each card's accumulated extended annual unit cost added to and recorded on the next item card, until the last item card has been accumulated. The accumulated annual cost recorded on the last item card (or bottom) should match the company's total cost of sales for the annual period studied.
7. Compute the "% of $ Sales" (H) for each item. This may be accomplished when the extended annual unit costs are accumulated, or as a separate manual operation. "% of $ Sales" is computed by dividing the accumulated extended annual unit cost (G) of each card by the accumulated extended annual unit cost "total" recorded on the last (or bottom) item card.
8. The information recorded on each item card may now be placed together, in proper sequence, on a typed listing—for management analysis, if desired.

```
        A629 404 - (A)

                 1 - (B)              .07% - (C)

           12,067 - (D)           $16.359 - (E)

         $197,404 - (F)      $ 197,404.000 - (G)

                                    1.70% - (H)
```

EXHIBIT 3-1:   **Preparing a Manual ABC Analysis on Annual Dollar Sales by Using 3" x 5" Cards**

Codes given above are assigned the following descriptions:
  A—Item (or Part) Number or Description
  B—Card Item Number
  C—"% Item Count"
  D—Annual Sales Units
  E—Unit Cost
  F—Annual Sales Dollars
  G—Accumulated Sales Dollars
  H—"% $ Sales"

The Distribution by Value Listing

The basic format of a distribution by value listing is shown in Exhibit 3-2. In this exhibit, the sample data shown illustrates an industrial firm with annual cost of sales of $11,601,431 and 41,930 items in inventory. Notice that 534 items account for 50% of the firm's revenue. Although fictitious, this dollar sales distribution is valid for industrial firms in general. This type of sequential listing vividly illustrates the ABC principle that a few items will generate most of the dollar sales revenue. An analysis of this listing will help determine where to place the ABC identification points for controlling the inventory investment. The selection of A, B, and C items is mostly subjective, but should be dependent upon whether different types of control are planned for each group, and what resources (such as control system, people, computer assistance, etc.) are available for controlling inventory activities.

PART NUMBER	PARTS COUNT	% PARTS	ANNUAL UNITS	$ COST (UNIT)	ANNUAL $ SALES	CUMULATIVE $ SALES	% $ SALES
A629 404	1		12067	16.359	197,404	197,404	1.70
C595 501	5	.01	2060	24.799	51,086	568,908	4.90
C589 532	18	.04	109	364.040	39,680	1,148,791	9.90
B502 600	25	.06	188	174.718	32,847	1,397,394	12.04
C626 189	41	.10	125	207.232	25,904	1,855,447	15.99
A734 038	50	.12	9	2560.111	23,041	2,075,895	17.89
C175 400	62	.15	302	60.841	18,374	2,313,793	19.94
C294 510	100	.24	859	16.343	14,039	2,916,125	25.13
D639 171	200	.48	47	182.979	8,600	3,997,545	34.46
C161 009	288	.69	12	524.417	6,293	4,636,474	39.96
C128 301	534	1.27	149	24.349	3,628	5,802,177	50.01
E085 036	937	2.23	57	40.982	2,336	6,961,561	60.00
F055 533	1588	3.79	8	169.375	1,355	8,121,798	70.00
F142 601	2092	4.99	151	6.483	979	8,701,934	75.00
G158 231	2800	6.68	3	228.334	685	9,282,183	80.00
F168 643	3168	7.56	33	17.576	580	9,513,915	82.00
D299 776	3608	8.60	2	242.000	484	9,746,143	84.00
K180 985	4139	9.87	1	397.000	397	9,978,016	86.00
J185 777	4797	11.44	1	315.000	315	10,210,348	88.00
H634 146	5632	13.43	2	122.500	245	10,442,339	90.00
S412 334	6138	14.64	4	53.250	213	10,558,242	91.00
H177 866	6730	16.05	1	182.000	182	10,674,331	92.00
B724 883	7428	17.72	26	5.885	153	10,790,367	93.00
A441 999	8262	19.70	463	.272	126	10,906,446	94.00
A348 287	9298	22.18	4	25.000	100	11,022,407	95.00
C999 888	10805	25.29	8	9.625	77	11,137,050	96.00
V143 994	12390	29.55	5	11.000	55	11,253,385	97.00
P282 768	14994	35.76	2	18.000	36	11,369,423	98.00
W228 962	19530	46.58	7	2.571	18	11,485,422	99.00
A334 670	38135	90.95	9	.111	1	11,601,431	100.00
T555 555	41930	100.00	0	13.000	0	11,601,431	100.00

EXHIBIT 3-2. Distribution by Annual Dollar Sales for ABC Analysis

Significant items can be plotted (from the distribution by value listing) as a simple curve, to show the visual curve representation, and to help determine where the A, B, and C identifying points should be. Although most individuals use arbitrary selections, some use the points where the center curve changes its path. Exhibit 3-3 shows the distribution by value curve. (Note the arrows where the curve apparently changes.) Percentage points were selected from data presented in Exhibit 3-2 and plotted here. Selecting ABC classification by change in direction of curve is one way. Mostly, an arbitrary selection is made on "gut feel."

Using the Distribution by Value Listing

The primary use of the distribution by value listing is to determine the best fit for Class A, B and C items. Once determined, inventory planning and order strategy development can be accomplished. An analysis of the distribution listing, and its visual curve, helped in the following selection:

Inventory Classification	Number of Items Selected	$ Revenue of Items	Inventory Control Method Selected
A	1,588	$ 8,121,798	Order Point Forecast/EOQ with tight scheduling (preferably on a demand period basis).
B	7,710	$ 2,900,609	Order Point Forecast with EOQ or a fixed time supply.
C	32,632	$ 579,024	Order Point Forecast/Fixed Point Order Quantity (usually a year's supply).

Setting Priorities. The ABC analysis allows priorities to be established for control of replenishment ordering, with top control on A items and less control on B and C items. *Class A* items should be under constant review. These items are the inventory "bread and butter" items, and require strict supervision control. Monthly (or demand period) schedule quantities should be planned as multi-shipments against a single order,

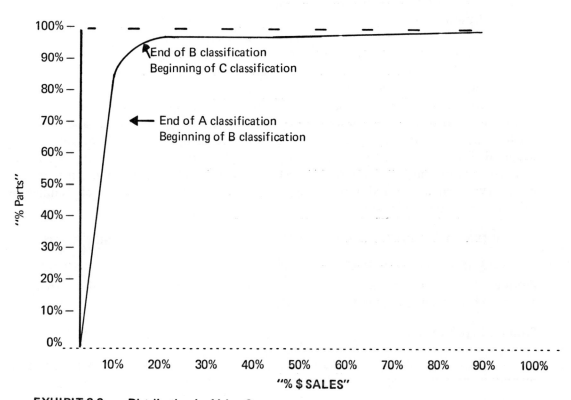

EXHIBIT 3-3.   Distribution by Value Curve

in place of larger EOQ (Economical Order Quantity) quantities. *Class B* items should be given normal periodic review based on order point forecasts, but perhaps ordered on a quarterly basis in place of EOQ. Order quantities could be released automatically on B items, by computer, if such a resource were available. Normal order control should be exercised on B items. *Class C* items are not critical in nature—from an investment viewpoint—so an arbitrary fixed time supply (i.e., a year's supply) order quantity could be permitted. This releases the C item's normal review time requirements for other ordering uses, and allows a good "buffer" stock on such parts. Since these C parts flucuate greatly in demand due to their low quantity sales, the chance for stock-out is lessened by ordering a year's supply at a time. A two-bin system is established by some companies to save additional time on C items, by not updating transactions. The order point quantity is physically separated in some manner to alert another "buy" requirement, when the physical order point quantity is first broken into. This permits a physical order point to be used in place of a record card's order point quantity. (Actually, a traveling requisition card should be placed with the items in stock and used to keep some type of statistical control for ordering purposes, where a two-bin system is used. Low control "emphasis" on C items should not imply "no control.")

Cases in point: A large multi-divisional manufacturer of electrical products and equipment uses the "ABC" method for classifying inventories—to control investment, storage assignment *and* obsolescence. Four inventory classifications are normally assigned, but more than four are used, depending on the manufacturing division involved. Item activity is used for investment control. Product classification and physical parts characteristics are used to control assignments of storage locations. Obsolescence is controlled by frequent appraisals, made in the form of perpetual *and* annual physical inventories, periodic sales verification and cycle time analysis. Adoption of the inventory classification and appraisal technique has increased inventory turnover from 30% to as high as 100%, varying according to the division being controlled. Obsolescence expenses have been reduced; and a 30% improvement in customer service performance was a typical result among all company divisions.

Another multi-divisional manufacturer (of temperature control systems) uses the "ABC" method to control investment and obsolescence only. Item value and usage are "ABC" variables. More than four classifications are assigned. Immediate savings also occurred for this company in the form of higher turnover of inventories, lower obsolescence expense and improved customer service—after implementation of the inventory classification and appraisal technique. System benefits were very similar to those given for the other company.

FINDING THE RIGHT ABC'S TO CONTROL STORAGE LOCATION ASSIGNMENTS

Several inventory classification methods are used for assigning storage locations. Product classification, numerical sequence, physical characteristics and sales activity all contribute their part as the most commonly used methods.

Product Classification

Product classification consists of more than one method itself. *Vendor product separation* of parts allows easy reference to general storage area location and affords a means to review (in the case of a manual system) all of a single vendor's items, visually, at one time. This aids in insuring "car load" discounts—or at least a method to meet minimum vendor order requirements when doing replenishment ordering.

Separation by *product function* is a method of storage location assignment by item function. Competitive "brand name" products can be found stocked together in full-line stores offering multi-brands. Examples would be on most items such as toothpaste, flashbulbs, clock-radios, etc. Where multi-brands are not carried in inventory, this method can still be used where product improvement creates the need for serialized components that otherwise perform the same function. Automotive parts and accessories like carburetors, air filters and fuel pumps are examples of product function separation on a single brand name. (This method can also be used as a sophistication of the vendor product storage method.)

Numerical Sequence

One of the most commonly used methods among smaller "parts" inventories is to assign inventory locations by numerical sequence. Each company has a standard "sort" sequence for preparing a merchandise catalog or price list. This "sort" method is used in the storage area as the assigned storage location. The master price listing becomes the location assignment guide. This provides a simple method for locating and finding a given item in stock without having to look up a storage location for it. You need only to memorize the "sort" sequence. For large inventories, this can become inefficient, as unused space must be left to allow expansion for those items not presently in stock. Adding items to the inventory, which fall in a specific part number group, can create a congested condition which necessitates moving many other items in order to make room within sequence. Storage equipment, to remain compatible in nature, can create a double location system because of size of items being stocked. Those items not able to fit physically into the storage bin in sequence, must be relocated into larger storage racks. Usually this means in another area of the storage facility, as butting different size racks together would disorient the aisle space and produce other inefficient conditions. Since hindsight is often better than foresight, there might possibly be three or four such areas of numerical sequence within a single storage facility. Using this method, new personnel, not knowing the numerical "sort" sequence as well as they should, can mislocate parts. When this happens, it's difficult to find such parts unless a physical inventory is taken of all parts. But—many parts men swear by their lives on this system of location control, even with all its faults. This system should, however, be restricted to non-retail establishments.

Physical Characteristics

The one factor that breeds more concern (and headaches) in storage assignments than anything else, is the physical characteristics of a part. The physical characteristics are many, and include:

- size, shape or color of items.
- weight or peculiar handling needs.
- damageability factors.
- inflammable nature.
- pilferage rating.
- shelf-life conditions.
- refrigeration needs.

The *sizes, shapes, or colors* of items create the need for many different types of storage equipment, such as cantilever racks, sturdy racks, vertical storage bins, etc., which in turn dictates special layout attention within the storage area. The *weight or peculiar handling needs* of certain parts might cause different receiving procedures to be followed. Such parts might be stored close to the shipping area to prevent unnecessary handling through the storage area during order processing. Because of this, the receiving of such parts might be through the shipping area. *Damageability factors* might dictate special pre-packaging prior to an item's stocking. Special storage equipment might be required to house such items (i.e., long, wide, flat aluminum skin material, cut to size, will "can" easily. Normal bins will not permit stocking. Special storage equipment is needed for these items). The *inflammable nature* of an item is important due to safety reasons. Separate, fire-proof areas are generally required for these types of items. Paints, thinners, acids, etc., are restricted from normal inventory stocking due to existing health and safety laws regarding special storage consideration. The *pilferage rating* of an item, if high, will cause an item to be stored in a lockable area. Such an area would be centrally located, in storage, for all items which might be theft prone. *Shelf-life conditions* urge special packaging and special storage equipment which will permit stock rotation so that the "first in-first out" technique can be applied. Easy location of such parts is mandatory, so that periodic stock checks can be made to determine if items are still salable or must be purged from inventory. *Refrigeration needs* present a unique situtation. A cold storage area must be made available for such inventory items which represent a special shelf-like item condition.

To use the physical characteristics of an item, in storage location, all affected items must be distinguishable by some form of assigned code. The code should condition the inventory strategies relating only to receipts processing and storage assignment of these items. The code should be kept simple in definition, but must be designed so that a priority system can be enforced (i.e., what happens when an item is both an awkward part and one which requires special equipment; or is a pilferage item that requires refrigeration; or is a shelf-life item that is inflammable?) A simple way of coding such items is to define the placement of such parts in a storage facility, and assign a code that represents a general area within the storage facility.

Sales Activity

The most commonly used method in location assignment is item sales activity. The greatest emphasis (in the inventory storage areas) is placed on order processing: picking orders, getting them to the shipping area, and quickly out the back door. Advocates of physical inventory layout and planning would have all items located closest to the shipping area. Large, heavy, awkward parts should be close to shipping. Parts easily damaged should be located close to shipping. And faster moving parts should be located close to shipping. But everything can't be located next to shipping, unless the volume of inventory items is small and the inventory investment is nil. So there must be trade-offs. Other concepts must be employed to overcome this situation. The use of electric picking carts, or automated item picking through the use of high rise equipment, has caused an increase in the density of item quantity within a given area of storage. The increase in density is in faster moving parts within restricted picking levels. Slower moving parts are removed into an area away from main aisles to prevent congested traffic. Consideration is given to a common efficient item flow from

PART NUMBER	PARTS COUNT	% PARTS	ANNUAL UNITS	CUMULATIVE UNIT SALES	% UNIT SALES
S11 882	1		218,446	218,446	4.21
AII 666	5	.01	68,432	541,108	10.43
S861 20	10	.02	39,544	801,855	15.46
M23 156	18	.04	30,243	1,078,514	20.79
A16 567	25	.06	26,400	1,273,068	24.54
S99 511	50	.11	15,668	1,767,843	34.08
*A629 404	70	.16	12,067	2,034,432	39.22
D500 445	140	.33	5,745	2,596,640	50.06
N308 630	267	.63	2,919	3,114,776	60.05
*C595 501	370	.88	2,060	3,367,541	64.92
A731 057	527	1.25	1,334	3,631,310	70.01
*C294 510	788	1.87	859	3,910,103	75.38
A510 905	1,149	2.74	528	4,149,465	80.00
*A441 999	1,267	3.02	463	4,207,843	81.12
S020 064	1,371	3.26	415	4,253,126	82.00
S626 316	1,655	3.94	321	4,356,969	84.00
C401 010	2,021	4.81	251	4,460,986	86.00
I591 591	2,489	5.93	200	4,564,700	88.00
J812 325	3,108	7.41	141	4,668,400	90.00
J600 832	3,513	8.37	117	4,720,264	91.00
K610 012	4,003	9.54	98	4,772,105	92.00
S042 080	4,598	10.97	78	4,823,998	93.00
L348 917	5,360	12.78	59	4,875,920	94.00
L051 910	6,373	15.20	44	4,927,774	95.00
S136 112	7,767	18.52	31	4,979,632	96.00
L031 318	9,807	23.39	21	5,031,516	97.00
N445 770	13,003	31.01	12	5,082,872	98.00
M231 024	19,075	45.49	6	5,134,734	99.00
M110 202	41,929	100.00	1	5,186,599	100.00
*T555 555	41,930	100.00	0	5,186,599	100.00

EXHIBIT 3-4:   **Distribution by Annual Quantity Sales for ABC Analysis**

all areas into the shipping area. Picking in the high density "fast moving" inventory area allows more picking to be accomplished by fewer people. The key to this concept is in item location by sales activity.

Distribution by Quantity Sales. We look at the ABC analysis again. This time, the descending sequence is by quantity sales for the last 12 months. Exhibit 3-4 shows the format of the distribution listing. (Asterisked items also appear on the sample distribution by value listing in Exhibit 3-2.) Sample data shown in Exhibit 3-4 illustrates the quantity sales associated with the distribution by annual dollar sales in Exhibit 3-2. This type of information can be used in assigning general storage locations. Notice that 140 items account for 50% of total quantity sales. The steps involved in preparing the distribution by quantity sales listing are essentially the same as for the dollar sales listing, except less data is required. Dollar extensions are not necessary. Annual unit sales (or uses) are accumulated on each 3" x 5" card instead of extended sales dollars. A sample card is shown in Exhibit 3-5.

S11 882   —(A)

1   —(B)   .002% —(C)

218,446   —(D)   218,446   —(E)

4.21% —(F)

EXHIBIT 3-5:   Preparing a Manual ABC Analysis on Annual Quantity Sales by Using 3" x 5" Cards.

Codes given above are assigned the following descriptions:

A—Item (or Part) Number or Description
B—Card Item Number
C—"% Item Count"
D—Annual Sales Units
E—Cumulative Sales Quantity
F—"% Quantity Sales"

The distribution by quantity sales listing presents a good method for deciding when, where and how to assign storage locations. However, a trade-off would occur in the movement of the slower moving items. When set sales rates are no longer met, such items should be removed from the high density picking area and relocated in storage. This rearrangement can be expensive if done frequently, but will pay off in the long run through more efficient picking of the faster moving items. An analysis of the distribution by quantity sales listing helped in the following selection:

Inventory Classification	Number of Items Selected	Quantity Sales Rate	Storage Assignment Area
A	1,149	4,149,465	High Density Area (Close to shipping)
B	5,224	778,309	General Storage (Shipping fringe)
C	35,557	258,825	Remaining Special and Outlying Storage —as applicable

A curve was not graphed on the distribution by quantity sales data, as capacity is the overruling factor. Unless new storage areas are to be assigned, the capacity of the current storage areas will decide the number of items to be located within a given area. The analysis resulted in the selection of only three areas. However, as few as two or as many areas as desired can be assigned, wherever a logical (or capacity) break is found in the listing.

Deciding Sales Activity by Bin Trips. Another, more beneficial, method of determining sales activity is by number of trips made to each storage location for a given item. This is quite difficult to arrive at with good accuracy, without the resourcefulness of the computer, but can be obtained in a manual method. The major failing of the distribution by quantity sales listing is that it doesn't accurately depict the picking trips made. A given item may sell a quantity of 2,000,000 per year. However, if this item is a common hardware item, it is possible that only ten orders were processed for this part in the last year. This item is, in reality, a slow moving item.

Companies using computers generally have historical data on the number of line items processed during a year's period of time (or more). This data would include the company's packing sheet numbers assigned to each shipment. The number of different packing sheets assigned for the same item (or part) number will, therefore, accurately describe the number of trips made to an item's location for picking purposes. A descending sequence by total number of bin trips, for all items in the inventory, will provide another ABC "type" analysis exercise.

Manual Preparation of Distribution by Bin Trips. An ABC "type" analysis can be developed for bin trips, manually, if inventory record cards are being used. If storage space is not a restriction, the complete ABC analysis can be calculated. Otherwise, a shortcut approach can be taken where we forget the "% Item Count," the "Accumulated Bin Trips" and the "% of Bin Trips." This leaves each item's "number of bin trips per year" as the guiding information. A descending sequence by this "number" will still give you the most frequently picked items at the front of the list, and the slower picked items at the back of the list. Where duplicate picking frequency exists on several items, the item's "characteristics" can determine placement within a given bin storage location. (See Exhibit 3-6.)

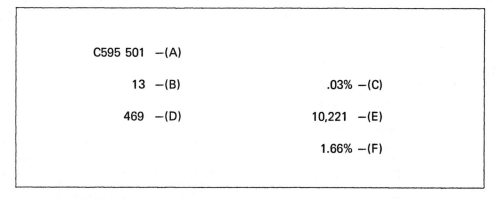

EXHIBIT 3-6. Preparing a Manual ABC Analysis on Annual Bin Trips by Using 3"x 5" Cards.

Codes given above are assigned the following descriptions:

    A—Item (or Part) Number or description
    B—Card Item Number
    C—"% Item Count"
    D—Annual Bin Trips
    E—Cumulative Bin Trips
    F—"% of Total Bin Trips"

When using the shortcut approach, everything except (A) and (D) can be omitted.

The number of bin trips is obtained by counting each separate customer order entry made on the inventory record cards. Depending on the sales activity of a given company, the ABC analysis can be overlooked on those items having less than a desired number of annual bin trips (i.e., less than six trips a year would not be considered in the analysis). This would reduce the amount of time required to prepare such a distribution listing, and would still show the most significant items. The main purpose of this listing is to show those items which are being picked most often, so that they may be located within an area which allows quick picking access and order flow to shipping. Exhibit 3-7 shows an annual distribution by bin trips listing. Sample data shown here illustrates the annual bin trips made in relation to the distribution by quantity sales listing shown in Exhibit 3-4. This type of information is more useful in assigning general storage locations than just quantity sales. Note the bin trips assigned to those two items having quantity sales of 30,243 and 251 (bin trips of 82 and 81 respectively).

PART NUMBER	COUNT	% PARTS	ANNUAL UNITS	ANNUAL BIN TRIPS	CUMULATIVE BIN TRIPS	% OF TOTAL BIN TRIPS
C595 501	13	.03	2060	469	10,221	1.66
S99 511	21	.05	15668	417	13,742	2.23
S11 882	63	.15	218446	289	29,198	4.74
C294 510	147	.35	859	212	50,669	8.22
D500 445	151	.36	5745	210	51,513	8.35
A11 666	296	.71	68432	157	77,995	12.65
A731 057	327	.78	1334	150	82,727	13.42
S861 20	527	1.26	39544	119	109,382	17.74
M23 156	1037	2.47	30243	82	150,426	24.40
C401 010	1055	2.52	251	81	151,900	24.64
J600 832	1284	3.06	117	72	169,763	27.53
K610 012	1310	3.12	98	71	171,555	27.82
N308 630	1525	3.64	2919	63	186,520	30.25
S626 316	1668	3.98	321	59	201,409	32.66
A16 567	1983	4.73	26400	52	213,721	34.66
A441 999	2057	4.91	463	51	217,538	35.28
I591 591	2109	5.03	200	50	220,279	35.72
S042 080	2251	5.37	78	47	227,721	36.93
L348 917	2620	6.25	59	42	258,773	41.97
J812 325	2904	6.93	141	38	265,383	43.04
S136 112	5159	12.30	31	21	328,752	53.32
L031 318	5238	12.49	21	21	330,507	53.60
A510 905	5325	12.70	528	20	332,289	53.89
L051 910	8574	20.45	44	12	402,837	65.33
M231 024	22772	54.31	6	6	488,123	79.16
M110 202	41929	100.00	1	1	616,592	100.00
T555 555	41930	100.00	0	0	616,592	100.00

EXHIBIT 3-7.   Distribution by Annual Bin Trips for ABC Analysis.

ADDING THE ABC'S FOR INVENTORY OBSOLESCENCE CONTROL

Constant review of the inventory investment is necessary to measure individual item movement taking place. When an item's movement slows, or stops, action is immediately required to prevent total loss of investment on this potentially dead inventory. A classification system on sales activity (based on an ABC analysis explained earlier) can be modified to convert to a movement code, to identify activity potential of each inventory item.

Development of Movement Code

Two factors are considered in the development of the movement code. The first factor is the ABC points selected from the distribution by quantity sales. The second is arbitrary points selected from the distribution by bin trips. These two factors illustrate what is being ordered most often, and what is being sold in the greatest quantities. Designing a code matrix on these two factors will enhance movement control over the entire inventory investment and generate a good basis for obsolescence control. The movement code is more suited for computer use. A frequent (quarterly) computer update can signal movement trends and reassign the movement code. A quick glance at a physical record card can usually give a good indication of *its* obsolescence factors, if it has been properly maintained. In Exhibit 3-8, the customer order frequency (or number of packing sheets) and the annual sales frequency (or quantity sales) were arbitrarily chosen factors for this matrix. These factors will vary greatly by type of industry and products measured.

CUSTOMER ORDER FREQUENCY	ANNUAL SALES FREQUENCY	CODING ASSIGNED	ACTION
100 – UP	528 – UP	A	None, except for surplus stock measurement.
44 – 99 (and) 1–43	44 – 527 1 – 43	B C	None, if an upward movement is indicated, except for surplus stock measurement. If, however, a downward movement is indicated, individual appraisal is made, with inventory "buy" action temporarily stopped. Surplus stock is measured and item disposition is planned.
0 – 0	0 – 0	D	Inventory planning is stopped. Disposition of stock is planned. Final disposition is based upon elasped time that code D has been assigned.

EXHIBIT 3-8. A Movement Code Matrix

Miscellaneous Code Use

It should be noted that the movement code could also be used for development of recommended inventory requirement listings for various distribution levels. The Class A items can be assigned as required stock for retail outlets. Class B (and A) items can be assigned as required stock for wholesalers. If the Class B items were too much for the wholesalers, an ABC analysis of just the Class A items can be made with recommended stock requirements split from this, etc.

4

Goal Keeping: The Key to a Results-Oriented Work Environment

Various inventory management goals are used to maximize productivity, customer service and profits. The four most essential goals are defined and analyzed in this chapter, with criterion furnished for their development and implementation. Illustrated methods are included for "goal measurement," and for measuring the effectiveness of the work environment. Operating results will be improved if these goals are used; and inventory management will additionally benefit from a more knowledgeable participation on the part of their employees.

SETTING GOALS IN INVENTORY MANAGEMENT

Operating limits, or guidelines, are an inventory management necessity. These limits can be placed low for inventory investment, or high as in a customer service level. But such limits are necessary, primarily in a results-oriented environment, to monitor the direction a company is headed in—and in making decisions on how the company is going to get where it wants to be. The four most essential goals in inventory management are customer service, average dollar investment, net sales and profits.

Customer Service

A goal should be developed for a satisfactory customer service level to keep and increase business without losing profits. This goal can be developed as a percentage goal. When unsolicited customer "noise" is accompanied by a decreasing drop in business, the service level percentage is normally too low. When unsolicited customer "noise" stops, the service level percentage is often too high. Results of both could indicate an unwarranted loss of profits.

Three Measurements of Customer Service. A three-dimensional view of the customer service goal is developed through the use of:

(1) percent of fill,
(2) elapsed out-the-door time, and
(3) solicited customer attitudes and suggestions.

53

"Percent of fill" measures inventory availability of items wanted. "Elapsed out-the-door time" measures reaction speed. Customer noise is measured by "solicited customer attitudes and suggestions."

Fill Rate: a Measure of Product Availability. The first measurement of customer service should be product availability. This is generally referred to as "fill rate," or "percent of fill" measurement. This relates to the number (or percent) of items (or dollars) ordered by a customer which can be shipped (or sold) at the time of request.

A small retailer of farm equipment and trucks uses "fill rate" to measure customer service on "after-market" repair parts, as a means to calculate lost sales. Customer suggestions are solicited with customer attitudes carefully measured to restrict or control these lost sales. Another company, a medium-sized wholesaler (of industrial supplies, heavy hardware and steel), uses "fill rate" to measure customer service, and applies judgment from this measurement to inventory-ordering decisions on product lines, based on the "fill rate" findings.

Methods for Determining "Fill Rate." Information requirements to provide this measurement include the total number of items sold, the total quantity for all items sold, the total number of items that can be shipped (or delivered), the total quantity for all items that can be shipped (or delivered), the total dollars sold and total back order dollars—for a specific reporting period. Several methods can be used in figuring the fill rate of customer service:

1. *Item fill rate* is calculated by dividing those items, with quantities shipped complete, by the total items sold—for those orders processed in a specified time period.
2. *Quantity fill rate* is determined by dividing total quantities shipped by the total quantities sold—for those orders processed in a specified time period.
3. *Dollar fill rate* is obtained when the total dollar value of items shipped is divided by the total dollar value sold—for all orders processed in a specified time period.
4. *Item-quantity fill rate,* a combined method, can be accomplished where items are the primary consideration and a percentage is added for the partial quantities filled.

FILL RATE METHOD USED:	TOTAL ITEMS ORDERED	TOTAL QUANTITY ORDERED	TOTAL DOLLARS ORDERED	ITEMS SHIPPED COMPLETE	ITEMS SHIPPED PARTIAL	QUANTITY SHIPPED COMPLETE	QUANTITY SHIPPED PARTIAL	TOTAL DOLLARS SHIPPED	FILL RATE % CALCULATED
ITEM	1500	– – – –	– – – –	1380	– – – –	– – – –	– – – –	– – – –	92.0%
QUANTITY	– – – –	75,000	– – – –	– – – –	– – – –	72,250	1,250	– – – –	98.0%
DOLLAR	– – – –	– – – –	$73,685	– – – –	– – – –	– – – –	– – – –	$66,317	90.0%
ITEM/QUANTITY	1500	75,000	– – – –	1380	50	72,250	1,250	– – – –	94.8%

EXHIBIT 4-1.   Fill Rate Methods

Exhibit 4-1 illustrates the calculations involved in obtaining "fill rate." In this example, item fill rate is calculated by dividing *items shipped complete* by *total items ordered* (92.0%). Quantity fill rate is calculated by adding *quantity shipped complete* and *quantity shipped partial* together, and then dividing by *total quantity ordered* (98.0%). Dollar fill rate is calculated by dividing *total dollars shipped* by *total dollars ordered* (90.0%). The item/quantity fill rate method is normally used with computer "power" as it is a more complex method. However, it is more accurate as it considers total effort. To calculate:

    a. Calculate the reciprocal of item fill. (100.0% less 92.0%)–*8.0%*.

    b. Calculate total quantity unshipped. (75,000 less 72,250 less 1,250)–*1,500*.

    c. Calculate total items unshipped. (1,500 less 1,380)–*120*.

    d. Multiply the total quantity unshipped (1500) times the total items unshipped (120)–*180,000*.

    e. Multiply *quantity shipped partial* (1250) times *items shipped partial* (50)–*62,500*.

    f. Divide the product of "e" (62,500) by the product of "d" (180,000)–*34.7%*.

    g. Multiply the reciprocal of item fill (8.0%) times the result of "f" (34.7%)–*2.8%*.

    h. Add the product of "g" (2.8%) to item fill rate (92.0%) for item/quantity fill rate–*94.8%*.

    Selecting "Fill Rate." The method used for determining customer service fill rate is not as important as the fact that this measurement is being used. However, consistency is important in preparing statistics to show the true trend pictures of (improved or worsened) service.

    There is no fixed fill rate that will satisfy all industries. The most useful guide, therefore, is the customer noise generated. A certain amount of customer noise will always be present—but when the intensity reaches "too loud a level" (too many phone calls, too many letters, too many fires to put out), the fill rate percent in existence is most likely inadequate. Record it as a minimum fill rate, and take steps to improve the service. When customer noise starts fading away, without a commensurate drop in revenue, record the level closest to a tolerable noise as the maximum fill rate percent. (Raise your rate above this maximum percent as much as possible, without decreasing profits beyond corporate limits, and you can pick up a competitive edge.)

    Place the upper and lower noise limit percents as vertical lines on a fill rate graph. The actual fill rate should be kept somewhere between these two lines, and should not exceed either. The higher limit would obviously please customers more, but the lowest rate possible, without losing to competition, is where the rate should be.

    A manufacturer in the copying, duplicating and facsimile "field" measures the percent of fill *in addition* to soliciting customer suggestions. Field inventories are measured by line items only, while manufacturing inventories are measured by an item-quantity combination. Future dollar sales, profits and cash flow requirements are forecast, and inventory turnover is constantly monitored. The cash flow measurement is considered a most meaningful measurement to this company. During one year, these inventory measurements increased the customer service level for field spares (at the customer level) by 2%; the company's interplant delivery service level was increased by 5%; and a 10% drop in worldwide non-equipment inventory resulted.

    The graph in Exhibit 4-2 shows a bar chart representation of fill rate performance by month. The upper (97.0%) and lower (92.0%) "noise" limits are shown as horizontal lines on this graph to monitor fill rate performance. These horizontal lines provide a signal trip that lost sales are occurring (below 92%) or that inventory investment is too large (above 97%). These percentages vary within company and industry.

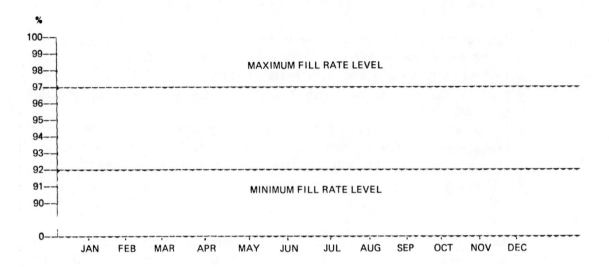

EXHIBIT 4-2:   Fill Rate Graph

Out-the-Door Time: a Meaure of Reaction Speed. Elapsed out-the-door time, as used here, includes the actual time from receipt of a customer's order (or customer selection of merchandise) to the point in time where shipment is made to the customer (or when the customer leaves with the merchandise purchased).

Convenience Important. Convenience must be considered a big part in out-the-door customer service. Leisure time is increasing today, yet there is growing impatience by the consumer towards long "check-out" times, or long delays in receiving mail-order merchandise. "Convenience" stores have sprouted up to permit extended buying hours on certain merchandise. Full-line stores are copying this concept. But the real answer is in giving the quickest possible processing of a consumer's purchase, not in offering a longer period of time in which the consumer has a choice to wait.

Nobody wants to wait to receive merchandise which has been purchased. Mail order houses reduce selling prices to help offset the customer's waiting time and to entice business. However, when this waiting time becomes unreasonable, customers go elsewhere to buy. Even a 100% fill rate on merchandise is not good, and future repeat sales will be lost, where the waiting time (out-the-door) is critical to the customer.

Time Is Critical. Time is a critical factor where each minute is costing dollars in lost revenue to a customer needing repair parts or supplies to continue business or perform a service. Time is also critical on seasonal items which are needed within the period for which they will be used. "Want" motivations will often create a critical time situation, too, where merchandise is required at point-of-sale or a sale is lost. Here again trade-offs do occur, so that temporary stock-outs are overlooked by the customer if the store has a good reputation for quick delivery performance on stock-out merchandise. Consumers don't mind waiting for brand name or quality merchandise if estimated delivery dates are reliable. (On made-to-order merchandise, the out-the-door time is measured by comparing actual delivery times to quoted delivery times.)

ORDER PROCESSING CONTROL SHEET
ELAPSED TIME "OUT-THE-DOOR"

_____

(DATE)

DAYS:	OCCURRENCES	
1–	~~卌~~ ~~卌~~ ~~卌~~ ~~卌~~ ~~卌~~ ~~卌~~ ‖	(32)
2–	‖‖	(3)
3–	‖‖	(3)
4–	‖‖‖	(4)
5–	‖‖	(3)
6-15–	‖‖	(3)
16-30–	‖	(2)
30-on–		—
TOTAL		(50)

EXHIBIT 4-3: **Control Sheet for Logging Out-the-Door Times on Customer Orders**

Recording Elapsed Time Out-the-Door. Measuring out-the-door elapsed time is simple, and the clerical time required for this purpose has a trade-off in the improved and more knowledgeable customer order control obtained. A copy of each sales ticket or packing sheet is reviewed after shipments are made, and an elapsed out-the-door time is logged on a simple control sheet. (Exhibit 4-3 shows how a clerk must look at each packing sheet or sales ticket, as shipments are made, to determine the number of days, or hours, the order has been in flow. A simple mark on the control sheet is sufficient to record each order movement.) The control sheet is formatted with several time categories to fit the particular business using it. For illustration purposes, we will use day increments of 1,2,3,4,5,6-15, 16-30 and 30-on days. Actual time segments will depend on how fine the measurement must be and what the operating goal is. (If a goal is set for 24-hour order shipments, then hours would replace days on the control paper.) At the end of each day, the various time periods should be totaled, and added to a daily reporting form for managing to review. (In Exhibit 4-4, daily totals are transferred to this report from the daily control sheet "log" for management information. Only the first two, and last, day(s) of the month are shown. Totals and percents are given for the complete month.

ORDER PROCESSING
ELAPSED TIME REPORT

MONTH & DAY	NUMBER OF DAYS TO OUT-THE-DOOR								TOTALS:
	1	2	3	4	5	6-15	16-30	30-on	
JAN 2	54	0	4	2	0	0	1	0	61
JAN 3	32	3	3	4	3	3	2	0	50
JAN 28	60	4	3	1	1	2	0	0	71
TOTAL	1210	86	72	14	15	29	14	0	1440
PERCENT	84%	90%	95%	96%	97%	99%	100%		

EXHIBIT 4-4:   **Elapsed Time Report**

It is important that the unit used for out-the-door times be identical to that used for fill rate measurement. (For example, if "items" were used for fill rate measurement, use "items" for measuring out-the-door performance also.) The % figures on the report are obtained by totaling each out-the-door time period for the month—and relating each as a "%" of the total—for all time categories together. An optional visual curve can be prepared by the "%" figures from the elapsed time report, each month, for quick management review. A goal line can be shown on the graph to permit easy reference to where "actual" should be. Exhibit 4-5 presents an easy visual guide to the monthly position of out-the-door times. A goal curve is permanently drawn on the graph to enable reference to be made of actual-to-target.

A System's Look at Elapsed Out-the-Door Time. The best performance in customer service should be in reaction speed—how soon shipments (or deliveries) are made—after receipt of a customer's order. From a system's point of view, the elapsed out-the-door time is a critical control item. A system review, with the customer in mind, can effect big improvements in customer service if seriously undertaken and carried out. A simple system review outline follows:

1. Separate elapsed out-the-door time into distinct elements, after customer service goals have been determined.

2. Keep records of all time elements. An order log should be set up if not now in use. The cash register tape or sales ticket normally provides this log for retail establishments. The order log in manufacturing and wholesale distribution serves additional purposes. It not only contains key information useful in measuring fill rate

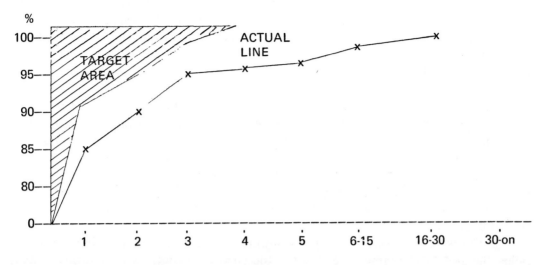

EXHIBIT 4-5: **Optional Elapsed Time Graph**

and elapsed out-the-door time, but it also usually contains all the essential information concerning a customer's order—and is usually organized to control the main elements in the total work flow. Such a record log contains:

    a. Time order was received.

    b. Customer's name or billing code.

    c. Customer's purchase order number.

    d. Method of shipment requested.

    e. Total number of items on order.

    f. Priority assigned to order.

    g. The time when packing sheets and/or pick tags were completed.

    h. The time when order picking was completed.

    i. Total items going on backorder status.

    j. The time when shipment was routed.

    k. The time when shipment left.

(The following optional items may be recorded in the log, but their use will largely depend on methods of measurement used:)

    l. Total item quantity on order.

    m. Total item quantity on backorder.

    n. Dollar value of order.

    o. Dollar value of shipment.

The record log should be arranged so total overall time can easily be determined.

3. Calculate the percent of total time each element is taking. The elements using the most time will afford better chances for time reduction results.

4. Rearrange each element into as efficient an operation as possible. Can any of the elements be shortened by allowing some of the work to be accomplished later (after order shipment) without jeopardizing control or overall costs? Correcting order errors prior to printing packing sheets can waste time. One manufacturing company decided to print the original customer order packing sheets with errors showing.

Inventory balance corrections and quantity updates were not made until it could be determined what merchandise was needed. Everything else available was shipped immediately. Errors were cancelled or later corrected before the next shipments were made. Up to 72 hours were reduced from elapsed out-the-door time on the items shippable. No additional work was involved. And orders were received in a more accurate condition after the system change was placed in effect.

Can aids be given to assist in faster flow times? In retail operations, increased use of the suggestion box concept is recommended. Boxes are located throughout the store, into which customers can drop paper slips suggesting items not found which they'd like to find stocked. Or an intercom system is used in place of these boxes. The intercom connects customers directly with customer relations office personnel to obtain immediate help. Promotional signs above the intercoms alert customers to use the intercom system. Records can be kept for a lost sales report resulting from use of the intercoms.

5. Check results. Has the elapsed out-the-door time decreased? Is more volume being handled in the same time flow? If the answer to these two questions is no, the system's review was not properly done. Additional people should be brought in for new ideas. Other businesses should be visited. In some cases, a talk with the company's vendors is valuable. Then—re-do the system's review.

The descriptive table in Exhibit 4-6 illustrates the similarities in the work flow elements between manufacturing, wholesale/distribution and retail establishments. The workflow elements for manufacturing and wholesale/distribution are company oriented, with primary consideration given for speed of merchandise flow "out." Determine the total allowable time for customer out-the-door order handling. Separate this time among the work flow elements. Establish individual time performance reporting. Adjust element times to meet out-the-door order handling objectives.

The work flow elements for retail establishments are customer oriented, with two primary considerations: speed and customer convenience. The customer must find merchandise in an easy and quick manner. Easy access to merchandise is necessary. Quick check-out, after merchandise selection, is the top convenience factor. Retail element times are set by the customer in finding and selecting merchandise. A shortened check-out procedure is therefore vital, and must be company controlled.

WORK FLOW ELEMENTS		
Manufacturing	Wholesale—Distribution	Retailing

1. Order processing
  a. Order taking
  b. Delivery quotation
  c. Material procurement
  d. Order scheduling/release
	1. Order processing
	  a. Order taking
	  b. Preparing packing sheets
	  c. Issuing pick tags
		1. Locating merchandise

2. Product manufacturing	2. Filling an order	2. Selecting merchandise
3. Inspection	3. Inspection	3. Check-out procedure
4. Packaging	4. Packaging	4. Packaging
5. Routing and shipping	5. Routing and shipping	5. Invoicing
6. Invoicing	6. Invoicing	

EXHIBIT 4-6:   Work Flow Elements

Solicit Customer Suggestions. Show concern! Solicit tips on how to improve customer service. Ask a customer questions that will require other than a yes/no response. Include short prestamped questionnaires, randomly, in sales packages or deliveries. But don't put the customer on the spot. If a restaurant waitress asked a selected group of customers why their tip was "so little" or "so large," she would receive obvious suggestions for improving or changing service. But the customers might be offended and not return. Some restaurants print an eye-catching request on the back of the meal ticket (which incidentally is laid face down on the top of the table in plain sight). The request? A simple: "Please tell us what you think of our service!" Ample space is given on the ticket to write down comments—and the customer isn't put on the spot. The comments received, regardless of how tips are solicited, will add up to another kind of statistics useful in measuring or directing customer service.

A northern manufacturer of paper and cellulose products measures customer service by only one method—by soliciting customer suggestions and monitoring the accompanying attitudes. A "Customer Service Index" is used which is based on stated service criteria. Customer service performance has increased from 10% to 15%—just by listening to the customer. This company also keeps a tight rein on profits. Inventory turn is monitored. Future sales, profits and cash flow requirements are all projected. These measurements are coordinated with customer service measurements, and resulted in a 20% reduction in inventory investment.

A manufacturer of film, cameras and photo supplies uses all three customer service measurements, and adds personal field visits. Fill rate is measured by an item-quantity combination *and* by dollars. Inventory turnover is controlled. Future sales dollars and cash flow estimates are made. "% of fill" is considered the most important measurement by this company, which through the years has maintained a continuously high standard of customer service for their industry.

Turnover: a Measure of Average Inventory Investment

Average inventory is greatly affected by the customer service goals established. A rise in service level for a properly controlled inventory will usually cause a rise in average inventory investment. Measuring average inventory investment by the turnover concept is a meaningful way of measuring inventory performance.

Setting the Turnover Goal. Average inventory is most often described as one-half of an established stock order quantity plus safety stock. The inventory portion referred to as "safety stock" is what provides (in theory) the service level potential. Since safety stock is a "plus" effect on average inventory, an "up" in service level will create a corresponding rise in safety stock, and in average inventory. This leaves "order quantity" as the only variable factor in increasing or decreasing average inventory—if the customer service level is kept constant. Therefore, you would expect the inventory turnover goal to be set at the ratio established when optimum replinishment inventory scheduling is in force. The inventory turnover goal, however, should be set at a higher (but respectable) rate than this, to offer the opportunity for creative responsibilities where they are needed—at the operating level. To achieve this higher turnover goal, a miraculous thing happens. A clean, fast moving "service" inventory comes into being.

Average Inventory Calculation. A simple method is used for calculating average inventory investment. Add each of the previous 12 months' ending inventory balances (for the preceding fiscal or operating year) to the inventory balance (at the beginning of the preceding year) and divide by 13. If the fiscal year is January 1 through December 31, average inventory would be figured as the following example shows:

Month	Cost of Ending Inventory	Cost of Gross Sales
December	$ 156,500	$ ────────
January	150,000	110,000
February	147,000	106,000
March	148,000	100,000
April	152,000	100,000
May	155,000	102,000
June	161,000	108,000
July	170,000	110,000
August	173,000	117,000
September	167,000	108,000
October	162,000	105,000
November	160,000	102,000
December	159,000	100,000
Totals:	$ 2,060,500	$ 1,268,000
Average Inventory	$ 158,500 ($2,060,500 divided by 13)	
Turnover:	8 times per year ($1,268,000 divided by $158,000)	

Estimating Average Inventory. If inventory figures are not kept on a monthly basis, but are obtained only at the end of each fiscal year by means of a physical inventory, average inventory should be manually calculated for each month to obtain a higher degree of accuracy in arriving at turnover. Each of the preceding fiscal year's month-ending inventory balances can be obtained as follows:

December ending inventory	:	$ 156,500
January estimated receipts cost	:	103,500
Inventory sub-total	:	$ 260,000
Less January estimated cost of sales:		110,000
Estimated January ending inventory:		$ 150,000

The above calculation is continued on to each succeeding month until estimated ending inventory balances are computed for all 13 months. These computed values may not be 100% accurate, as *some* amount of guessing may be required—due to actual figures not being recorded. However, the resulting inventory turnover ratio obtained will be more accurate and meaningful than one obtained by using an average of just the beginning and ending fiscal year inventory balances.

Using Turnover. The inventory turnover ratio is a good method for measuring inventory effectiveness. It also provides a means to project future storage and expense requirements in relation to anticipated sales growth. Simply reverse the measurement procedure! Divide the projected cost of sales for next year by the most recent actual turnover ratio, and the future inventory investment can be estimated. If the projected inventory level should create too great a demand projection on cash flow, steps can be taken (in advance) to lower the proposed total investment. These steps might include a move to standardize products, discontinue slow moving items, combine inventories, reduce the customer service level offered, etc.

The Need to Forecast Sales Activity

A sales forecast is necessary to permit measurement of actual sales activity. The forecast is an important variable in those management decisions such as facility expansion, introduction of new products, increasing current production volumes, changing customer service performance, increasing inventory investment, strengthening the company organization, etc. What would happen if sales dropped in half today? If sales doubled tomorrow? Reactions to such drastic changes in sales activity must be decisive, well thought out and made quickly to prevent unnecessary losses in profits, customers or business growth. These reactions can and should be planned ahead through adequate and accurate sales forecasting. The planning function is normally responsible for these forecasts.

The Three Sales Forecast Goals. A sales forecast should extend over a normal business growth cycle. It should provide budgetary support. It must remain subject to current changes so that it can be easily revised. It should reflect optimistic sales, but it must be realistic, and correctly show current and future sales trends.

A common approach to sales forecasting, by planning personnel, is to prepare three related sales forecasts to serve as goals: current, intermediate and long range—since it's obvious a single forecast can't accomplish all that is desired.

Long Range Sales Forecasting. The long range forecast will generally cover a period of three to ten years, but must be equal to the corporate long range planning period. This permits management decisions for future new programs to be proposed and time-phased completely (organization-development-implementation), in the same planning period. The newer forecast information supports these programs; verifies whether such programs should be continued, speeded up, slowed or discontinued—by showing anticipated changes in sales that weren't known previously, and in a timely manner so that overall losses will be minimal and profits will be maximum. Long range forecasts are to be revised each year. The first year (corresponding to the company's next fiscal year period) is normally shown in weeks or months; the second year in months or quarters; and the remaining years in annual amounts.

Intermediate Sales Forecasting. Intermediate sales data allows expense budgeting support for a company's fiscal year planning period. Operating plans are fixed, based on dollar projections from this forecast, and provide management a method by which to measure actual sales dollars.

Intermediate sales forecasting will generally cover a period of from three months to three years, to provide a link between, and lend credibility to, the long range and current sales planning. There should be a consistency between the overlapping projected dollars. Like long range planning, an intermediate forecast is made each year. The fiscal year is shown in weeks or months, with all other periods shown in months or quarters.

Current Sales Estimate. This forecast is the most time consuming, and the most demanding, as far as accuracy is concerned. Overall sales are forecasted on a 30-60-90 day basis, while a forecast is made on each individual inventory item to reaffirm or change the reorder points. Current sales estimates are prepared at the end of each demand period, and provide the actual dollar data to be used in measuring current sales activity. The overall 30-60-90 day projections act to improve the intuitive method for short range estimates, and increase insight in measuring a company's sales.

Measuring Sales Activity. Daily sales comparisons are made to the 30-day projection to discover any drastic changes in activity which might invalidate the current year's forecast. All sales forecasts should, therefore, share a common characteristic, i.e., they must all be figured in the same unit: net sales dollars, number of orders, items, pounds, etc. Although dollar sales are universally correlated to almost any business activity, sales analyses can be made on other units; i.e., a leading automobile manufacturer uses a daily forecast of "pounds" to select the number of men needed for peak or slack activity periods.

If the measurement on current sales activity shows an unexpected deviation in sales, reasons should be found immediately. If sales fall short of forecast and lag behind for a sustained period of time, the inventory investment and customer service performance should be investigated. A drop in "fill rate" or "out-the-door" performance could tell the story. If the change continues on a semi-permanent basis, then a new 30-60-90 day forecast should show this. Budget revisions will become necessary, and the intermediate sales forecast will need amending.

Measuring Profits

It has been said many times that the primary aim of any business is profit. Since a business could not last long without profits, the importance of profits cannot be ignored, and the measurement of profit should become paramount. Proper measurement should be made in three ways: the corporate profit goal, the inventory manager's goal, and actual. These should, of course, be at least the same. However, the corporate profit goal must be met; the inventory manager's profit goal must be obtainable; and, the actual must be explained if it falls below either of the other two.

The Corporate Profit Goal. The profit goal set by corporate is based on certain guidelines established for inventory management. These were mentioned earlier in this chapter as average inventory investment, inventory turn, the customer service level desired, and sales dollars. An acceptable gross margin, or contributed profit, must be allowed for in the setting of selling prices. However, over-investment, surplus inventory or bad customer service can reduce profits with as much effect as inadequate gross margin. The corporate profit goal should be met automatically if the guidelines are correctly established and followed, and forecasts are met.

The Inventory Manager's Profit Goal. The inventory manager has the ability to manipulate the established guidelines to obtain the ultimate profit. Quantity price break "buys" and optimum scheduling on purchases will reduce unit costs and provide better customer service, and will lower inventory costs if correctly accomplished. Increased service on faster selling items and lowered inventory support on slow movers can also increase profits. An inventory manager will normally set a profit goal which is higher than the corporate goal. He can experiment with new, and perhaps better, management techniques; he can still meet the corporate profit goal; and he stands a good chance to better it.

Reporting Actual Profit. Actual profits should be compared to the corporate profit goal, with a written report submitted on a weekly or monthly basis. This report should show the actual profit comparisons. Stock build-up for seasonal or promotional considerations or new product support should be identified. Any significant change in customer service should also be given and qualified.

Less-than-normal profits should bring about a change in one or more of the inventory management guidelines established by corporate, whereas surplus profits would permit strengthening these guidelines to add more inventory, decrease turn, increase customer serivce and/or permit write-off capability on slower moving stock. An overall appraisal of the profit picture should be a part of the report—with recommendations for guideline changes.

5

Inventory Planning Controls: The Sextant to Working Value and Investment

This chapter is premised on the primary planning functions. A program is outlined and supported for minimizing inventory investment dollars. Basic order strategies are analyzed for supporting customer demand. Demand patterns are described to permit a simple item forecast method to be used on most, if not all, independent demand items. Sales dollar forecasts are classified and discussed as long range, intermediate and current planning forecasts, with a linear regression forecast method (called the "least squares" technique) illustrated in detail for easy use. The "least squares" technique provides a simple but accurate forecast means to determine future sales.

Minimizing investment dollars can best be achieved through:

(a) Accumulative use of sales forecasting
(b) The development of order strategies
(c) Use of marketing research data
(d) Proper systems innovations
(e) Publishing policy and procedure information
(f) Constant *performance monitoring.*

MINIMIZING INVENTORY INVESTMENT DOLLARS

An inventory can be measured in many ways: inventory investment to current assets ratio, return on investment, investment turnover rate, item turn or others. However, the real key is in minimizing the inventory investment by continually measuring its working value. This is done by measuring for the absence of dead stock or slow moving merchandise. The working value is higher when the level of dead stock or slow moving merchandise is low, because excess non-moving merchandise restricts working capitol and prevents maximum customer service. Dead stock is unwanted merchandise, and therefore has no working value. It is this part of the inventory that must be reduced and controlled.

Identify Unwanted Merchandise

Classify the inventory to identify unwanted merchandise. A method of classification must be accepted which is consistent with corporate policy and which will lend itself to repeated use. The most popular inventory classification methods used are presented in Chapter 3. Select from one of these methods, or develop one. The method used should include characteristics such as total number of items stocked, annual sales dollars and/or quantities, pricing data and available inventory levels. Items showing a decreasing sales trend should be isolated and closely watched. Those meeting a suggested maximum period for no sales become immediate candidates for write-off and disposal.

Practice Write-off

A write-off program is simply planning ahead of time to get rid of something when it stops selling—to free invested capital for needed merchandise. Write-off reserve is often determined as a set percent of net sales. However, the reserve could be established as a percent of net operating profit. In either case, net profit should occur before write-off is approved or a net operating loss would be recognized. The size and value of unwanted inventory will determine how often a write-off is needed. If unwanted inventory does not exist, then the write-off reserve can be carried over to the next month, or time period used, or added back into net profit. Theft or inventory losses are considered a loss of profit—why not' ordering errors, obsolescence or unwanted merchandise?

Plan Orderly Removal

Unwanted merchandise should be removed from active inventory immediately after write-off assignment is made. This is necessary to make room for faster moving merchandise and will encourage more rapid disposal decisions. Most inventory personnel tend to become "string savers," which is not at all bad, but this thwarts write-off decisions and actually delays the disposition of write-off material. If write-off material is kept, a second inventory control system is started to keep track of the items. As long as sporadic sales continue to offset the cost of keeping the write-off material, it will never be disposed of. This will seriously hamper an on-purpose continuing program of write-off. It would be best to rethink the write-off decision criteria to select only dead stock for actual write-off—if the wrong material is being picked. Then, what is written off will be disposed of. Bad inventory decisions must be observed with disposition made on non-moving stock. Data should be accumulated on why bad decisions were made. Until scrap dollars accumulate, a concerted effort will probably never be made to determine why such bad decisions are being made.

Establish Preventive Controls

The classification system which identifies unwanted merchanise can be used to prevent such types of merchandise from getting into future inventory. Historical data will show what parts become unwanted. Scrap dollars will vividly illustrate how much. "Why" must be determined. Even if the only correlation found is age, if you discover the characteristics that identify unwanted merchandise, you have the criteria needed to establish preventive stocking guidelines.

Regular Inventory Appraisals

The time between write-offs is the minimum time period in which an inventory classification should be made. (Constant inventory review is recommended if time is available.) During inventory appraisal, determine if any significant changes in merchandise sales have occurred. Is the working value of the inventory higher or lower than the last appraisal? Figure working value by dividing the total inventory dollars less unwanted merchandise dollars by the total inventory dollars:

$$\text{Working Inventory (\%) Value} = \frac{\text{Total Inventory Dollars less Unwanted Inventory Dollars}}{\text{Total Inventory Dollars}}$$

This percentage should be plotted or recorded after each inventory appraisal, to gauge any trends in the working value of the inventory. A complete inventory appraisal is difficult where large inventory arrays are not supported by EDP equipment. Select a manageable group of items, by product classification, and periodically appraise them. When indications of significant dead stock build-up occur, plan for a complete appraisal.

DEVELOPING BASIC ORDER STRATEGIES

Inventory planning becomes increasingly difficult as the different kinds of order strategies used grow in number. Otherwise, you could have as many order strategies as you have different parts in inventory. The number of order strategies should be limited as much as possible without becoming inflexible. Ordinarily, at least three general types of order strategies are present in any finished goods inventory. These three are required for new merchandise, replenishment and warranty support ordering. This is because:

—new merchandise ordering is handled separately as historical sales data is not available;

—replenishment ordering is largely based on historical sales data:

— warranty support generally covers a known need and results in mostly "one-shot" buys to satisfy such demand.

New Merchandise Order Strategy

The decision to stock new merchandise is the governing reason for its order strategy. This decision is strictly subjective, if the merchandise has never been marketed before. Therefore, it is important to know the estimated market potential and expected consumer acceptance of the product in advance of buying. (This kind of marketing research data is usually available from the vendor, along with established or proposed advertising campaign support data or incentives. Consumer acceptance statistics are often prepared from the advance research work accomplished. Vendor reputation for honesty and reliability will aid in weighing the use of such information.)

The order strategy for buying new merchandise should permit an acceptable ROI (Return on Investment). Where vendor returns are authorized on first shipment orders of new products, a breakeven point on sales must be known to aid in determining the initial order quantity. The following variables will be needed for determining both ROI and the breakeven point:

A— Total "proposed" investment dollar value;

B— Average annual inventory maintenance expense—expressed as a percent (including charges for interest, handling, theft, damage, taxes, obsolescence, return of parts to vendor, etc.);

C— Number of days vendor will allow merchandise to be held prior to return, divided by 30 to be expressed in months (used for breakeven point only);

D— Unit selling price of new merchandise;

E— Unit cost of new merchandise;

F— Unit gross dollar mark-up (or the difference between selling price and cost);

G— Breakeven quantity (or number of units that must be sold within the time period specified by C [above]—to prevent an operating loss from occurring);

X— The number of months before merchandise will be sold (used for ROI only).

Breakeven Formula. Using the above variables, an order strategy formula could be developed for determining the breakeven quantity—where the return of unsold merchandise is allowed by vendors. This formula is represented as:

$$\text{Breakeven Quantity} = \frac{ABC/12}{F}$$

Assume: A is $200; B is 24%; C is 2 (or 60 days divided by 30); D is $10; E is $8; and F is $2 (or D-E).

Substitute for the letters in the formula to obtain:

$$G = \text{Breakeven Quantity} = \frac{\$200 \times .24 \times 2/12}{\$2}$$

$$G = \frac{\$8}{\$2} = 4$$

Therefore, a quantity of four would have to be sold within 60 days to break even with total expenses, after the remaining inventory is returned to the vendor. If the calculated breakeven quantity cannot be sold, the item should not be considered for inventory.

Net Return on Investment Formula. If return options are not offered by the vendor, a net ROI should be calculated for the dollar investment considered, and it should be compared with the desired net investment return percent established by Corporate decision. This order-strategy would use a formula represented as:

$$ROI = \frac{F - BX(E)/12}{E}$$

Substituting for the letters in the formula (while using the preceding example data), we have:

$$ROI = \frac{\$2 - .24\,(\$8)/12}{\$8} = \frac{\$2 - \$.16}{\$8} = 23\%$$

where "X" (the length of time before merchandise will be sold) is set equal to one month.

"X" can be varied to include actual investment time period expected, so the true net return on investment may be shown. For example, if in the above formula, the time period were extended to two (2) months, then:

$$ROI = \frac{\$2 - .24(2)\,(\$8)/12}{\$8} = \frac{\$2 - \$.32}{\$8} = 21\%$$

An item should not be considered for inventory if the net return on investment is expected to be less than acceptable by Corporate objectives.

Case in Point: A textile manufacturer uses breakeven point caluculations and return on investment figures when considering the addition of new inventory items, with order point-EOQ controlling replacement inventory purchases. Order strategy does vary, however, with the demand patterns. Dollar sales are forecast for the current, intermediate and long range planning periods. (Long range planning is largely based on intuition while other forecasts are made statistically.) The "least squares" projection method is used on dollar forecasts, and correlates well, as 70% of their total items fit a trend pattern. This company acknowledges inventory planning as essential to their obsolescence program. The working value of their inventory is measured and charted, to gauge any trend pattern in unwanted material, with immediate reviews made to determine why unwanted material has happened. Future planning is modified on the basis of these findings. Measuring the inventory's working value has improved inventory management communications and coordination, has pinpointed non-profitable items for discontinuance, has led to establishment of preventive controls for inventory buying, has allowed standardization of products, and has even permitted the combining of inventories.

Replenishment Order Strategies

Two basic order strategies are used in reordering currently stocked merchandise. This is because dependent demand items require a different order strategy than independent demand items.

Dependent demand items are needed to support the sale of an item of which they are a component. Such items do not sell independently as an end item. Or, if they do, the extent of end item sales is an insignificant percentage of the total usage. Dependent demand items usually are concentrated in manufacturing activities where an explosion of needed items (into the components making up the item) determines the ordering needs.

Independent demand items are those items which sell individually, even though they might also be used as a component part in another item. Independent demand items are normally concentrated in finished goods inventories such as are found in wholesale distributor warehouses or retail stores.

Dependent Demand Ordering. Dependent demand order strategy is generally referred to as Material Requirements Planning. It is time-series oriented. The important characteristic is determination of when the item will be needed instead of when an order should be placed. Each different sub-assembly or assembly requires a corresponding known or "fixed" number and quantity of different detail items. The detail items require a known or "fixed" amount of raw material support. Knowing when a quantity of assemblies are needed—whether automobiles, airplanes, houses, desks, books, etc.–determines the logistics for detail and/or raw material support. Subtracting the overall assembly time period from the completed assembly need date will set the requirements date for finished details going into such an assembly. Subtracting appropriate procurement times for the dependent details results in the need time for raw material.

Ordering costs and inventory carrying costs are balanced by combining quantities needed for future periods of time (additional lot releases), and comparing total procurement costs with total inventory carrying costs for the different quantities and corresponding periods of time considered. Material Requirements Planning is normally related to production control areas of manufacturing, and will not be detailed here.

Independent Demand Ordering. The order strategy for independent demand items consists of an item forecast, a forecast error allowance and the calculation of an order quantity. (These three factors are covered in detail in Chapter 9. Although order strategy is developed by Planning, the execution is accomplished by a requirements estimator.) The demand forecast is normally made statistically (although judgment can be, and is, often used), but should not be any more sophisticated than necessary to get the job done. A large, multi-product, finished-goods inventory with an inventory appraisal system, and with restrictive management guidelines, can be quite effective in meeting low dollar inventory *and* high service level targets—with just a simple "average" forecast method. Why forecast for items that should not even be considered for inventory stock?

Demand Patterns Condition Item Forecasts

Sales activity, either by product line or by item sales, develops into a demand pattern if associated with reoccurring increments of time, such as weeks, months or years. This time increment should be set as the standard review period. The stock levels, or status of merchandise, should be reviewed at the end of each such period. This review period should remain constant to permit consistent periods of demand to be recorded, so a more accurate sales pattern will develop.

The types of sales activity occurring must be known and pre-assigned to a specific demand pattern, if a good sales forecast is to be obtained. This allows a simple coding technique to identify merchandise by individual demand pattern, and therefore to signal that an adjustment is, or is not, necessary to the basic forecast. Four general demand patterns exist. These patterns include normal demand, trend demand, seasonal (or cyclic) demand, and the remainder which have no apparent explainable demand pattern at all. A demand table is summarized in Exhibit 5-1, following a general description of each demand category.

Normal Demand Items. Items with normal demand lack any increasing or decreasing quantity trends over a period of a year. (A 12-month period of time is necessary for determining most trend patterns, especially for seasonal demand items. A 12-month period is also normally used for demand averaging. However, a period equal to even months of lead time is found reasonable for setting an item's average sales rate, if such an item is not cyclic in nature, and if coding for demand pattern is applied.)

Normal demand items have sales activity which is consistent, in quantity, with the average sales quantity found. There may be random quantity fluctuations, above and

DEMAND PATTERN	CHARACTERISTICS	FORECAST METHODS	ORDER QUANTITY
Normal	No definite trends. Has random fluctuations about an average demand, but otherwise is consistent in behavior.	Demand averaging. Simple moving average, and with or without exponential smoothing.	E O Q, or time supply.
Trends. Either with increasing demand, or with decreasing demand.	Sustained overall gain or loss in demand activity about an average demand.	Simple demand averaging and double smoothing, or linear regression and %'s.	EOQ, or sales estimating.
Seasonal. Either with increasing trend, decreasing trend, normal seasonal, or once-a-year repeat sales.	Over-emphasized, repeating demand "peaks and valleys" over a given time period. Seasonality can be easily explained.	Base series, or base index.	Time supply, or sales estimating.
No pattern discernible	Highly fluctuating demand with many periods of no demand. Could be due to promotional effects, fads, new items, national disasters, etc.	None with any accuracy.	Personal judgment.

EXHIBIT 5-1:   **Demand Pattern Table Showing Different Forecast and Order Quantity Methods**

below the average sales rate, but there is no apparent sustained increasing or decreasing trend. These items can be forecast through simple averaging of demand, whether a 12-month trailing moving average (where all past demand periods are treated equally), or a 12-month moving average (with different emphasis applied to the individual past demand periods) is used. The latter is with "exponential smoothing" (which applies to the weighing of months differently), and provides a method to minimize data storage requirements where computer equipment is used, and computer storage space is limited.

Trend Demand Items. Items with a sustained increasing or decreasing sales activity over several review periods, or with an overall sales increase or decrease one year to the next, can be considered a trend item. They may resemble normal demand items by also having fluctuating sales above and below the average sales rate; but when consecutive average sales rates are compared, a noticeable increase or decrease is found. Trend items can be forecast best by computer, through use of a linear regression formula, or by demand averaging with "double exponential smoothing." (Double smoothing reacts quicker to demand changes than single smoothing, but requires *two* smoothing factors to be kept—an important factor in computer use. Smoothing is applied to base indices as well as to average demand.)

Seasonal (Cyclic) Demand Items. Cyclic items have a "peak and valley" situation which reoccurs. When such items normally have sales restricted to a single month or a maximum grouping of two or three consecutive months each year, they can be considered a seasonal item. Other cyclic items may reverse trends once or twice a year or once in two or more years. Where seasonality can be explained, a base series or base index system can be used for forecasting. Cyclic sales occur for many reasons. Two general reasons are:

1. Double selling seasons happen because different product lines sold have potential sales in different time periods of each year (i.e., air conditioning or heater parts).
2. Participation in the world-wide market generates sales, for one season's use, at different periods of the year (i.e., the United States and Australia). Conceiveably, overall dollar sales could represent normal demand, when in fact cyclic sales are occurring and are camouflaged by the effects of world-wide sales.

Order point—EOQ, min-max seasonal market estimates and fixed time supply techniques are used in replenishment stock buying by a leading automobile manufacturer. The reorder method used per item will vary as to classification and demand pattern involved. Order point-EOQ, min-max and fixed time supply order strategies are generally associated with support of normal demand pattern items, with sales estimating applied to trend or seasonal demand pattern items. 20% of all inventory items are seasonal (or cyclic), 60% fit in a trend pattern, and only 20% remain as normal (horizontal) movement items. Because of the large group of trend demand items, the "least squares" forecast method is used on item demand. Dollar sales are forecast for the current, intermediate and long range planning periods. Sales planning is also accomplished statistically, with intuitive judgment added only to the long range projections. The company considers breakeven point and return on investment on new items.

Human Judgment Needed

An automatic forecasting method does not allow for human judgment, and can create an excess inventory where judgment is completely excused. A single forecast method won't work for every situation. A method should be selected which is simple to understand, easy to work with, flexible for differing conditions, and highly responsive to customer needs.

FORECASTING SALES

The inventory planning function provides an overall dollar sales forecast for logistical use in provisioning for adequate inventory support. Item forecasts are not individually accomplished by the planning function, but the guidelines used and the order system followed are designed by planning to permit compatible item estimates. The method of forecast is important, but not as important as consistency of use and compatibility between the many forecasts made. There must be a common basis for determining future sales, whether they are current, next year's, or down the road a few years.

The Big Three

The long range forecast is usually made intuitively rather than by statistics, although definite statistical background information is necessary to support the end result. Market information, consumer trends, inflation, and any known correlative data are used to present the long range forecast. In the final analysis, though, an arbitrary decision will be made, which will be based primarily on management judgment.

The current 30-60-90 day projections are, like the long range planning, also an intuitive exercise. Constant estimating of monthly sales, with good experience developed in measuring forecast error, tends to build up the intuitive capability in 30-60-90 day forecasting.

The intermediate forecast is usually statistical in origin. It is a vital work tool. Operating budgets are prepared on the basis of this forecast and fixed to match the anticipated sales trend depicted. Intermediate planning must be well supported statistically. It must be optimistic and accurate. The first year of this forecast should equal the first year of the company's long range plans. And the first three months should correspond with the current 30-60-90 day projection.

The "Least Squares" Forecast Method

The intermediate range forecast is the nucleus of planning. This is mainly why it must be detailed, and accurate. Because of the detail involved, it's important to understand how a forecast is made. The *least squares method* is a simple method to understand, and one which provides good accuracy in forecasting. This method sums the squares of all points (of prior history) plotted on a graph, so that is a line were drawn which would best fit all points on the graph, the difference between the sum of the squares of the points below and those above the line drawn are minimized. The mathematics involved simply creates a line, for all points on the graph, which best fits all points.

Preparing for the Least Squares

The linear regression forecast method, of least squares, cannot determine if cyclic or seasonal effects are in the quantities for which the "best fit" line is made. Therefore, it is necessary to deseasonalize data which is used, if less than yearly time increments are being forecast. This will permit a more accurate trend picture to be known.

1. Obtain enough prior history data to support a forecast. A minimum of twelve periods of data should be used to forecast a same future period of time. However, forecasts can be and sometimes are made on much shorter past history periods than this, but is not recommended.

2. Make sure the time periods (i.e., months) are compatible. Each monthly period should be set equal to another. The best way to do this is to adjust for actual work days within each month. A 21-work day month standard is normally used.

3. Adjust the periods to a common point in time. Inflation adds a false picture to a forecast. Relate all periods to a common "year" dollars, or units based on these common dollars, to prevent any false trends being accepted.

4. If the forecast is for a month period of time, deseasonalize the months to show the true business trend.

5. Plot adjusted data on a time and dollar, or time and quantity graph. Using mathematics, calculate the formula which represents the "best fit" line to make your

forecast. Sometimes a sight line, drawn without benefit of mathematics, can give a good approximate fit—and forecast. However, the least squares method is not too difficult, and can easily be processed within a half-hour period, using a common desk calculator. A least squares line worksheet (Exhibit 5-5), a supporting graph (Exhibit 5-6), and a forecast worksheet (Exhibit 5-7) are given to illustrate the necessary steps. The five year's sales values used in these illustrations were 85, 100, 107, 112, and 119.

Restating the Forecasts in Months

Most statistical forecasts, other than item forecasts on inventory items as shown in Chapter 9, are made to support intermediate planning. They therefore usually cover a year period of time. Relating this one-year projection back into monthly projections is necessary for continuous management review and response. The exercise is time consuming, but is simple, providing known data is available concerning prior sales, work days, and seasonal indices. The steps involved include:

1. Multiply the year forecast value by an inflation factor, if dollars are being projected.
2. Divide the inflation-adjusted forecast by 12 to obtain an average monthly value.
3. Assign the actual work days to each of the future 12 months being forecast.
4. Divide each average monthly value by a constant 21 and then multiply times the actual work days for each respective month.
5. Multiply each work-day-adjusted, monthly forecast, by the seasonal index for the respective month, rounding as necessary.

Exhibit 5-2 explains how to develop the seasonal indices. Work steps include:

1. *Sales* are divided by *# Work Days*, and then multiplied by a constant 21 to arrive at *Adjusted Sales*.
2. *Adjusted Sales* are added together and divided by 12 to find an average adjusted sales per month.
3. Each month's *Adjusted Sales* is then divided by the average monthly adjusted sales to obtain each monthly seasonal index.
4. Indices are added to a seasonal index table for accumulating monthly averages.

ANNUAL SALES FOR YEAR (−4)

MONTH	SALES	# WORK DAYS	ADJUSTED SALES	SEASONAL INDEX
JAN	4	21	4.00	56.4%
FEB	6	20	6.30	88.8%
MAR	7	22	6.68	94.1%
APR	6	21	6.00	84.5%
MAY	4	20	4.20	59.2%
JUN	5	20	5.25	74.0%
JUL	7	21	7.00	98.6%
AUG	10	23	9.13	128.7%
SEP	12	21	12.00	169.1%
OCT	10	22	9.55	134.6%
NOV	8	22	7.64	107.6%
DEC	6	17	7.41	104.4%

EXHIBIT 5-2:   **Developing the Seasonal Indices**

Exhibit 5-3 shows a seasonal index table, in which seasonal indices are averaged for each month. Example results shown in parenthesis are for the month of January.

1. Add all indices for a given month together (2.965).
2. Subtract the highest and lowest index percentages, where big differences exist. This can be ignored where uniformity limits the percentage spread to within 2% for all years concerned. The highest percentage for January is .641 and .559 is the lowest. The previous total of 2.965 less this 1.200 is (1.765).
3. Divide the remaining total by the number of years still included. The total of 1.765 divided by 3 is (.588).
4. The seasonal index to use for January is 58.8%.

YEAR	JAN	FEB	MAR	APR	MAY	JUN	JUL	AUG	SEP	OCT	NOV	DEC
−4	.564	.888	.941	.845	.592	.740	.986	1.287	1.691	1.346	1.076	1.044
−3	.599	.880	.915	.838	.629	.755	.958	1.313	1.677	1.371	1.029	1.036
−2	.559	.939	.960	.894	.587	.704	1.006	1.225	1.676	1.279	1.068	1.104
−1	.641	.917	.854	.673	.785	.961	1.268	1.602	1.325	1.021	1.055	1.056
CURRENT	.602	.949	.959	.903	.632	.738	1.004	1.191	1.606	1.246	1.054	1.116

EXHIBIT 5-3:   **Seasonal Index Table**

Exhibit 5-4 lists the seasonal indices, calculated for sample data covering a five-year period, and explains how to correct for index error caused by averaging. In Exhibit 5-4, work steps are:

1. The seasonal indices, for each month of the year, are added together and divided by 12 to obtain a "mean" month percentage figure. (Refer to Exhibit 5-3 to see how to obtain for a given month.)
2. Subtract the mean month percentage figure from 200.0%, and multiply times each month's completed projection to correct for seasonal index error. The example here has a mean month percentage (1200.3% divided by 12) of 100.025%. This shows that the projected annual sales total is off .025%. This figure is insignificant on low quantity units, but is significant where millions of dollars are concerned.

MONTH	SEASONAL INDEX	OUTER % LIMITS DEDUCTED (HIGH LIMIT − LOW LIMIT)	
JAN	58.8%	(64.1%)	(55.9%)
FEB	91.4%	(94.9%)	(88.0%)
MAR	93.8%	(96.0%)	(85.4%)
APR	85.9%	(90.3%)	(67.3%)
MAY	61.7%	(78.5%)	(58.7%)
JUN	74.4%	(96.1%)	(70.4%)
JUL	99.8%	(126.8%)	(95.8%)
AUG	127.5%	(160.2%)	(119.1%)
SEP	165.3%	(169.1%)	(132.5%)
OCT	129.0%	(137.1%)	(102.1%)
NOV	105.9%	(107.6%)	(102.9%)
DEC	106.8%	(111.6%)	(103.6%)

EXHIBIT 5-4:   **Determining a Seasonal Indices Correction Factor to Apply to Projected Sales**

The least squares line worksheet, shown in Exhibit 5-5, permits relocating the origin of the independent variable data to its arithmetic mean. The independent variable (time) is normally entered as X on the worksheet, while the corresponding dependent data (sales) is entered as Y. The arithmetic mean of X (in this case 3) is determined by adding 1, 2, 3, 4 and 5 together and dividing by 5. Locating the origin at year 3, consecutive minus and plus values are substituted for the remaining time periods of X, and recorded in the adjacent X' column.

LEAST SQUARES LINE WORKSHEET

(TIME) X	X'	(SALES) Y	X'Y	X'^{2}
1	−2	85	−170	4
2	−1	100	−100	1
3	0	107	0	0
4	1	112	112	1
5	2	119	238	4
6				
7				
8				
9				
10				
11				
12				
	0	523	80	10
N = 5	(ΣX')	(ΣY)	(ΣX'Y)	(ΣX'^{2})

$$\frac{\Sigma Y}{N} = \frac{523}{5} = 104.6$$

$$\frac{\Sigma X'Y}{\Sigma X'2} = \frac{80}{10} = 8$$

EXHIBIT 5-5:   A Sample Least Squares Line Worksheet
(This least squares projection was based on the following five year's sales data: 85, 100, 107, 112 and 119. The answers for average annual sales and the line's slope are circled above.)

Two other columns ($X'Y$ and X'^2) are added to the worksheet to record those values when:

1. The independent variable is multiplied times its corresponding dependent variable value ($X'Y$); and,

2. The independent data value is "squared," or multiplied times itself, (X'^2).

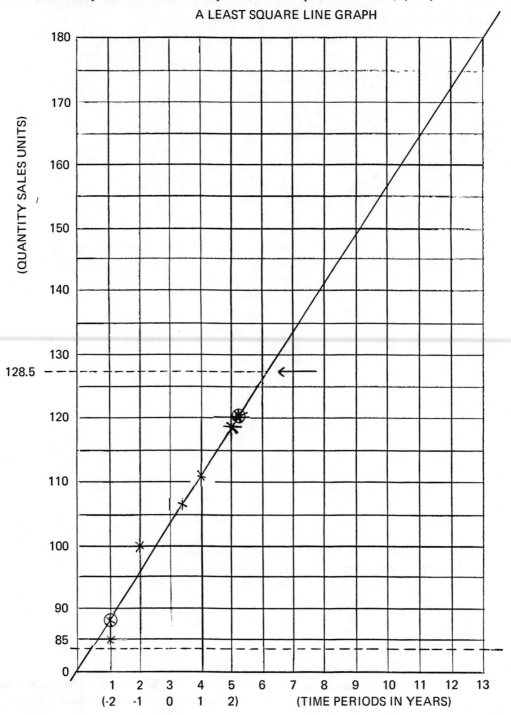

EXHIBIT 5-6:   A Simple Graph

The bottom row of the worksheet is for recording the sums (or totals) of each column.

The two points required for drawing a straight line on a graph may be calculated by using the formula:

$$\frac{\Sigma Y}{N} + X' \left(\frac{\Sigma X' Y}{\Sigma X' 2}\right)$$

Substituting formula values obtained from the least squares worksheet, and the X' values of -2 and 2 in the above formula, we arrive at the numbers 88.6 and 120.6 as our two required points. These two points can then be plotted on a graph as shown in Exhibit 5-6. (NOTE: any two of the X' values on the worksheet could have been used instead of -2 and 2 which were selected.) The graph shown here visually supports the least square line worksheet (Exhibit 5-5). The annual sales data used for the forecast (85, 100, 107, 112, and 119) are shown plotted above. Two points were solved for a straight line from data on the least squares line worksheet, and the straight line was drawn on this graph to extrapolate next year's sales (shown as 128.5).

XX–XX–XX
_____
(Date)

FORECAST WORKSHEET

FISCAL YEAR __XXXX__

1. Least squares (unit)–(dollars) projection   128.5
2. Judgment factors:
    —Production changes and new model relationship   ----
    —Economic factors   ----
    —Proposed future programs   ----
3. Total (unit)–(dollars) projection   128.5
4. Total (unit)–(dollars) projection divided by "12"   10.7
5. Monthly (unit)–(dollars) projections:

MONTH	# WORK DAYS	ADJUSTED TO WORK DAYS	SEASONAL INDICES	RESTATED PROJECTION
JAN	21.	10.70	58.8%	6.29
FEB	20	10.19	91.4%	9.31
MAR	22	11.21	93.8%	10.51
APR	21	10.70	85.9%	9.19
MAY	20	10.19	61.7%	6.29
JUN	20	10.19	74.4%	7.58
JUL	21	10.70	99.8%	10.68
AUG	23	11.72	127.5%	14.94
SEP	21	10.70	165.3%	17.69
OCT	22	11.21	129.0%	14.46
NOV	22	11.21	105.9%	11.87
DEC	17	8.66	106.8%	9.25

EXHIBIT 5-7:   Restating the Forecast in Months

Exhibit 5-7 shows the results of restating an annual forecast into months, using a five-year period of sample data. In this example, next year's sales were extrapolated as 128.5 units from the least squares graph, and were placed on the worksheet for #1. Since no judgment factors (#2) were anticipated, the total unit projection (#3) remained at 128.5 units. A monthly average of 10.7 units was obtained for #4. This average was then adjusted to actual work days, and then by each respective index, to arrive at the restated projection. Rounding will be required on the restated projection. An allowance for anticipated price changes should be made where dollars are being projected.

6

Customer Order Processing: Catalyst for Inventory Action

This chapter provides an in-depth look at the customer order processing system. Good perspective views are given on the customer name and address file, the customer billing number system, order processing priority assignments, the sales order form needs, the part number master file (with each field of information described), the invoice form use, and backorder control. In addition, vital processing problem areas are given special treatment. Read the workable suggestions given for such factors as inventory allocation methods for "ship complete" orders; "order edit" parameters; item substitutions; uses of special processing codes; order quantity changes; pricing considerations and control; receipts allocation to backorders; and discrepancy processing. Use the methods offered here, and gain a more accurate, efficient and profitable customer order processing system.

Five distinct functions can be seen in customer order processing:

1. Order taking.
2. Creating the packing sheet.
3. Order handling.
4. Invoicing.
5. Backorder item processing.

The order processing system must consider each of these functions, be flexible in the handling of order deviations and peak loads, and furnish exception information for spotting or correcting system failures.

PLANNING AN ORDER PROCESSING SYSTEM

(a) Develop a customer name and address file.

(b) Establish a customer billing number system to control item (a), and to organize order taking.

(c) Initiate an order log for order control purposes.

(d) Decide on company sales order numbers and packing sheet number.

(e) Assign priorities to order processing.

(f) Select (or design) a sales order (packing sheet) form set.

(g) Design a record file for historical activity records for each item in inventory.

(h) Select an invoice form "set" to control order billing.

(i) Introduce an invoice numbering system.

(j) Adopt a method for keeping track of back orders and arranging to either ship or cancel them.

The Customer Name and Address File

This file, in a manual order processing system, is simple and flexible. Name and address cards are prepared for each approved customer. The cards are normally small, up to 3" x 5" in size, and can be situated in a file drawer or in a "dial-a-file" moving or stationary card holder. Organization here, as in a computer supported system, is the key to efficient use. The answers to the following questions might be more critical in building a computer file, but should be considered in a manual system design too:

1. What line length, and how many lines, should be allowed for each name and address? The line length and total lines should be the same for each customer. These two variables are big factors in deciding card or file size.

2. What code system should be used to identify each customer? A code may be used to identify the level of distribution, such as a wholesaler, a retailer or a direct customer. If wholesale or retail contracts are separated into distinct groups, perhaps the type of contract would be a good code variable—for each level of distribution. The coding can describe discount structure allowed each customer, for determining correct billing prices.

3. Are C.O.D. customers allowed? If so, then a code should be used to identify whether a customer is on C.O.D. status, or open account.

4. What mailing zone is the customer located in? Many companies wait to figure this out when mailing an order, and don't realize the time-saving capability. When labels are prepared, the code can be there on the label.

5. Should a code be used for controlling complimentary copies of catalogs, literature, etc.? Where various groups of wholesalers or retailers are permitted, it is possible that some literature would not be mailed to all customers, or extra copies would be mailed to preferred customers. A number showing the exact copies to mail would be sufficient. Sometimes the customer identity code (number 2 above) is also used to determine this answer.

6. Should sales data be captured for each customer? This is not too appropriate for a manual system, as there is not enough room on a card to record very many quantities. A supplementary list or record would have to be maintained to collect sales data, which is usually extracted from inventory control record cards or the order log. Where computer name and address files are used, it is worthwhile to capture sales data like:

    a. Gross sales dollars, items, quantities and orders.

    b. Adjustments for corresponding dollars, items, quantities and orders.

    c. Returned goods authorized in dollars, items and quantities.

Items, quantities and orders would be obtained during packing sheet printing. Dollars would be obtained during invoicing. Adjustments would be captured during credit memo processing. These figures could be arranged in more sophisticated detail recording to obtain performance reporting; and warranty returns, net sales information, number of orders received per reporting period and number of items per order— for statistical purposes in determining depth of customers's inventory planning accomplished. If merchandise return programs are permitted, and are based as a percentage of net sales, a running account of acceptable dollars returned would be available immediately— for random merchandise return at the customer's discretion, and by computer control.

System Number	Description	Sales Volume ($1,000,000)	Daily Volume Orders	Line Items	Time Available for Processing	Availability of Information
1A	Manual	Under $5	Under 100	Under 500	Any	Immediate
1B	Manual/machine output	Under $15	Under 250	Under 2000	Any	Immediate
2	Central computer centralized entry	$10-$100	100-500	500-2500	Over 2 days	Call back
3	Central computer field entry	$20-$100	Over 250	Over 2000	Over 1 day	Call back
4A	Computer network batch mode	Over $75	Over 500	Over 2000	Over 1 day	Call back
4B	Computer network on-line mode	Over $75	Over 500	Over 2000	Same day	Immediate
5A	Time shared system batch mode	Under $10	Under 250	Under 2000	Over 1 day	Call back
5B	Time shared system on-line mode	Under $25	Under 500	Under 2500	Same day	Immediate

EXHIBIT 6-1: Criteria for System Selection. (By courtesy of Marketing Publications Incorporated, Customer Service Newsletter, Vol. 1, No. 2, September 15, 1973.) The above table was compiled on the basis of experience with 20 to 30 order processing installations, in firms ranging from $10 to $150 million.

System Number	Time Required in Months Design	Installation	Data Processing Capability Required	Pre-Installation Costs(a) (One-Time) ($1,000)	Operating Cost Per Order (c) (d)	Flexibility	Availability of Packaged Systems
1A	1	1	None	Small	$ .25 to $ .50	High	n.a.
1B	1-2	2-3	Low	$1	$ .50 to $ .75	Med to High	n.a.
2	2-3	5-7	Med-high	$50-$100	$1.50	Low-med	Yes-$5,000 and up
3	3-4	6-8	High	$75-$125	$2.00	Low-med	Yes-$5,000 and up
4A	5-7	9-10	Med-high	$300 and up	Over $2.50	Low	Yes-$100,000 and up
4B	6-8	10-12	High	$500 and up	Over $3.50	Low	Yes-$200,000 and up
5A	3-4	3-4	Medium	$5 and up(b)	$ .75 to $1.00	Med to high	n.a.
5B	3-4	4-6	Medium	$10 and up(b)	$1.00 to $1.50	Med to high	n.a.

(a) Assume that hardware is leased, not purchased.
(b) Costs vary with applicability of packaged systems. Pre-installation costs may be absorbed into monthly operating charge.

(c) Based on average order of three-line items.
(d) Assume computer installation used 50 percent on order processing systems.

EXHIBIT 6-2: System Characteristics. (By courtesy of Marketing Publications Incorporated, Customer Service Newsletter, Vol. 1, No. 2, September 15, 1973.) The data set forth here are intended as a guide, and individual applications may vary considerably. Certain figures, like cost-per-order, are necessarily based on averages.

1A. *Manual.* Entire system handled by clerical/administrative employees using only typewriters, calculators, catalogs and files.

1B. *Manual with Machine Readable Output.* Same as manual system except that typewriter and/or calculator may be connected to a punched tape or card output device to facilitate further processing or transmission.

2. *Central Computer, Centralized Entry.* Customer orders are immediately keypunched and entered for complete or partial computer processing into orders, shipping documents and invoices. Associated processing handles accounts receivable, sales history, inventory, etc.

3. *Central Computer, Field Entry.* Orders received at field sales or service location, transferred into machine readable form and transmitted to central computer for processing as in (2).

4. *Computer Network.* Orders received and processed in field sales or service office by local, on-site computers. Data transmission to central computer utilized for off-line functions and files. Field computers may be full-scale, general purpose, or special purpose mini-computers. Field operations may be: 4A. Batch mode

4B. On-line mode.

5. *Time Shared Systems.* Similar to (4) computer network, except that the field computers are general purpose machines operated by an outside service and accessed by the sales office through terminals.

May be operated in: 5A. Batch mode

5B. On-line mode.

Frequently these systems are offered by proprietary services on a per-transaction rental basis.

EXHIBIT 6-3: Summary of Criteria and Basic Characteristics of Order Processing Systems. (By courtesy of Marketing Publications Incorporated, Customer Service Newsletter, Vol. 1, No. 2, September 15, 1973.)

A Customer Billing Number System

The accounting department usually develops some kind of billing code for each customer. This billing code can be used, or a uniform billing code numbering system can be developed which will afford better customer identity than just a number. For instance, a different code system might be used for export customers as compared to domestic customers. Geographical location might be used instead, or become a part of the coding system within each of these identifiers. If regions are used by a company, perhaps using the region number would be a benefit. Retailers might be further identified under each region or wholesalers, as:

```
A   B   CCC
            Retailers
        Wholesalers
  Regions or geographical locations
```

The name and address file records in a manual system are normally arranged in alphabetical sequence, for obvious reasons. However, in computer files the filing is usually by billing code sequence. Time can be saved when billing codes are used in place of the name and address information on the customer order form. A chart would be necessary for order-taking use, in support of a computer file, but is easily memorized due to the "meaningful" billing codes used. (The billing code is also referenced on the manual name and address file cards.) Numbers should be used in the billing code, wherever possible, in place of alphabetic characters.

Case in Point: A container manufacturer in the Northeast maintains a separate name and address file on computer, with a billing code assigned to each customer. This billing code is eight digits in length, and reflects regional geographical locations as well as various distribution levels such as branches, zones and dealers. A Midwest parts distributor uses only five digits to accomplish the same identity. Both companies save 75% of the time normally required to handwrite the customer's name and address. Order taking and processing are shortened and customer phone bills are reduced. Long distance callers agree with the billing code systems, and identify themselves immediately with a billing code number when placing an order.

The Order Log

A record log, for customer orders, is outlined in Chapter 7. Many uses exist for this record log. A quick look will give the general location of the order in flow, whether in picking, in shipping, or in transit to the customer. Other control advantages would include verification that an order was received; what kinds of orders are being received (priority type); size of orders and their relation to other orders overall; number of backorder line items (for manual performance reporting); determining what order processing times are involved; etc.

Sales Order and Packing Sheet Numbers

All documents should be easily referenced, especially where some type of control activity is involved. This is the reason for sales order and packing sheet numbers. The sales order and packing sheet number can be the same, where backorder items are not permitted and are cancelled, with the customer having to reorder at a later date. However, where backorders are permitted, control is mandatory. They must relate to the original sales order number they were placed on. A different packing sheet number is usually required to identify each individual shipment made against a specific sales order number. (The shipping date can be used for the packing sheet number, if internal company accounting will accept this control. Otherwise, a separate packing sheet number will be required.) The packing sheet log in a manual system is generally kept and controlled by the shipping department, if the forms do not have preprinted packing sheet numbers assigned. Packing sheet numbers are assigned automatically, under computer control, when packing sheets are printed by a computer.

Order Processing Priority Assignment

Orders requiring more consideration than others are often marked to get them through the system quicker. This could be by the color of the sales order form, by different color coded or worded notes attached to an order, or by different forms. During manual processing of order data, new orders are sequenced by priority before pre-posting occurs, to give preference to certain customers or for favoring emergency conditions. This priority system would have at least three priorities: confirmation (or computer by-pass) orders, emergency orders, and regular orders. A further sophistication could include shipment destination, a further breakdown of normal orders by shipment method, etc. The same priority message is required when using a computer system, although it may be recognized differently (appearing as a number code on the input order or as a check mark in one of many "ballot boxes" on the order form).

Case in Point: One of the largest manufacturers of electrical equipment and appliances has supported customer order processing with computer resources for almost 18 years. Because of large business volume (now currently at 14,000 orders and 65,000 line items per month), setting priorities on order processing was taken over by computer. Six variables are considered in their order priority system. These variables, listed by importance in descending sequence, are emergency status of order, customer, type of order, method of shipment, extended dollar value and line item size.

The Sales Order Form

A sales order form must be selected, or designed, to use in order taking and shipping. Three copies are essential. An office copy is needed for later file reference and for controlling backorders. An accounting copy is required to control customer invoicing. A packing sheet is needed to accompany the order shipment. Sometimes more copies are used, so that the office receives an extra copy when the order is prepared to start working on backorders immediately; a customer acknowledgment copy is optional to notify a customer that his order is in process, where ship time takes more than a few days; or an optional copy for traffic control is used.

WATCH THIS: The order processing system should be improved to maximum efficiency instead of substituting more form copies. Each form copy handled involves costs in time and labor. Paper scarcity and costs are both increasing, and should be considered.

The order form's design should include those criteria outlined in Chapter 16. It should also allow for "header" information such as "bill to" and "ship to" names and addresses, customer purchase order number, date, method of shipment desired, person initiating order; and order "line item" data such as item number, quantity, part number, description, model or serial references, pricing data and an estimated shipping date "field" for backordered items (if backorders are permitted). If a qualified company forms design man is not available, the services of a local forms supplier should be used. Most forms suppliers are competent in forms design and offer free assistance in the design work involved.

The Part Number Master File

In a manual system, the part number master file is made up of inventory control record cards (Kardex, Diebold, visual record cards, etc.). In a computer file, these inventory control record cards are essentially the same, except they are an electronic representation contained on internal computer storage. Most of the data requirements listed here will be found on a physical inventory control record card. If not, they should be considered as add-on items. These data are arbitrarily grouped into four categories: control, pricing, activity and ordering data.

Control Data. This category consists of:
Part number. A maximum of 15 digits should be considered.
Description. Limited in length unless the description is also the part number.
Unit of measure. Can be limited to a two-digit code abbreviation.

Cross-reference part number and reason code. Superseding/superseded alternates (substitutes), identical items, or replaced items must be coded to allow proper reduction of stock balances to reduce obsolescence, or to purge stock of bad items.

Storage location. The physical location of any item must be known under a formal storage location assignment system.

Status code. This code can equate a part's characteristics to manufactured or purchased, active or inactive, in production or not.

Commodity code. The actual code, or a machine code equivalent, for the Commerce Department commodity code. Used for export business. Not necessary for domestic (only) sales.

Product code. An identification as to type of product or function, or can be assigned to show commonality of usage.

Date out-of-production. If spares support is continued on out-of-production items.

Date of last sale. Recorded during each posting operation.

Date of last receipt. Recorded during each posting operation.

Date of last adjustment. Recorded during each posting operation.

Pricing Data. This category consists of:

List price and discount code. Used for both retail and discounted sales. A discount chart would list all discount codes and respective percentages allowed. If primary business sales were to a retailer, an optional dealer price could also be shown. However, list price and discount code permits an easier extension by accounting people when preparing invoices, and for their verifying prices where cash sales occur.

Current replacement cost. Not added if a constant gross margin pricing concept is used. This data should be placed close to the order requirements information, as it is used in calculating E.O.Q. quantities.

Average cost. Normally handled by accounting, this information (as well as current replacement cost) requires a periodic update. Many firms figure average cost whenever new quantities are received. This data is highly confidential, if used, and should be placed on the card where it can not be abused.

Catalog code. Price information is controlled by this code to signal new prices or price changes. This permits either a new price catalog or a price update listing to be printed.

Activity Data. This category consists of:

Beginning shelf balance. Shows quantity balance physically in storage at the beginning of a demand period.

Adjustments. Inventory quantity reductions or increases for the current demand period. Stocking errors and miscount corrections, returned goods, variances (if not booked), can be handled separately—or together in a common entry field.

Receipts. For the current demand period.

Cumulative demand. Combined sales and/or usage quantity for the current demand period.

Current shelf balance. This quantity balance is the actual quantity of parts on a shelf location, except for allocations made without printing a packing sheet. This quantity is important to internal auditors. It permits reconciliation of allocated items not physically picked. Cross-footing of other activity data balances will be necessary to arrive at this figure.

Allocation quantity. Shelf quantity assigned to demand which won't have an immediate packing sheet printed. Usually for ship-complete orders which restrict shipments until all backorders are fillable.

Backorder quantity. Unfillable demand, or fillable allocated quantities, for the current demand period.

Total backorder quantity. All backorders, including backorders for the current demand period.

Ordering Data. This category consists of:

On hand balance. Current shelf quantity less backorders.

Total open order quantity. Total quantity of all open order schedules. If a separate order file is not maintained, and computer storage is no problem, all schedule quantities could be kept in the part number master file.

First due (date) order quantity. Where all schedule quantities are not kept on the part number master file, the first due dated order date should be referenced. This date could be used for estimated shipping date for backordered items, if schedule quantities are adhered to and are accurate.

Lead time. Time requirements to replenish inventory. Includes both administrative and vendor lead times. A quantitative figure in tune with the length of a demand period used. If a 4-week demand period is used, the lead time would be in increments of the 4-week period. A 10-week lead time would be shown as either 10 weeks or calculated at 2.5 demand periods, depending on computer programming logic.

Old demand average. A moving weighted demand forecast for the last demand period.

New demand average. A moving weighted demand forecast for the current demand period.

Old safety stock average. Increments of MAD (Mean Absolute Deviation) based on service level desired. This is a moving weighted error forecast for the last demand period, based on previous MAD's.

New safety stock average. A weighted moving error forecast for the current demand period, based on the old safety stock average and the current absolute deviation.

Order point forecast. New demand average extended for lead time requirements plus new safety stock average. Expedite cards can be issued against open orders when the on-hand quantity falls below a set percentage of this order point calculation.

Order point restriction code. A fixed order point quantity code for by-passing or creating an early order forecast.

Order quantity restriction code. A fixed order quantity code to restrict EOQ to a set period minimum or maximum quantity, etc.

E.O.Q. (Economical Order Quantity.) A mathematical quantity which considers the balancing of ordering and carrying costs related to inventory. This quantity is updated each demand period, and is to be used when replenishing stock, unless order quantity restriction codes are used.

Order strategy codes. Vendor minimum quantity buy items must be identified as either a combination dollar amount, or a single item fixed quantity or dollar amount. An alert is needed for items which are going to be superseded (obsoleted), where future stock buys are not recommended. Serialized or other made-to-order items, shelf-life, kit only items, high dollar (ABC classification) items should all be identified if different order strategies are desired.

Base indices. Moving weighted monthly percentages of annual demand. These data are required for trend or seasonal items, but will probably be stored with the forecast model program.

Procurement codes. Each buyer can be assigned a code, or approved vendor codes can be assigned to each part number to assist in preparing computer printed purchase orders.

Computer record lengths must be the same for each item contained in the part number master file. Record length should be kept to a minimum for lower machine costs. Only those items necessary to provide adequate inventory management, and order processing activities, should be kept within this file. Adequate growth space should, however, be allocated as part of the record for anticipated program plans, to prevent costly file conversions later.

The Invoice Form

The invoice form, in a manual system, could be a part of the order form used. Where limited copies (three) are used for the customer order form, an additional three copies could be added to the form set as invoice copies. All relevant information is present on the form except for extensions of individual dollar amounts. Price extensions are easy as list price and discount code is given for each item ordered on the order form. Discrepancies are worked before accounting is given their copies, so billing information is correct. Complete shipping information is on the invoice form. The only thing left to do is extend unit prices and total them. In this manner, the invoice and packing sheet number can be the same.

In computer systems, feedback information is needed to alert the computer that a shipment has been made. Discrepancy information is given and machine handled prior to invoicing, so that the invoice suspense file will be correct when the invoice is printed. The invoice number used by the computer can also be the packing sheet number assigned for the shipment being invoiced.

Backorder Control

The customer items ordered which cannot be shipped must either be backordered or cancelled. When backorders are allowed, some method is required to keep these backorders current—and on backorder until shipped. Since more variable information is needed than can be placed on the part number master file, a separate backorder file might be designated. The backorder file should contain all header control information contained on the sales order, such as sales order number, "bill to" and "ship to" names and addresses, and customer purchase order number. Line item data requirements would add item number (sequence on order), quantity ordered, unit of measure, part number, description, model and serial number given (if required), and pricing data. Where variable data links are possible between data files, some of this information could be deleted as file requirements, but the data must be available for use. In manual systems, individual backorder cards are prepared with this information for each customer backorder and filed in part number sequence, by order priority.

STARTING THE ORDER PROCESSING FLOW

Order taking begins with receipt of customer order information. Customer orders can be received verbally (in person), as mail orders, or through tele-communication devices. A standard sales order source form is prepared (for the customer order) as input for computer processing. This source document, or the one received as a mail order, is considered the customer's purchase order. Order information is visually checked and entered in an order log, with a corresponding order log sales order number cross-referenced on the sales order source form. The form is then ready for keypunching as input data for the computer.

Source data entry equipment is used to input order information via a keyboard method instead of by a source document. The programmed interactive "conversational" instructions, provided by the source data equipment, prevent information from being missed as an order is entered for editing. The source document is created as a computer print-out list where mail orders are not received.

The source document is usually a single-part form that contains all necessary order information in a preselected format for use in keypunching data, as input to a computer. It is sometimes identical in format to an actual sales order form "set" used; i.e., confirmation (or computer "by-pass") order forms, which are handwritten orders processed prior to pre-posting, are a multi-part form "set." One copy of the confirmation form is used as a "source" document, for adjusting inventory quantities *after* the order is shipped. (In manual systems, a packing sheet is created from this "source" document prior to entering information in the order log. The packing sheet is then manually processed against inventory records prior to processing an order shipment.)

CREATING THE PACKING SHEET

Logic guidelines are needed to guide the computer in editing the customer's order and in printing sales order packing sheets. The logic guidelines must cover all error conditions, as an order could still be wrong even by passing all editing logic—if all error conditions were not edited. "Header" and "line item" edit guidelines are kept separate for a purpose. "Header" errors, without corrections, should prevent a customer's order from being processed; whereas "line item" errors could be present, but still permit the sales order packing sheet to be printed.

"Header" Edit Guidelines

"Header" information consists of all billing and shipping data, and includes sales order number, "bill to" and "ship to" name and address codes, customer purchase order number, transportation method requested, and special notes or instructions. These "header" data must be checked, with a "hold" placed on packing sheet printing until errors are corrected.

"Bill To" and "Ship To" Must Be Compatible. Both "bill to" and "ship to" name and address codes should be present. These codes should be compatible with each other and with the sales order number assigned. (A sales order number *must* be assigned.) For example, where sales order numbers are prefixed differently for export orders than for domestic orders, an export sales order prefix should not be assigned where a domestic "bill to" name and address code is used. Where drop-shipments out of a franchised area are not authorized, the "bill to" and "ship to" codes should match the same area. Where drop-shipment is authorized to a non-established customer, and a special "ship to" code is used to indicate this, an edit check must be made to insure that notes information is entered to supply the drop-ship name and address.

P.O. Number Is Authority. A missing customer's purchase order number indicates an edit error. The P.O. number authorizes the process of shipment and billing. A customer's liability is limited where this number is missing.

Shipping Method. A shipping method must be identified, either by a selected code or by an abbreviated description. If the computer is not instructed to add "best way" for transportation method where a shipping method is not indicated, then an error condition should be noted.

C.O.D. Control. The name and address file, for the "bill to" code entered, will identify if the customer is on C.O.D. status, if such information is not also manually entered (as an over-ride). C.O.D. status would cause the packing sheet to be printed with F.O.B. point equal to "factory," and freight charges to be "collect." A special code could be used to override the C.O.D. status, if cash is paid in advance at time of order taking. Edit logic would check notes information to insure that a check (or money order) number is entered with the other order data.

Transportation Expense. F.O.B. point and charges need not be keypunched, or otherwise entered, as most shipments other than C.O.D. will normally be F.O.B. "factory," and charges "collect"—unless, of course, the company's selling price includes prepaid transportation to destination. Some exceptions do exist, as shipments to government air bases, and Parcel Post or UPS shipments must be prepaid. Changes in charges and F.O.B. point, after the packing sheet has been printed, will happen and can be marked by hand on the packing sheet. Invoices should correctly show final decisions.

"Line Item" Edit Guidelines

Line item data consist of the actual order information. These data must be verified to insure that the proper quantities get picked, shipped and charged; and they include the sequenced line item number, the part number, description, unit of measure, quantity ordered, and the model and serial numbers given (if required). Each order's line item (of input information) should also contain the "header" control information of sales order number, "bill to" and "ship to" codes and customer purchase order number. (This primarily applies to card input systems where cards must undergo sorting or are sometimes misplaced. This allows all of an order's information to be placed together again. Where source data entry equipment is used, this repeat information is not necessary, as it is under program control.)

Part Number Is Key. The part number check is mandatory, and is usually the first item check made. An unmatch on part number would prevent any other editing against the part number master file, as the part number record wouldn't exist. (The unmatched part number could be a good number that has not yet been placed in the file; strictly a bad number ordered; or it could be a keypunch error. Review is necessary.) Some service bureaus use an item number equivalent in place of part number, for matching purposes on turn-around data. This reduces keypunch volume and still offers good control, but can't apply where part numbers ordered are not selected from an itemized table.

Order Quantity. Quantity ordered should be checked against high and low parameters. The high check would be based on normal demand quantity (i.e., an order for 10,000 each on an item that sells only 50 each per demand period should, if not a keypunch error, be reviewed with the customer). The low check would either be one each, or would be set equal to a minimum quantity sold. If company policy is not to increase a customer's order quantity to a minimum quantity offered, then the item should be cancelled.

Unit of Measure. If the "input" unit of measure differs from the unit of measure on the part number master file, it should be reviewed. The computer can assign the unit of measure; however, some problems could exist—i.e., where an item is sold 100 each to a package with a unit of measure of "package" and a customer orders 1000, does he want 1000 packages or 1000 each? If the computer changes the quantity to 100,000 each, to match the computer unit of measure, the inventory balance would probably be wiped out, backorders would occur, and at least one customer would be dissatisfied.

Nomenclature. Description is normally not entered as part of an item's information, due to its unimportant status when a part number is used. The description on the part number master file is used when printing the packing sheet. This reduces keypunched input volume.

Model/Serial Number Reference. A check is made to see if model or serial number requirements are necessary. If required, and not given, the order item is in error. If company policy won't allow item cancellation, review with the customer is necessary. Normal procedure is to automatically let the item cancel and cause a customer reorder with proper support data.

Line Item Sequence Number. Each part number contained on an order should be identified by a sequenced item number. The computer can assign sequential item numbers at the time the packing sheet is printed, but assigning the item numbers on the order form (before order entry) allows for some additional control checks—those of missing or duplicated item numbers.

Edit Corrections

Everything that could result in a wrong shipment or billing should be reviewed and corrected. This should be done immediately on both "header" and "line item" errors; however, it is not necessary that the packing sheet be held up from printing until "line item" errors are corrected. As long as "header" errors don't exist, the packing sheet could be printed, with ship action taking place on all error free line items. Items in error can be reviewed and corrected during the initial packing sheet shipment.

Order Processing Guidelines

The packing sheet can be printed after order editing has been satisfied. During printing of the packing sheet, certain rules should be followed. Guidelines are given here to insure proper order processing.

Order Priority Followed. A priority system is necessary when printing sales order packing sheets, so that discrepancies are kept to a minimum and emergency orders are given preference. The first-in/first-out concept should be retained, but emergency orders should receive special treatment. A simple priority system would process confirmation orders first, with emergency orders second and regular orders last.

Confirmation orders are those orders which are processed before preposting can occur. They are called "by-pass" orders because they are filled manually, without regard to inventory balance posting. By-pass orders are common in both manual and computer supported systems. It is imperative that these orders get posted before other inventory action, because they represent potential discrepancies for other orders if stock balances are not corrected first. *Emergency* orders should be pre-posted next, as they are more urgently needed than the remaining regular orders. Where minimum quantity levels exist on some items, a stock order should not take priority over a part needed for an emergency situation. All *regular* orders are then pre-posted. In a computer supported system, priorities must be finitely assigned so that all orders can be sequenced by code without leaving an order out. It is probable that more than just these three priorities will be assigned, but the priority system should be kept as simple as possible to administer.

Confirmation Order Processing Is Unique. The packing sheet for a confirmation order must be identical to the shipping information as shown on the order form, regardless of superseding codes, cancel codes or other coding which normally would stop shipment or cause a merchandise substitution. Quantity allocations are to be made identically as on the order form. Errors require immediate attention and should be reconciled with the confirmation order. Top processing priority is given, as item quantities shipped have not yet been deducted from inventory balances. Disregarding these shipped quantities can create discrepancies on other orders.

Ship Complete Orders. Some orders, where all items are requested to be shipped complete, pose extra problems in order processing—if backorders exist. Two basic ways of handling these orders are available:

1. Machine allocation only. Quantity adjustments are made, but packing sheets are not printed. Inventory items are not physically picked.
2. Machine allocation with packing sheets printed. Inventory items are physically picked from stock.

"Machine allocation only" will reduce inventory quantities, but will also create a risk of a discrepancy inventory situation later when the order is completely allocated and ready to pick from stock. An emergency order might occur and might be shipped one of the allocated parts; a conscientious expeditor will overlook a machine allocation; or an inventory balance might have been inaccurately stated.

Case in Point: A manufacturer in the Northeast, with multi-billion dollar annual sales, not only schedules order shipments on request, but also permits "ship complete" order processing—where nothing is shipped until everything can be shipped. These two shipment methods comprise a volume of some 78,000 line items per year for this company. With such large line item quantities requiring single shipments, a staging area was out of the question for storing items picked for a "ship complete" order. Therefore, the "machine allocation only" method was selected to allocate available stock. Physical picking of stock does not occur until the entire order is allocated to ship. The computer offers tight control of these allocated items, restricting discrepancy occurrences on these orders to only a fraction of one percent. Supporting this control is a direct allocation method, by which nearly 30% of incoming receipts dollars are directly allocated to specific customer orders.

"Machine allocation with packing sheets printed" will also reduce inventory quantities, but this method prevents late inventory discrepancies from interfering with a shipment. Discrepancies can be caught early in order processing. However, where backorders exist, a staging area is necessary to house the picked parts, and could pose other problems where extra storage space is not available.

Only Valid Items Are Processed. The edit performed on order line items will determine if items are valid. During order processing, one of three steps must be taken if unmatched items are found:

1. The customer order should be restricted from processing until the items in question have been identified or corrected.
2. The customer order is processed. Unmatched items are cancelled with the customer reordering the items properly.
3. The customer order is processed. The unmatched items are coded as "in supense" to the customer; and are reviewed, then cancel-coded or corrected on the next packing sheet issued on the order.

Parts Substitution. The edit performed on order line items will determine if a part substitution is necessary. A cross-reference system can identify those items which are, or will become, superseded or superseding. The cross-reference code will explain the reason for change; will prevent replenishment buying on the superseded item; yet will still permit exhausting old item stock before substituting a newer product. Two basic decisions arise:

1. If the new item is ordered, and the old item being superseded is still in inventory, substitution of the old item is made. (If the entire quantity ordered cannot be supplied with the old item, a decision is automatically made either to ship what is available and cancel any quantity balance remaining, or to withdraw and ship the new item. Backorders should be for the new item only.)
2. If the old item is ordered, it is withdrawn and shipped, unless the old item is being obsoleted or is no longer in stock. Inventory is usually purged when an obsolete code is assigned. The new item is substituted where old item stock is depleted. The quantity rule in (1) applies where a quantity balance is available on the old item. Backorders should be for the new item only.

Two problems relate to these decisions. The item ordered can be one that requires model and serial references, or pricing differences may be involved. The items (which require model and serial data) will vary in color, size, function, etc., and cannot follow normal item substitution procedure. The code assigned will cause order item cancellation, if reference data is not contained on the order. Backorders apply to specific model and serial numbers. Price differences are often controlled where old item substitution is being made. However, when older stock is gone, and the new item is being substituted, the new price is generally used. Material change or product improvements usually require price changes which are followed unless company policy does not allow such changes.

Special Coded Items. Special codes are used to handle processing deviations that become necessary. These codes would apply to items which are no longer available; items that have become discontinued; items sold only in certain configurations (such as details, assemblies, or kits only); items sold in matched sets; items requiring special pricing considerations; and special lead time items. Other reasons also exist. Items are cancelled from the customer's order where coding information is printed in the company catalog or price lists. Items requiring special price consideration, such as made-to-order parts, are generally not cancelled. Instead, a processing procedure is followed which permits a price quote and delivery commitment to be given to, and approved by, the customer. However, disapproval, or lack of approval being received within a specified time period, will cause item cancellation to occur if desired. Items drop-shipped from another depot, or direct from vendor or factory location, are cancelled from the original order and placed on a separate order basis. The separate order is required if the depot, vendor or factory bills direct; or to keep separate records on drop-shipment business costs.

Standard Quantity Sizes. Items may be coded to sell in certain quantity sizes only. When this occurs, the customer quantity is increased to the minimum quantity offered, or is increased to the next greater increment of the packaged quantity. (Special processing might be approved under certain conditions, such as in confirmation order processing where the exact quantity shipped must be reduced from stock balances.)

Pricing Packaged Items. Pricing can become a problem when dealing with packaged items. Package size can vary, and can be either odd or even lot quantity. One approach is to price packaged quantities by the hundred, regardless of quantity contained in the package. This has a unique advantage to retailers, who can determine the suggested unit list prices simply by moving the decimal place on the list price two places to the left. A deviation to this procedure is made when the list price, per hundred, becomes greater than a certain dollar value. When unit price is large enough, the parts are priced by the unit. The "price-per-hundred" concept is needed where low-priced items are concerned. When special processing of an item occurs (quantity shipped is below normal package quantity), the extended price may fall below a penny. A special procedure should be followed to replace the calculated price extension by $.01, or a minimum dollar amount, when this happens. Normally, a no-charge shipment is made to keep costs down, but this situation should not be overlooked.

Picking Tags. Some method of finding stocked items is required, where assigned storage locations are used. One method is to sort and print order items in storage location sequence per order, with the storage locations printed. This method makes it difficult to find a particular part number on a packing sheet, and allows abnormal handling (or abuse) of the packing sheet form "set." Another method, more favored, is to prepare picking tags for each line item which has a shipped quantity. Packing sheets are printed in part number sequence, or as ordered by customer, with additional picking tags printed in storage location sequence. This method offers a means to locate individual parts in storage; provides an identification tag to be placed on the package (for internal inspection purposes as well as for the customer's benefit); and permits printing summary picking tags (per order and per "batch") containing machine accumulation of total customer orders and line items to be picked per storage zone. The summary data points out where potential picking bottlenecks might occur, to permit better manhour allocation for picking.

See Exhibit 6-4 for a typical sales order packing sheet summary tag. This tag shows detail order "header" information, in addition to the number of line items to pick from each warehouse picking zone, for each sales order printed in a "batch." A batch summary tag is printed at the end of each batch of customer orders. It shows beginning and ending sales order and packing sheet numbers for the batch instead of "header" information. Batch summary information shows where the picking manhours are needed. The card shown in Exhibit 6-4 contains:

(A) Company sales order number.

(B) Company packing sheet number.

(C) Date packing sheet was printed.

(D) "Bill to" name and address code.

(E) "Ship to" name and address code.

(F) Customer's purchase order number.

(G) Shipment method requested by customer.

(H) Summary data on line items to pick.

A1987 (A)	XX–0029234 (B)			XX–XX–XX (C)
50100 (D)	50131 (E)	1239A (F)	UPS (G)	TOTAL – 100
				ZONE "A" – 34
				ZONE "B" – 22
				ZONE "C" – 28
				ZONE "D" – 16
				(H)

EXHIBIT 6-4:   Sales Order Packing Sheet Summary Tag

CONTROLLING CUSTOMER ORDER DISCREPANCIES

Basic order-handling steps are covered in other chapters of this book; however, one important aspect needs specific coverage here: discrepancy processing. Inventory discrepancies exist where less stock is found in a storage location than is allocated on the picking tag being filled. This discrepancy initiates many actions:

1. The employee filling an order records the discrepancy quantity on the packing sheet, and on the picking tag. A new handwritten picking tag is created for the partial quantity picked.

2. The shipping inspector verifies that the quantity shipped is corrected on both the sales order packing sheet and the picking tag.

3. Discrepancy information is "inputted" to the computer via source data entry or off-line keypunch equipment. This input data permits a quantity update on the customer order packing sheet prior to invoice processing; creates a backorder quantity; flags the part number master file of the discrepancy situation to prevent further picking errors; and causes an inventory request listing (and individual request cards) to be printed, for use in discrepancy inventory verification.

4. A physical inventory is taken upon receipt of the inventory request "turn-around" cards. The inventory balances are recorded on the cards, with the cards (or input data) being returned to the computer facility. Physical inventory quantities are also recorded on the inventory request listing. The listing is retained on file to audit discrepancy frequencies.

5. The physical inventory count is entered on the part number master file as the current shelf balance. (Quantity difference between prior shelf balance at the time of

discrepancy and the physical inventory count is recorded as a variance adjustment.) The discrepancy flag is removed from the part number master file, and normal record activity is resumed. The discrepancy packing sheet number can remain in the file, but will be insignificant without the flag. (When flagged, multi-discrepancies of the same part number and with earlier packing sheet numbers are printed on the discrepancy inventory request listing but only one inventory request card is prepared for the part number.)

INVOICING THE PACKING SHEET SHIPMENT

Customer billing is initiated by shipping information picked up from the sales order packing sheets processed. Discrepancy information accompanies this shipping data, and is machine updated prior to customer billing to prevent invoice errors.

Invoice Control Card

An input invoice control card is created from shipping data placed on the sales order packing sheet. All order "header" control data is picked up, plus actual method of shipment used, final charges and F.O.B. point, bill-of-lading number and special charges. This card is matched to the "invoice suspense" file, with matching line item data pulled for invoice printing.

Invoice Editing

Editing of invoice data is required prior to invoice printing. Most of the editing is accomplished by comparing "header" data (on the control card) to the invoice suspense file. Price data, however, must be edited specially. Most companies use existing prices in force when a shipment is made, as the billing price. These prices are picked up from the part number master file and placed in the invoice suspense file when packing sheets are printed. Occasionally, some prices might be missing when packing sheets are printed. This causes the invoice suspense file also to have prices missing. The part number master file is checked on each invoice item that has a price missing, with printing cancelled on any packing sheet which still has any items unpriced. A price request follow-up listing should be printed after invoice editing, for use in obtaining needed prices. The invoice control card can be duplicated (or machine rejected) for use as a turn-around card, to initiate customer invoicing after needed prices have been obtained.

Pricing Control

Price changes should be updated only in the part number master file, where previous selected prices existing on packing sheets must be retained—as with export order shipments where prices are quoted from the packing sheet and fixed by a letter of credit. Special prices, such as made-to-order prices, are updated in the invoice suspense file only—to permit invoice printing without publishing the price. New prices are updated in both the part number master file and the invoice suspense file, as both files will have missing prices—if any sales have occurred.

PROCESSING CUSTOMER BACKORDER ITEMS

Backorder items are important to customer order processing. Backorder costs can be great, because tight control must be employed to keep backorders current, and because many shipments might be necessary to complete a single customer order. A daily backorder additions-listing will alert inventory personnel of new backorder quantities. A master backorder listing will contain all backorder quantities existing on all part numbers. A method of receipts quantity allocation will determine who gets what, when more is on backorder than is received for shipping. A method of changing customer orders will allow cancellation, or quantity reduction, of backorder items which cannot be supplied, and will facilitate the handling of discrepancies.

The Daily Backorder Additions Listing

New backorders are listed each day. Each backorder item has its order "header" data and "line item" data printed on the listing. In addition, existing open order information is given showing the total quantity on order (with due date and order memo numbers an option). Coding information identifies the purchased or manufactured status, the lead time, the buyer and/or vendor and any special inventory control order strategy. Management review of this listing can show ordering performance (percentage of items covered by open orders at the time of backorder); why backorder items weren't covered by an open order; which items should be cancelled; etc.

The Master Backorder Listing

A listing of all backorder items together shows the current backlog. This backorder listing becomes a control device. The format is about the same as the backorder additions listing, except that each part's assigned storage location is also given. Spot inventories can be taken on emergency backorders to verify correct zero stock balances. Care must be taken not to overlook any machine allocations. Expedite priorities can be developed from this listing. Procurement performances can be measured. Direct allocation of receipts can be made using data from this list. The general age of backorders can be easily determined.

Receipts Allocation

A certain percent of the inventory items will tend to appear continually on backorder. Enough quantity cannot be obtained (most of the time) to prevent a backorder situation on them. When receipts arrive, more quantity is on backorder than can be shipped. A method to direct allocate receipts is necessary to determine which quantity is to be shipped first. The backorder listing is normally printed in order priority sequence within part number sequence. Without a special method to allocate receipts, backorders will allocate to ship in this sequence. Special emergency conditions might change a low priority order to a higher priority. A new emergency order might be received which is not even in the backorder file. These conditions require special allocation.

Sales order number, item number and model and serial number references can be placed on a receipts document (or input information), to signal that the receipt quantity is to be specially allocated as designated. Any excess quantity after the direct allocation is made is to be allocated by the computer in the file sequence of the remaining backorder items.

Customer Order Alteration

The order processing system should allow customer order items to be added to an order, reduced in quantity or cancelled. New order edit, discrepancy processing, arbitrary cancellations or superseding of certain items command this capability.

In Exhibit 6-5, which illustrates an operating flow chart for customer order processing, the customer order is the catalyst for inventory action. The order processing system must consider the functions of order taking, creating the packing sheet, order handling, invoicing and backorder processing. The system must be flexible in handling order deviations and peak loads, and furnish exception information for spotting and correcting system failures.

JUSTIFYING A COMPUTER SUPPORTED SYSTEM

Customer order processing is a prime consideration in the inventory management system. A simple, quick, order flow should be planned for both manual and computer supported customer order processing. Much more detail will be involved in the computer supported system. Unless a "real time" system, with source data entry, is being used; it is doubtful that a computer supported system can beat the speed of a simple manual system for a single customer order. But the main justification of a computer support system is in volume processing. And nothing can handle order volume better than a computer, if the order processing system is properly planned.

A data linking system for computer "chaining" (offering controllable computer access to and from variable data files), could be adopted, to provide establishment of variable data files and permit divisional, depot or other distributional integrated inventory control programs to support customer order processing. However, the customer, company convenience and cost should all be considered in planning order processing.

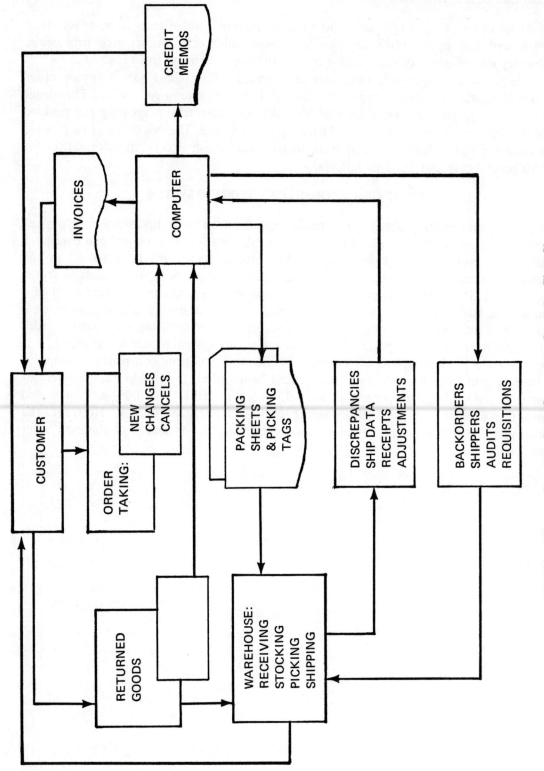

EXHIBIT 6-5:   Customer Order Processing—Operating Flow Chart

7

Realizing Efficient Inventory Withdrawals Through a Dynamic Paperwork System

Withdrawals processing involves the integrated use of a paperwork system for activating material movement; a communication means for liaison between order processing and shipping; material handling methods/equipment for physical location and movement of merchandise; and an audit system to monitor material movement results, flow efficiency and picking performance.

These interactive functions are outlined and discussed here to help in upgrading the importance of picking parts. Withdrawal forms are illustrated for company sales, shipment returns, intercompany material transfers, employee stock requisitions, and stocking-error corrections. A checklist is prepared for handling inventory discrepancies or losses. The significance of these different picking forms is accented to justify their usage. A warehouse control point is suggested, and implementation methods are offered. A summarization of customer order data provides the needed characteristics for developing an order priority system for use in order-picking assignments. Equipment needs are stressed; but a simple approach to the productivity problem is outlined, and it is suggested that it be used first. The addition of "picking with common sense" is added to the basic parts-picking functions, with guidelines given. And finally, a new way to measure parts-picking performance is recommended.

A STREAMLINED PAPERWORK SYSTEM CONTROLS THE WITHDRAWALS PROCESS

A paperwork system is required to initiate and control movement of merchandise, once merchandise is recorded as part of inventory investment. Inventory withdrawal forms provide this physical control over merchandise movement, and simplify the withdrawals processing.

Security Benefits

The paperwork system contributes to inventory security. Some companies rely heavily on paperwork as a major part of their inventory security program. Special forms, created to cause a specific type of inventory movement, identify the transaction being processed. Merchandise accompanying a form must be correctly identified and counted, because audit or security checks are made on merchandise in flow.

A Sales Record Provided

Inventory withdrawal forms are used either as a tool for, or a product of, record keeping. Record keeping is vital to withdrawals processing, with greater care needed where transactions are recorded prior to sales. Accurate posting of all withdrawals will permit recorded knowledge of what is in inventory without requiring a physical stock check. The time taken to pre-post record quantities does create a slight customer delay, but the delay would be much longer (without pre-posted record keeping) if a physical check shows nothing is in stock. Withdrawal quantities are lost if they are not recorded. This could mean future lost sales, also, because less inventory is being bought than is actually being sold. A form document will guarantee a record of all sales—if used.

MANY DIFFERENT FORMS GUIDE AN INVENTORY'S MOVEMENT

The different material movement forms in use today can be separated into those used for sales, shipment returns, intercompany material transfers, employee stock requisitions, stocking-error corrections and inventory discrepancies or losses.

Over-the-Counter Sales

The form used for over-the-counter sales should be designed for quick preparation and use. Such a sales form must have only essential information on it. It must be processed quickly and with the least amount of bother to the customer. Speed is the essential element of this form. The form could be the perforated tag attached to the merchandise, a cash register ticket, or a fast snap-out form. (See Figure 7-1.)

The size of the form is kept small due to the limited information required. The buyer's name and address are needed (if perforated tags and/or cash register tickets are not used) as well as the merchandise number or description, unit sales quantity, and pricing information such as unit prices, extended prices, summary price and applicable tax. A check number should be cross-referenced on the sales ticket if sale is made by check.

This form is not used for picking parts, unless customers are restricted from physical selection of merchandise, as the retail customer normally selects and controls the movement of merchandise sold on over-the-counter sales tickets. The ticket therefore does not have to show merchandise storage location, weight, size, etc., unless such information is a part of the article's description. Supplementary picking tags (to find material), shipping labels (to ship material), and/or freight bill preparation (for transportation routing and charges) are not required.

Record keeping is accomplished *after* sales are made. Forms are usually batch processed after each day's sales—to update inventory balances, prepare sales data information, payroll commission reports, etc. Online hook-up of "point-of-sale" terminals will allow "real time" processing of this sales information and can signal advance stock replenishment needs to prevent lost sales.

ORIGINAL

RS510-2D

Customer's Order No.						Date		19	
Sold to									
Address									
Sold by	Cash	C.O.D	Charge	On Acct	Mdse Ret	Paid Out	Ordered by		
Quantity	Description					Price	Amount		
						Tax			
Thank You Present this bill with claims or returned mdse.						Total			

No. 03601

Uarco Business Forms

Rec'd by   RS 510-2

EXHIBIT 7-1: An Over-the-Counter Sales Order Form. Designed for quick preparation and use, the form shown here is a manually prepared machine pull-out form. (By courtesy of Uarco Incorporated Business Forms, Barrington, Illinois.)

Return Shipments to Customers or Vendors

The form used for return of customer property does not require updating of inventory balances. Some type of paperwork is necessary to authorize return shipments of merchandise (resulting from vendor over-shipments, wrong material received, returned goods beyond warranty, etc.). Information is needed to define what merchandise is to be shipped, whose property the material is, where shipment is to go, how it is to be shipped and responsibility for transportation charges. (See Exhibit 7-2.)

Picking tags are not used as the merchandise is readily accessible when form is prepared, and the form is attached to the merchandise for forwarding to the shipping area directly. Shipping labels and a freight bill of lading will be required. A copy of the shipping authorization form accompanies the shipment as a packing sheet. After the

```
_____ COMPANY
                        SHIPPING  AUTHORIZATION
DATE_____                                        N⁰  11065
SHIP TO_____

    _____      _____ Expense_____  ROUTE COPIES:
    _____      Vendor Expense_____    No. 1 WITH MATERIAL
                         Vendor Code No._____      TO SHIPPING_____
VIA_____       Sent from Dept. No._____  No. 2. SENDER'S FILE_____
                         Return to____ Yes__ No__  No. 3 WRITER'S FILE_____
TRANSPORTATION CHARGES___ Return to Stockroom or Dept.
    DECLARED VALUE_____                          PUR. ORDER NO._____
```

Item No.	Qty.	Code	Part No. & Description

Reason for Shipment _____

_____

_____

Approved By _____ Dept. _____
                          Full Name

EXHIBIT 7-2:   Shipping Authorization Form. This form, used to return shipments of merchan-
                  dise, does not require inventory balance update as merchandise being shipped is
                  already customer property.

shipment is made, one copy of the form should be routed to the person (or department) authorizing the shipment. One copy should be forwarded to the accounting department. An optional copy can be retained in the shipping office for future claims processing or shipment tracing. (See Exhibit 7-3 and 7-4.)

The shipping authorization is handled by the parts pickers only where return is not customer property. In this case, a material transfer form is also required with the shipping authorization, for parts picking and inventory balance updating.

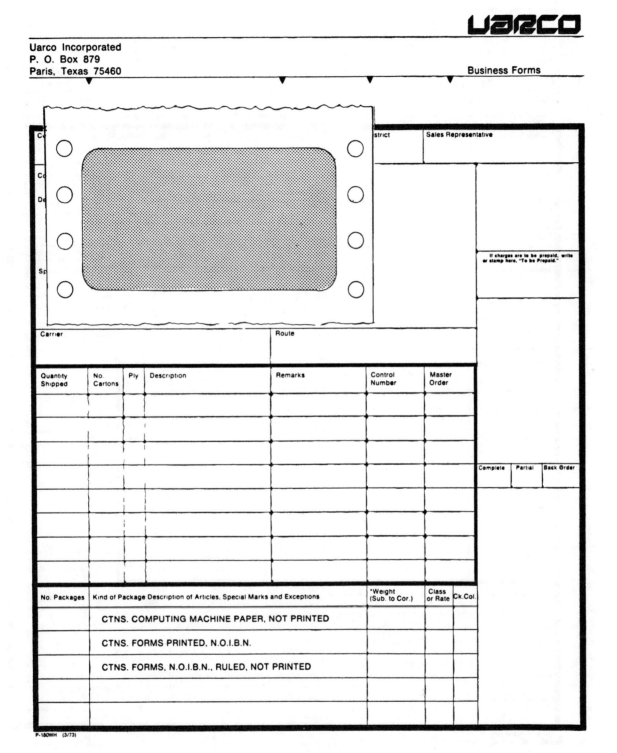

uarco

Uarco Incorporated
P. O. Box 879
Paris, Texas 75460

Business Forms

No. Packages	Kind of Package Description of Articles, Special Marks and Exceptions	*Weight (Sub. to Cor.)	Class or Rate	Ck.Col.
	CTNS. COMPUTING MACHINE PAPER, NOT PRINTED			
	CTNS. FORMS PRINTED, N.O.I.B.N.			
	CTNS. FORMS, N.O.I.B.N., RULED, NOT PRINTED			

P-180WH (3/73)

Permanent post-office address of shipper: P.O. Box 879 Paris, Texas 75460   **PACKING SLIP**

EXHIBIT 7-3: Packing Slip (or Packing Sheet). Sometimes used as a shipping authorization. The one shown here has a stencil label attached to the front of the form. (By courtesy of Uarco Incorporated Business Forms, Barrington, Illinois.)

†The fibre boxes used for this shipment conform to the specifications set forth in the box
maker's certificate thereon, and all other requirements of Consolidated Freight Classification.

Straight Bill of Lading - Short Form
ORIGINAL - NOT NEGOTIABLE

Carrier: _____

Shipper's No. _____

Carrier's No. _____

RECEIVED subject to the classifications and tariffs in effect on the date of the issue of this Bill of Lading

At **Paris, Texas** _____ 19____

From **UARCO** Incorporated

the property described below in apparent good order except as noted (contents and condition of contents of packages unknown) marked consigned and destined as indicated below, which said carrier (the word carrier being understood throughout this contract as meaning any person or corporation in possession of the property under the contract) agrees to carry to its usual place of delivery at said destination, if on its route otherwise to deliver to another carrier on the route to said destination. It is mutually agreed as to each carrier of all or any of said property over all or any portion of said route to destination and as to each party at any time interested in all or any of said property that every service to be performed hereunder shall be subject to all the terms and conditions of the Uniform Domestic Straight Bill of Lading set forth (1) in Official Southern Western and Illinois Freight Classifications in effect on the date hereof if this is a rail or rail-water shipment or (2) in the applicable motor carrier classification or tariff if this is a motor carrier shipment

Shipper hereby certifies that he is familiar with all the terms and conditions of the said bill of lading including those on the back thereof, set forth in the classification or tariff which governs the transportation of this shipment and the said terms and conditions are hereby agreed to by the shipper and accepted for himself and his assigns

Customer's Order No.				Uarco's Order No.	District	Sales Representative

Consigned To

Destination

Special

Subject to Section 7 of Conditions of applicable bill of lading. If this shipment is to be delivered to the consignee without recourse on the consignor, the consignor shall sign the following statement:
The carrier shall not make delivery of this shipment without payment of freight and all other lawful charges.

_____
(Signature of consignor.)

If charges are to be prepaid, write or stamp here, "To be Prepaid."

Carrier				Route		

Received $
to apply in prepayment of the charges on the property described hereon.

Quantity Shipped	No. Cartons	Ply	Description	Remarks	Control Number	Master Order

Agent or Cashier.

Per
(The signature here acknowledges only the amount prepaid.)

Charges advanced: $

Complete	Partial	Back Order

C.O.D. AMOUNT

$

If the shipment moves between two ports by a carrier by water, the law requires that the bill of lading shall state whether it is "carriers" or "shippers" weight. NOTE - Where the rate is dependent on value, shippers are required to state specifically in writing the agreed or declared value of the property. The agreed or declared value of the property is hereby specifically stated by the shipper to be not exceeding

No. Packages	Kind of Package Description of Articles, Special Marks and Exceptions	*Weight (Sub. to Cor.)	Class or Rate	Ck.Col.
	CTNS. COMPUTING MACHINE PAPER, NOT PRINTED			
	CTNS. FORMS PRINTED, N.O.I.B.N.			
	CTNS. FORMS, N.O.I.B.N., RULED, NOT PRINTED			

Per
'Shippers imprint in lieu of stamp, not a part of bill of lading approved by the Department of Transportation

UARCO Incorporated **Shipper, Per** _____ **Agent** _____ **Per** _____

Permanent post-office address of shipper: P.O. Box 879 Paris, Texas 75460

ORIGINAL

EXHIBIT 7-4:   Freight Bill of Lading. May be prepared as a standard form, or may be part of another form. This "Straight Bill of Lading—Short Form" was a part of the packing slip shown in Exhibit 7-3. (By courtesy of Uarco Incorporated Business Forms, Barrington, Illinois.)

PARTS AND ACCESSORIES

SALES ORDER	BILL TO	SHIP TO
DISC.	TERMS	OTHER →

☐ TELEX
☐ MAIL
☐ PHONE
☐ WIRE

BILL TO		SHIP TO	
	1		1
	2		2
	3		3
	4		4
	5		5

DELIVER VIA	ORDER NO.	DATE	F.O.B.

ITEM	QTY.	U/M	PART NUMBER	DESCRIPTION	MODEL	SERIAL	PRICE	DISC.

CONFIRMATION

SIGNATURE _____

EXHIBIT 7-5: Telephone or Mail-in Order. This will vary in size and design. The telephone order shown here is also a "Confirmation" or machine by-pass order. (It by-passes inventory posting.) This order form is processed before any inventory postings are made.

Telephone or Mail-in Orders

There is equal concern with the speed in form preparation and in picking merchandise where telephone or mail-in orders occur. Speed in form preparation is important, however, and becomes critical with peak order volumes. These orders require more information than do cash sales tickets as they also require picking and shipping action. Information must be added to identify where material is stored so it can be found. The terms of sales and shipment data, such as where to ship, how to ship and when to ship, are also needed. A telephone or mail-in order will vary in size and design. The telephone order shown in Exhibit 7-5 is also a confirmation or machine by-pass order (it by-passes inventory posting). This order form is processed before any inventory postings are made.

The form size will increase to allow space for added information. The number of form copies will change due to more operations being performed after order taking, and because an audit trail must be left to account for additional work performed. Picking tags can be created to permit sorting of storage locations on items sold for quicker, more efficient picking of merchandise. Otherwise, storage locations can be noted on the form itself.

A picking tag can be a continuous form blank tag as shown in Exhibit 7-6, on gummed or self-adhesive labels, punched cards, etc. Computer sorting of customer order items into storage location sequence, before printing, can allow big time savings. Computer printed pick tags must show complete "header" and "line item" data, such as:

(A) Quantity and unit of measure.

(B) Part number.

(C) Item description.

(D) Storage location assignment.

(E) Company sales order number.

(F) Company packing sheet number.

(G) "Bill to" name and address code.

(H) "Ship to" name and address code.

(I) Customer's purchase order number.

(J) Shipment method requested by customer.

15 EACH	RGB100 5	Wheel	AE-01-03
(A)	(B)	(C)	(D)
A1987 XX-0029234			
(E) (F)			
50100 50131 1239A UPS			
(G) (H) (I) (J)			

EXHIBIT 7-6:   A "Continuous Form" Picking Tag

Manually prepared picking tags will omit most of the above data, with only the first line being given, if storage locations aren't assigned on the packing sheet itself.

Shipping labels and freight bills will also need to be prepared. They can be a part of the order form used, or can be prepared after the order is ready to route and ship.

Material Transfers to Another Company Department or Division

Transfer of material between company departments or divisions might require more than a single form because of different divisional operating procedures. Manufacturing companies which have government or military sub-contracts might demand different information on material transferred for this purpose than for normal commercial applications. A multi-purpose form can be designed, however, which can be used for material transfer to all departments and/or divisions alike. The use of more than one type of form for intercompany transfers of material should be discouraged. Account distribution coding for cost-of-sales can be applied to the form to allow different charges, or processing of data, to be accomplished.

Exhibit 7-7 shows a material transfer form used to move material from one company division, or department, to another. This can be a multi-purpose form for transfer to several divisions from a single distribution point (such as a company's finished goods inventory facility). This form does not generally require pick tags due to low volume of line items being transferred. Storage locations are added to the form before the material is picked for transfer.

Case in point: This form (Exhibit 7-7) is used for picking parts, but picking tags are not created due to the small quantity of items requested at one time. Picking tags could be used where item volume dictates. Shipping labels and freight bills will be required, depending on the geographical location of divisions, when freight carriers are used. Two copies of the material transfer form should be forwarded when the material is transferred (one copy to the receiving division's accounting department, one copy with the material to the using department), with one copy retained for inventory balance updating and then to be filed.

Employee Requisition for Material

Material required for use by company personnel must be requisitioned out of the material stockroom. In most manufacturing companies a requisition card, or "short form," is available at the plant stockrooms for use in obtaining supplies or materials. Some companies restrict the kinds of material obtainable in this manner, and require restricted material to be obtained on a material transfer form.

A "material and parts requisition" form, as shown in Exhibit 7-8, is used to obtain parts from another company department or division. The form shown is computer prepared, with inventory adjustments made prior to physical requisition.

The "requisition card" or "short form," as shown in Exhibit 7-9, is manually prepared at a company stockroom for needed work-in-process material or supplies. Inventory adjustments are made from this form after physical requisition occurs.

Requests should be originated by inventory control personnel, whenever possible, to control total material going into the shop work-in-process areas, and to prevent previous allocated quantities being taken. Inventory control personnel can update inventory balances from the material transfer form before requisition occurs.

SERVICE PARTS TRANSFER ORDER   No. 58029

SERVICE PARTS CENTER

REQUESTED BY_____ APPROVED BY_____ DATE_____ 19___

TRANSFERRED TO: DEPT. OR STOCKROOM NO._____ FOR_____

COMMERCIAL DIV. (RGB) 40_____ COMMERCIAL DIV. 41____SPECIAL CODE_____

MILITARY DIV. (RGB) 42_____ MILITARY DIV. 43_____MARKETING DIV. 47_____

PART NUMBER	DESCRIPTION	BIN LOCATION	UNIT MEASURE	QUANTITY SHIPPED	QUANTITY RECEIVED

1. Accompany Material To Rec. Dept. – Forward To Rec. Div. Accounting Dept.

2. Accompany Material To Rec. Dept. – Retain And File There

3. To Be Forwarded To Service Parts Scheduling – Forwarded To Comm. Div. Accounting

FORM # 1089

EXHIBIT 7-7:   Material Transfer Form

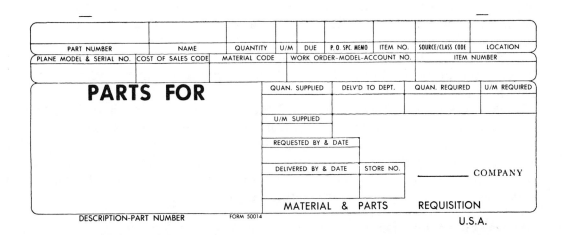

EXHIBIT 7-8:   **Material and Parts Requisition Form**

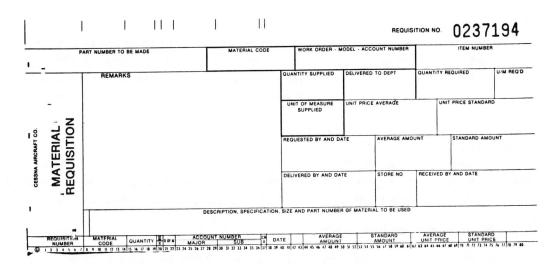

EXHIBIT 7-9:   **Requisition Card—Short Form**

Restrictions should be placed on what type of material can be checked out, and quantity limitations per requisition should be set so that personal excess material doesn't get into work-in-process areas (unknown by others) and create a possible surplus material condition within the stockroom after future replenishment buys.

Emergency shop need for material can be processed at the stockroom, but information is forwarded to inventory control personnel as soon as stockroom records have been updated.

Both the material transfer form and the requisition card, or short form, will be used by parts pickers. The routing for the material transfer form was explained earlier. The requisition card, or short form, is routed to the inventory control area, after material has been picked and stockroom records are updated, to adjust the company's overall inventory balances for the materials withdrawn. The card, or short form, is then forwarded to the accounting department where it is retained.

Stocking-Error Corrections

An article found to be in a wrong stock location can easily be restocked without paperwork, but unless inventory personnel are aware of this restock situation, correct stock balances cannot be maintained and inventory records will be in error. The stocking-error correction form, which controls such corrections, is initiated by the warehouse control person, and sent to inventory control personnel after restocking occurs.

This form can also be initiated by inventory control personnel when it is desired to break down an assembly(or parts kit) into detail parts, due to an emergency need of detail parts not otherwise available, or to permit sale of details where the assembly or kit itself is not selling. The form is two-part in format, as one area is allocated for information which will cause a quantity reduction to inventory, while the other area provides information which will cause a quantity addition to inventory. Inventory balance adjustments will be based on the picker's count quantity taken when a restock is requested or a stocking error is found. A stocking-error correction form (Exhibit 7-10) is prepared when mislocated inventory items are found. This form is usually initiated by warehouse personnel, and used for inventory update after restocking occurs. A variance adjustment is made to each affected part's shelf balance.

Inventory Discrepancies and Losses

Inventory discrepancies and losses happen for many reasons. Parts can be miscounted when received from vendor. Parts can be misplaced or stocked in wrong storage locations. Parts-picking counts can be wrong. Pilferage or theft can occur. Parts can become damaged. Carriers can inadvertently pick up too many cartons of material. Shipments can be misrouted or lost. Human error—which creates most inventory discrepancies—cannot be eliminated completely, but should be controlled. Inventory procedures should be reviewed periodically. Precedural revisions should be made when inventory discrepancies approach or become larger than 2% of the line item volume picked, or of the total revenue dollar value—whichever comes first.

If company policy is not to "book" inventory variances between inventory periods, then a negative variance adjustment can be made to reduce stock balance to zero. Otherwise, a material transfer form should be initiated as a scrap ticket. If the loss is attributable to damage, a material transfer scrap notice should be made regardless of inventory variance policy.

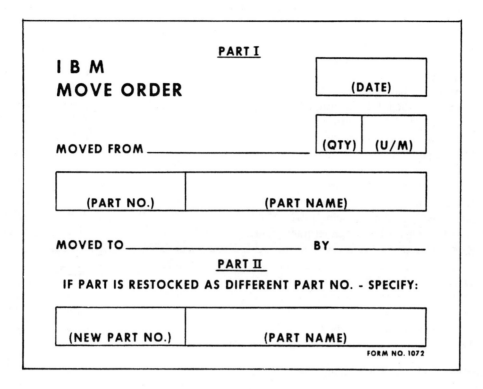

EXHIBIT 7-10:   Stocking Error Correction Form

The inventory discrepancy form acknowledges an inventory error condition. If damaged parts exist, this fact is noted on the discrepancy form. Where damage is noted, a material transfer scrap notice is initiated by inventory control personnel. Coding is contained on the material transfer form to handle a scrap transaction, as well as all other types of material transfers made.

Discrepancies not caused by damage will be handled on a variance adjustment after inventory control personnel have verified the discrepancy by a physical inventory procedure. This is normally a precautionary step because the variance adjustment will cause a stock-out condition to exist.

A list similar to the one shown in Exhibit 7-11 should be required on all stock discrepancies found. Information captured on this document will show a measure of picker's performance, flow problems in the receiving-stocking areas and paperwork processing problems.

EACH WITHDRAWAL FORM IS FLAGGED TO A SPECIFIC ACTION

Different picking forms mean different parts flow or action to the warehouse. Telephone or mail-in orders and/or pick tags signify customer sales. Material transfers indicate scrap or transfer of material to another department or division. Employee requisitions require manual record posting action by the picker. Stocking-error corrections need an inventory restocking action. Discrepancies require a thorough stock investigation.

DISCREPANCY CHECK LIST

PARTS PICKER _____	PART NUMBER _____	ORDER NUMBER _____

1. Is part on back order?   YES _____ NO _____
2. Does tub file have additional locations?   YES _____ NO _____
3. Are parts in the tub file's location?   YES _____ NO _____
4. Was part picked for a confirmation order?   YES _____ NO _____
5. Is picking tag for an emergency order?   YES _____ NO _____
6. Do receipts show in open order transactions?   YES _____ NO _____
7. Are receipts on the warehouse log sheet?   YES _____ NO _____
8. Are receipts on a stocking cart?   YES _____ NO _____
9. Are parts at the location on the log sheet?   YES _____ NO _____
10. Are parts in the pre-packaging area?   YES _____ NO _____
11. Is picking tag for unstocked returned goods?   YES _____ NO _____
12. Sign and give to Inventory Control _____
    Date _____ Time received by Inventory Control _____
13. Does the computer show receipts?   YES _____ NO _____
14. Does the computer show adjustments?   YES _____ NO _____
15. Does the computer show rejections?   YES _____ NO _____
16. Is on-hand balance minus or zero?   YES _____ NO _____
    Date _____ Time returned to Warehouse _____

EXHIBIT 7-11:   Discrepancy Check List

A COMMUNICATION INTERFACE PERMITS FOOLPROOF WAREHOUSE ORDER CONTROL

A system for information flow between order taking, inventory control and shipping personnel is necessary to establish a control point for withdrawals processing; to permit an immediate information flow for changes in order priorities; and to install an effective follow-up system. The warehouse control point established should be the only contact area in the warehouse for communication needs. Paperwork arrives there to initiate withdrawals-processing action. Picking assignments are supervised from there. Priority changing on order picking is controlled at that point. Communication interface needs beyond this point should be performed by the warehouse order control person.

A telephone or two-way communication system should be required between the warehouse order control point and the order taking, inventory control and shipping areas, to supply the communication needs. Walkie-talkies or two-way communications systems are efficient in a large storage area or where a zone parts-picking concept is used. Where zone picking is not established, a more complex method of controlling and assignment of orders is necessary, but communications needs will be the same. Walkie-talkie units should be considered for use by pickers in large storage areas.

An open two-way communication system (intercom) can be effectively used where storeroom areas are small in size. The unit situated in the storeroom is "live" so that information can be spoken from any point in the storeroom by the control person (or pickers) without having to go to a manual unit to answer. Or the unit can be turned on by the control person when he is to be away from his desk.

Order-Picking Assignment

The warehouse order control person makes picking assignments to all order pickers. The communication interface takes over after a picker has left on a picking assignment. A continual check is made on manpower requirements, as new orders arrive, to confirm that all orders received for a given day will be processed. Determination is also made as to which orders will be picked first. A situation will ordinarily exist where more orders (and items) are required to be picked than can be handled by the number of pickers available. A priority system must be acknowledged which will permit correct decisions to support the most satisfactory and timely order picking possible for that which is picked.

Creating a Priority System

An order priority system is developed from a list of order characteristics which can be given priorities. These characteristics would include such things as:

1. Type of order—such as customer sales, intercompany material transfer, employee requisitions or shipment returns.
2. Date order was called in or received.
3. Expedite nature of order—such as emergency, regular or special build order.
4. Method of shipment requested—such as air or surface transportation.
5. Order terms—such as C.O.D., prepaid or open account.
6. Total extended dollar value of order.
7. Customer value based on repeat business and expected purchase volume.

An order priority system could be developed by selection of a combination of the above characteristics. A sample order priority system with only seven priorities might be as shown below:

PRIORITY SEQUENCE	DESCRIPTION OF ORDER PRIORITY
#1	Emergency customer sales order—air shipment
#2	Emergency customer sales order—surface shipment, *or*, Regular customer sales order—air shipment
#3	Regular customer sales order—surface shipment, *or*, Special build customer sales order
#4	Intercompany transfers
#5	Employee requisitions
#6	Vendor shipment returns
#7	Customer shipment returns

Case in point: The important thing to consider in an order priority system is that priorities can vary among companies, or among divisions within the same company; that they are only a management tool for selecting the sequence of order processing. They can also vary in number or complexity, depending on whether computer resources are available for setting priorities. One multi-divisional company in New York set priorities independently, by division, as shown in Exhibit 7-12.

	DIVISION			
PRIORITY RANKING:	1	2	3	4
Customer	1	3	1	
Dollar Value	2	1		
Date Entered	3			
Type of Order	4	2	3	
Urgency of Need				1
Line Item Size		4	2	
Is a Computer used?	YES	YES	YES	NO

EXHIBIT 7-12:   One Company's Order Priority Ranking System—by Company Division

EQUIPMENT CONTRIBUTES TO PRODUCTIVITY

Many companies with large warehouse areas and low picking volume are still being supported, most of them profitably, by the use of handcarts or pushcarts in the parts-picking activity. Productivity gains can almost be guaranteed by replacing manual carts by electric parts-picking carts, tractors or high-rise equipment—if picking activity is high enough for any kind of a trade-off. Beyond productivity improvements, motorized equipment also reduces walking fatigue. Fatigue affects parts-picking productivity and creates an atmosphere which slows performance and allows picking errors to occur.

Cost reductions are being established frequently today, by replacement of internal combustion equipment with new electric material-handling equipment. Much of this is due to the added cost effects of solutions to the growing pollution problems, which are forcing many companies to look at electric equipment benefits more carefully. Additionally, employee morale and performance are improved by reduction or elimination of disturbing noises, fumes and toxic materials put out by the older gas or butane driven equipment.

How to Improve Flow for Equipment Use

An analysis of the existing warehouse flow should be mandatory before cost justification of new picking equipment is made or plans are even suggested. In most cases, cost improvements can be easily discovered, as original warehouse order flow systems are often neglected after implementation—and future planned improvements aren't always made. A review of the current inventory classification should illustrate if rearrangement of material by activity will help create a more favorable flow for cost justification. Parts pickers know the areas and can be a big help here.

The change-over from handcarts or pushcarts to electric picking carts could be accomplished in most companies with little or no change required in the physical characteristics of the warehouse layout, but lack of sufficient aisle space will severely limit the use of motorized or automatic parts-picking equipment. Aisle dimensions must be compatible with picking equipment before any change is considered. Where extensive bin rearrangement is required to correct for aisle space needs, a new improved warehouse flow layout, at that time, will maximize productivity increase, and will offer a nonrestricted view of the advantages of using electric material-handling equipment.

A Simple Approach to the Productivity Problem

The present productivity level in withdrawals processing should be reviewed to substantiate if equipment is the only thing at fault. Review the number of items being picked per manhour. How does this rate compare with last month? Last year? Study reasons for low picking performance. Is employee morale low? Why? Is new employee training adequate? How are working conditions? Is warehouse lighting good? Do shadows tend to confuse material identification? Are aisles easily traveled? Is a material location system being used? Are picking tags correctly sorted? Can material be found easily? Is material stocked within a normal reaching height? Are materials clearly marked and properly stored? Can material be packaged more efficiently prior to picking?

Sometimes the results of a simple approach, initiated by the preceding questions, can be more astonishing in increasing productivity than a sophisticated approach based on a fully automated operation concept. If lack of proper equipment is still found to be at fault, start a cost justification study immediately.

PICKING TAGS SPEED UP THE ORDER FLOW

Picking tags furnish a good method for locating items in inventory, especially where storage areas are large and high volumes of line items are picked daily. Picking tags are printed in stocking sequence so that an efficient one-way traffic flow to the shipping area is followed. Tags contain the item information needed to locate the storage area and to identify the material and quantity to be picked. Tags are attached to the picked material to become an identification means for the customer. Inspection checks of tags and material, while orders are in flow, are compared to order paperwork to verify that proper amount of material and correct items are being selected.

COMMON-SENSE OBSERVATIONS CAN ENRICH THE WORK SETTING WHILE IT IMPROVES PICKING PERFORMANCE

Basic parts-picking procedure includes selection and use of proper equipment for order-picking assignments; locating merchandise in a safe efficient manner as quickly as possible; picking correct quantities of the right material; wrapping and/or tagging material picked; delivering completed order and material to the warehouse control area; reporting all discrepancies on any order assignments completed; and correcting all picking errors found on assigned orders. Picking with common sense should also be incorporated as a basic procedure.

Common-sense observations will enrich the basic parts-picking procedure and, if exercised with corrective follow-up measures, will insure the safest, most efficient and productive order-picking operation possible.

Some common-sense considerations are:

1. *Use acceptable inventory stocking methods.* Are all inventory items classified uniformly, such as by dollar or unit sales activity? Are storage containers coded to reflect the material's classification? Are materials in inventory controlled by a storage location system? Are picking tags provided for order processing? Are storage containers placed upside down when stock is exhausted? Are special storage facilities such as gravity storage racks utilized? Is material handling equipment such as handtrucks, portable hoists and conveyors or motorized picking equipment an integral part of the storage concept? Is an adequate communication system available for use?

2. *Keep merchandise effectively arranged.* Are heavier parts stored on floor level? Are materials, too large or awkward for one picker to handle, located so that they are easily accessible to the shipping area? Are slow moving items using up prime storage space? Are the fast moving materials located close to the shipping area? Are they situated close to or facing the main picking aisle? Are they stored at waist high level for easiest picking?

3. *Maintain inventory items in a properly stored condition.* Are the storage containers too close together to remove material easily? Are the containers too small for the inventory quantity assigned? Is material stored in such a manner that damage will result when picking occurs? Are similiar material or part numbers located so close together that picking errors might happen?

4. *Practice safety.* Are safety shoes or hardhats required to be worn? Are convex mirrors located strategically to spot material handling equipment approaching from an adjacent aisle? Are training programs available, and adequate, for operation of the material handling equipment?

Reactions to common-sense observations, by the pickers, could help bring about long needed remedies and improve the overall picking performance.

BASING WORK PERFORMANCE ON CREATIVE RESULTS

Healthy competition among workers is good, but the means for this competition between pickers—performance reporting on line items picked—must be placed in correct perspective. No two orders are identical. They do not contain the same type or quantity of line items. Distances required to complete an order will vary. Material handling needs will differ.

Rating the Quantity Results

Production-type picking standards can be applied to order processing. Two results can be expected—if time standards must be met as condition of employment, or if salary is based on a "production standard-incentive plan":

(1) An increase in overall picking output, and
(2) Common-sense observations by employees, to find system remedies to permit improvement in picking performances.

A time standard based purely on the number of items picked per hour is not the answer. Several different factors will be required, resulting in several time standards, or in a multi-variable performance formula being developed. Seven important factors to consider are:

(1) Total number of orders processed
(2) Types of orders

(3) Total items

(4) Total quantity

(5) Classification of parts

(6) Distances traveled

(7) Equipment usage needs

Rating the Quality Results

Publish daily results for overall average picking performance, so each person can measure his own performance. Publish actual individual picking results, if permitted by, or not applicable to, union agreements. This should cause healthy competition among employees. But don't put too much stress on quantity volume alone—condition line item performance with variable picking results. Rate the number of picking errors, the quantity or dollar value of merchandise damaged during picking, and the volume or quality of suggestions offered. Let the pickers know that more is involved in the job than just picking merchandise.

8

Simple Packaging and Marking Methods Cut Costs in Shipping

Inventory management results can be improved in the shipping function in these areas:

 .... loss of materials

 .... money

 .... customer goodwill.

Sound common-sense systems that are easily implemented are offered in this chapter for effectively reducing dollar costs—specifically through focusing attention on theft, carelessness or misrouted packages. Many other profit-leak areas are also examined.

LOSS OF MATERIALS

Loss of materials can come about in several ways. Pilferage, damage by carelessness or misrouting of shipments are the most important material loss factors to control.

Pilferage

The biggest stopgap to loss of company material through employee theft is the physical control which can be implemented through a good security program. However, some things can be done without the "smell" of security control and still have a profound effect. For instance, the physical location of the shipping area can (and should) be completely removed from the company's receiving area whenever possible. It's much too easy to lose merchandise that has just been received, when the receiving and shipping areas are located together. Most of these losses happen through accident—a freight carrier picking up too many parcels or a shipper erroneously bundling up too many parcels together. Why make it easy for freight carriers to take extra packages during pick-up? If physical separation is not possible, at least exercise accountability over outgoing shipments. Check the freight carrier's bill of lading, the customer order (and order markings on each box) being picked up, and take a physical count of the packages assigned on each shipment.

Scrap Control

Another loss tightener would be to provide physical control over scrap items. One manufacturing company has automated its scrap procedure so that a conveyor system moves all scrap material from selected areas to an internal scrap compactor. The entrance to the compacting area is by locked doors. Periodically the manager of scrap disposal unlocks the doors and triggers the conveyor system from an operating panel inside the locked doors. This moves the scrap material into the compacting area. A qualified check is made of all material entering on the conveyor. Once inspected, the scrap material is automatically compacted and made ready for later pick-up through controlled exit into pick-up containers. This may be too costly for most medium or smaller size companies; however, the intent behind the system deserves a lot of merit:

1. All material is carefully checked for proper scrap approval.
2. Material exits only through a secure method—locked doors.
3. Scrap material leaves as true scrap material—in this case compacted.

No real chance exists for planned theft through such a system. Any material leaving is destroyed, and has no further use as originally intended.

Inspection

Item inspection of customer orders prior to movement into the shipping area affords a good method of correcting the inadvertent (or otherwise) loss of company materials. Proper inspection placed at this point will insure that only the items and quantities ordered are actually released for shipment processing. With the added function of directing specific orders to specific packaging sites, only a single order at a time can be packaged by one clerk. This does away with mistakes caused by having multi-shipments available for packaging with accidental placement of more than what was ordered into a shipment. (Order inspection prior to preparing for shipment also provides a means to monitor order-picking performance and errors in the warehousing arrangement and stocking procedures.)

A good inspection procedure for the order inspector to follow would include:

1. Complete inspection, if adequate manpower exists, with material identification, description and quantity being compared with the attached picking tags, as well as obvious damage or defective merchandise condition being spotted.
2. Verification that the items inspected are for the order-packing sheet assigned.
3. Determination of which order items require the recording of individual model or serial numbers, and confirming that these are on the packing sheet.
4. Correcting order-picking errors before order release into the shipping area. This is normally controlled through a PA or intercom system into the warehouse or order picking areas. Individual pickers (each assigned a number used for identity on packing sheets), are directed to the inspection area to place overage quantities back into warehouse stock; to obtain additional quantities needed due to picking shortages, or to initiate discrepancy action to correct paperwork for the specific quantity available to be shipped; to be alerted on damaged material picked (since if not caught by the picker when selected for the customer order it will be deemed as a picker damage condition); or for replacing a wrong item picked with what was really ordered.

5. Keeping a log on picking errors showing order packing sheet identification, errors found, type of errors, correction taken and picker responsible.

6. Approving the customer order for release into shipping, and directing the order to an individual packaging clerk. Usually, the latter function of order assignment is accomplished by a shipping room group leader or supervisor, depending, of course, upon the volume of orders being assigned. In larger companies, carousel conveyor systems (or feeder lines) are established to control the movement and assignment of packaging and crating responsibilities. Much should be said for restricting multi-order shipments from being grouped together at a single packaging station at the same time, unless some form of physical separation capability exists. With or without this control, it is of paramount importance that certain packaging/crating procedures be used which will add control to mispackaging of parts. These procedures should include the following two important factors:

   a. A visual check on item and quantity, and model or serial number recordings, to determine accuracy of items being packaged. (Necessary primarily where complete inspection is not permitted prior to release to shipping.)

   b. Noting the box number on the packing sheet (for each item) where more than a single box, carton, or bundle is being used for a single shipment order. This is generally necessary due to multi-packages being required for item separation by freight classification, to prevent unnecessary freight charges. (Where more than one "package" is being used, it is not necessary to mark the box number for those items which are going into box "one"—onto the packing sheet. Only the remaining box numbers need to be noted.) Box number assignment is necessary to permit a separate invoice to be prepared by box, where required by certain foreign countries in their import regulations. Box number assignment also provides a method for verifying shortages on high value items, by repackaging a like order shipment in a same size box and checking both weights.

Exhibit 8-1 shows a decision chart for inspection of customer order prior to release for packaging and shipment. A similar kind of check is made by shipping personnel, during packaging, when recording box numbers on the customer order-packing sheet form.

Carelessness Wastes Money

Handling merchandise through the shipping area can cost money if not properly practiced. Many customer returns are initiated because merchandise is damaged due to careless stapling, nailing or other fastening of the package. Lack of proper packaging material, or poorly designed shipping cartons, also account for merchandise being damaged during shipment.

Merchandise flow into and through the shipping department must be compatible with the types or kinds of merchandise being moved. Proper handling equipment is as necessary in the shipping area as elsewhere in a warehouse. Faster, more efficient methods of packaging or crating merchandise have led to large savings in supply usage, but when carelessly accomplished can turn into a disaster. Packaging and readying merchandise for shipment generally takes up to twice the time as for order picking, and the time factor becomes critical in the systems flow through the warehouse. However, merchandise safety should not be jeopardized in the search for efficiency.

Estimating Packaging Needs

A packaging or crating clerk must be a good estimator. He should be able to determine how many cartons are needed for an order shipment, and what sizes they

Inspection Decision Chart

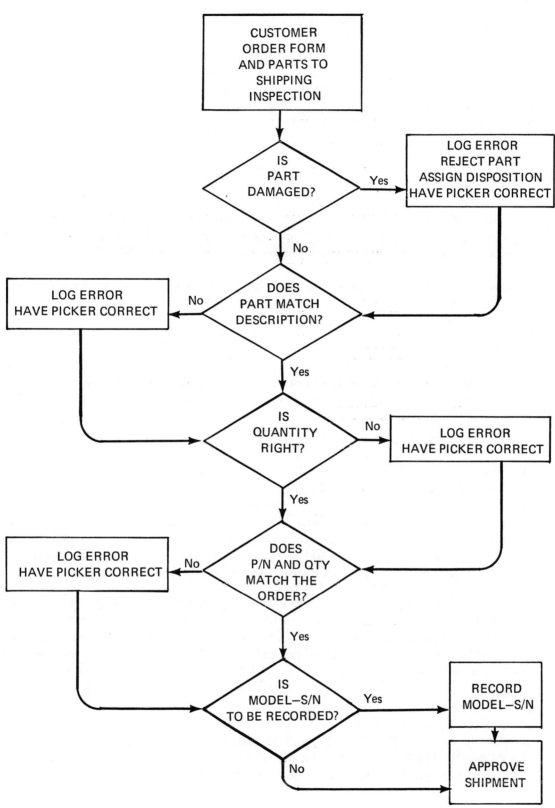

EXHIBIT 8-1:

need to be, simply by looking at an order shipment and considering the item's various freight classifications.

Packaging material and cartons can be selected prior to actual order packaging with the cartons assigned customer order markings when they are "built up" for use. The customer order identification should consist of sales order number, packing sheet number and box number. (Box number one should be assigned to the largest carton used for a specific shipment, as the box identification—for all items in box one—does not need to be marked on the packing sheet, and can save considerable packaging time by its omission.)

Shipping Methods

The shipment method is usually specified by the customer and is printed on the packing sheet. This prevents the wrong type of packaging material from being used (i.e., air cargo permits lightweight cardboard container usage, whereas ocean freight requires sealed crating or otherwise "watertight" containers). Routing is selected after the size, weight, number and types of packages are known. See Exhibit 8-2.

While a shipment is being routed, the bundles, cartons, boxes or containers making up the shipment (which are otherwise ready for pick-up) can be placed in a hold area to wait for the completed packing sheet.

"Ship-To" Labels

As routing information is assigned to the packing sheet, pre-typed or preprinted labels are either pulled from a label holder, or are created for each bundle, box, carton or container in the shipment being routed. Some companies use continuous-form (computer printed) packing sheets that have marking stencils attached. These stencils are printed with the "ship-to" name and address at the time the packing sheet is printed. Other companies print "ship-to" information on self-sticking labels, which are used in place of stencils as part of the packing sheet. Those companies not using a packing sheet with an attached label or stencil select from pre-printed labels kept on file by customer name, or manually prepare labels as the need occurs. Shipment volume, the kinds of shipments made, and the total number of labels used will help to determine which method is best for a given company. Where labels (or stencils) are part of a packing sheet, they are ready to be used when the cartons are set up for packing or crating a shipment. Immediate application of labels helps to prevent misshipments.

A Number Code. Where labels are applied to cartons *after* routing is assigned, the cartons are moved into a hold area until the labels, packing sheets and other required paperwork are available. Some method is required to prevent loose cartons from being placed with a wrong shipment, or to prevent overlooking all the cartons assigned to a single packing sheet. Where stencils are used, the total number of cartons to be stamped (a number code) should be added to the stencil. The number of boxes or cartons on a particular shipment should be coded to reflect the total pieces being shipped (i.e., the first of four cartons on a single shipment is marked "Box 1 of 4"; the second marked "Box 2 of 4"; and so on). If separate labels are provided they should be individually marked for the overall number of pieces in the shipment—as just explained. This simple marking device will save many misrouted cartons.

CARRIER	COST	SUITABILITY	PICKUP FROM SHIPPER	DELIVERY TO PURCHASER
Air express	Very expensive.	Good for high-priority shipments requiring speedy service.	Yes, but may vary according to the situation.	Yes.
Air freight	Expensive. Minimum charges required.	Provides fast service to airport cities only. Delivery to other towns is extra.	Yes, at extra charge.	Yes, at extra charge.
Freight forwarder	Low cost on shipments over 65 pounds.	Handles shipments of any size. Consolidates small shipments. Provides quick delivery at reasonable rates.	Yes.	Yes.
Motor truck	Low cost on shipments over 65 pounds	Provides fast door-to-door service for small and large shipments.	Yes.	Yes.
Parcel post	Most economical for shipments under 40 pounds.	Good service, no minimum charge. Restrictions on size, weight, and merchandise accepted.	No pickup. Shipments must be taken to post office.	Yes. Unlimited delivery area.
Railway express	Expensive, but very practical for shipments too large or heavy for parcel post and too small for motor freight.	Fast door-to-door service for large and small shipments of all types of merchandise. Will accept many commodities that other carriers will not take.	Yes.	Yes.
Rail	Economical.	Almost any type of commodity in any amount, size, or weight accepted. Great variety of freight-handling and moving equipment available. Many different services offered. Regular delivery service slow, particularly for less-than-carload shipments.	No regular pickup service. Shipper pays extra.	No regular delivery service. Purchaser pays extra.
Water	Cost is less than for any other method of transportation.	Good for transporting large, heavy, and bulky shipments. Delivery is slow by comparison with other shipping methods.	No.	No.

EXHIBIT 8-2: Comparison of Shipping Methods. (By courtesy of McGraw-Hill Book Company.) Elias S. Tyler and Eugene J. Corenthal, Materials Handling: Traffic and Transportation (copyright © 1970 by McGraw-Hill, Inc.), p. 74.

CONTROLLING MONEY LOSSES

The biggest loss attributable to shipping costs is in supplies. Improper use of shipping supplies can lead to a fast shrinking of profit. Standard size containers should be picked when packaging certain types and sizes of shipments. One distributor, notified of a lost shipment, duplicated an emergency shipment to his customer. A later check on carton size, weight and postage showed that although the same individual packed both shipments, a larger carton size was used on the duplicated shipment—amounting to $1.49 more for the larger carton, extra packaging and additional mailing costs.

Training Aids

There should be enough consistency in carton selection for use in mailing material so that even though it is processed at different times by different personnel, a standard size selection could be possible—to avoid waste through unnecessary supplies usage. The company training department can be a big assist here. Training programs can make each clerk proficient in the use of shipping supplies. The cost of the training program, administered just to shipping personnel for this subject, can effect a trade-off in cost reductions—and keep on bringing in many years of extra return on investment.

Error Control

Potential merchandise damages should be monitored by looking for poor packaging before the shipment leaves. Individual corrections made should be recorded. An expense summary should be provided for each shipping clerk, showing dollar mistakes made. This type of measurement can pinpoint repeating problems and permit correction and/or development of training programs that are badly needed—or will ultimately encourage replacement of personnel.

Freight Rate Classifications

Other losses can occur in shipping by ignoring freight classifications on items shipped where a company prepays customer orders. Companies that use computer power to control order processing can easily print a commodity code, or freight classification, which would enable like items to be packaged together for minimum freight charges, providing that a rail or truck shipment method is used, and the shipment weight justifies such packaging separation.

Freight classifications are based on a percentage of a standard rate per 100 pounds. Some items might be shipped at 85% of a standard freight rate (or less), while other items might require as much as a 200% or 300% freight rate adjustment. Big accumulative savings are available by using freight classifications on large, heavy shipments of goods, by separating and marking the packages or cartons by compatible classification codes within a single shipment. (Such identification makes it easy for the carrier to prepare needed paperwork also.)

The current lack of concern by most companies, in using freight classifications for packaging merchandise, is because most shipments are sent collect, with the customer paying the extra freight charges. By ignoring freight classifications, fewer supplies are used in packaging a shipment, so company costs are kept low if shipments are sent collect. However, looking at it from another viewpoint, shipments should be monitored to see what incoming freight loss happens because freight classifications are being ignored by the shipper. Incoming losses should be directed to the shipper, with lower shipping cost methods requested, where significant freight dollar loss is apparent.

Carrier "Paperwork" Responsibility

The carrier is responsible for creating many kinds of forms used in moving goods, for certification of receipt and in invoicing for freight services rendered. Two basic pieces of paper will be looked at here: the bill of lading and the freight bill.

The bill of lading proves ownership, based on f.o.b. point, and therefore requires both the shipper's and the carrier's signatures. This "waybill" is prepared by the carrier to identify a shipment while in transit.

A freight bill is used as an invoice by the carrier to bill for the shipment service given. Its preparation is also the responsibility of the carrier.

The preparation of the bill of lading and the freight bill is slowly being taken over by the shipper, as a prime means to gain favoritism from carriers in delivery pick-up, closer coordination or improved delivery speed. The result has been (and is) added hidden costs to the shipper.

A Combination Packing Sheet/Bill of Lading. The companies which use a computer in customer order processing can benefit greatly by designing a combination "packing sheet/bill of lading" form which will permit machine preparation of the bill of lading. Many different kinds of bill of ladings exist: air or surface; collect or prepaid; and special forms like an ocean bill of lading, or a uniform-through export bill of lading. However, since the carrier has the true responsibility for preparing these forms, a standard company bill of lading form could be designed to replace all other forms, and added as part of the customer order packing sheet. The computer can prepare most (if not all) of the information required on the bill of lading, and can save many company manhours (and dollars) by eliminating the proper selection and preparation of such forms (so freely supplied by the carriers). The carrier can remake this standard form onto his own company's document if it is necessary.

As far as preparing the freight bill goes—don't! The carrier can also do this job—and should. It's part of the freight expense for moving goods. Why pay twice? Where computers are not used, simply let the freight carrier prepare both the bill of lading *and* the freight bill—or look for a carrier that will.

A large manufacturer of lock nuts considered using such a combination form. A significant time savings more than offset the added form's cost. The form is used for truck shipments only at this time. No change in service priority has been experienced, and no complaints have been voiced by the freight companies involved. The company is completely happy with the results of the combination form.

Another company (which manufactures and distributes drug and toiletry preparations), uses a similar type form. Their bill of lading is accepted by all the freight carriers (who cut their own freight bills), even though the airlines voiced early preference for specific air bills. The carrier's freight bill number is applied to the company's bill of lading form number. An operating cost reduction has resulted for this firm also.

Stencils Add More Benefits. As stated earlier, another time savings experienced by many companies is the attachment of a shipping address stencil on a packing sheet form. The attached stencil is available for use when a shipment is boxed. It prevents the delay experienced where labels or stencils are provided by the shipping office after packaging occurs, and it provides added control over misshipped or lost boxes. Most companies using such stencils are completely satisfied with their use. (Case in point: a multi-divisional manufacturer of electrical equipment and appliances, with multi-billion dollar annual sales, has used this system for many years. The machine-prepared stencils *definitely* created an overall cost reduction for this company. Aside from the computer's small size print not being as large as they would like, the company is genuinely satisfied with this type of marking system.)

Self-Insure Technique

Insurance costs to cover shipments for the last 12 months should be reviewed. Is there a high dollar expense allocated for freight insurance? Have insurance claims paid for any lost shipments or damaged goods?

Most companies experience a low volume of lost shipments or damaged goods. Where this can be proven, it is worthwhile to underwrite the insurance costs—or at least think about it. Lower air express shipment rates can be obtained on shipments totaling less than $50, if you forget the carrier's insurance premium. (Anything valued over $50 must be insured for its true manufacturing replacement value; however, a shipment can be deliberately valued less than its true value to prevent paying insurance.) REA (truck and air) rates can be reduced 30 cents per hundred dollar valuation by not paying insurance. Truck rates are also lower where a signed release valuation exists: where only a token dollar amount per pound is paid by the carrier for damage or loss. Volume shipments by truck will provide good savings if the self-insure method is practiced. A large Midwest drug distributor has annual dollar savings in the five-digit figure, simply by underwriting their shipment insurance.

CREATING CUSTOMER GOOD WILL

The shipping function can promote customer good will by packaging to keep freight costs low; by adequately protecting merchandise during shipment; and by providing multiple use cartons for continued use on in-store merchandising. These are assigned job duties that must be improved on. However, other methods should be implemented to gain customer good will, and thus to increase sales potential.

Solicit Shipping Improvement Suggestions

A pre-stamped card (or questionaire), placed in randomly selected shipments, can help to gain customer good will—by showing concern in asking for valid suggestions on reducing order shipment errors, or for solving customer criticism. It also can verify the adequacy (or inadequacy) of company inspection results by providing post-inspection benefits by a critical inspector: the customer himself.

UPS Is Competitive

Fast delivery speed and low cost can always generate customer good will. In the areas where United Parcel Service (UPS), an independent parcel carrier, is operable, dependably fast service has been experienced at competitive low prices. In some areas, UPS has beat air express service on both counts. This "surface" service should not be overlooked when routing customer order shipments.

The "Added Touch"

Seven additional items can be practiced which will allow the shipping function to continue or increase good company relations with customers, while gaining a "good will" image within the industry. These seven items are considered an added touch, because they either permit savings to the customer or provide special service consideration being sought. Such items would include:

1. Notification to customers when emergency shipments will be delayed.
2. Consideration for late customer cancellation of items already boxed for shipment.
3. Special order-processing consideration to route shipments for meeting specified carrier shipment schedules.
4. Priority order processing followed, so that emergency orders will be handled before stock orders.
5. Permitting orders to be held for completion before shipment is made.
6. Bunching backorder shipments together to a "same" customer to save on freight costs.
7. Following good routing procedures to insure both fast service and lowest costs.

9

Inventory Answers for "When" and "What to Order" Require Flexibility, Judgment and Control

Answers are detailed for the two basic questions required by the requirements estimator: when to order, and what to order? A control method is developed (and offered to the reader) which can provide open order accuracy, automatic expedite capability and control over order cancellations, changes and receipts after orders have been released. The "when to order" is answered by the development of an order point system. The order point system is defined, and simplified examples are given, both on the formula itself and in its calculation. Two methods are described which can permit needed flexibility in the normal order point system. Both manual and automated order release capability are described, and system flow charts are provided. The "what to order" is answered by the economic order quantity (EOQ) formula. Exceptions (to the EOQ results) are listed to allow the use of individual judgment in inventory procurement. EOQ variables are described.

RELATING "WHEN TO ORDER" TO EXPECTED DEMAND DURING THE PROCUREMENT LEAD TIME

Many methods can be used to determine when to order merchandise for inventory. Where stock records are not kept, a periodic physical inventory will be required, with ordering accomplished as a result of the stock count. A string, wrapped around a quantity of parts, can cause an order to be generated when the string is broken so that parts can be used or sold. (It's more common to use separate storage locations, or partitions at the same location, than to use string. This "when to order" method is referred to as a bin reserve, or two-bin system.)

Where stock records are maintained, either internally within a computer or manually on item record cards, a quantity balance is used to signal for a reorder. This allows parts to be ordered on an exception basis when the assigned quantity is reached. The order point method is the most universally used tool for developing this quantity guide, and for determining when to order replenishment stock (for independent demand items) in a finished goods inventory.

130

The Order Point System

Several variables must be considered in the determination of when to order replenishment stock:

— How long does it take, normally, to receive a part from a vendor after it has been ordered? (Vendor lead time.)

— How long does it take to complete replenishment review and ordering? (Administrative lead time.)

— What quantity is being sold? (Averaged demand.)

— What extra stock is needed to cover unexpected items such as vendor shipments lost in transit; time lost while vendors are on strike, are behind in production output, or their manufacturing facilities are closed; when unusual demand occurs; etc.? (Bin reserve or safety stock.)

The order point method, in manual systems, considers these variables in a simple formula: $\text{ORDER POINT} = \overline{X}_{LT} + 2MAD_{LT}$

$\overline{X}$ is a mathematical definition for a quantity average—in this case an average usage per demand period.

$\overline{X}_{LT}$ represents this average usage over a lead time (LT). Lead time consists of both vendor and administrative lead time.

$2MAD_{LT}$ is the representation for the service level factor. It is two times the Mean Absolute Deviation (MAD) over a lead time (LT). MAD (or $MAD_{\overline{X}}$) is the sum of the absolute differences of $\overline{X}$, and the demand periods used to calculate $\overline{X}$, divided by the number of demand periods used. (One standard deviation is approximately equal to 1.25 Mean Absolute Deviation. Therefore, 2MAD is roughly equal to a 95% service level. The MAD coefficient can easily be altered to fit inventory level restrictions. MAD is an easy method of calculating safety stock requirements statistically.)

Controlling Order Points in a Manual System

The order points are usually calculated only once per year with manual systems. Monthly reviews are recommended (where practical), but are sometimes not justified because of time requirements or low sales volumes. An attempt should be made to refigure order points if and when stock-outs occur, if monthly review is not justified.

Computer Smoothing

The order point used by a computer is essentially the same as the one used in manual systems, except for changes caused by the "smoothing" factors. Smoothing factors are used to give more preference to certain demand periods over others, and are necessary to adjust for error in the forecast. Normally more weight is given to the most recent month's demand, with prior months receiving less consideration. If a smoothing factor of 10% is assigned to the current month's activity, the remaining 90% would be applied to the last average calculated (which is usually based on a 12-month moving average). For example, given a 12-month moving average of 120, and a current month activity of 150, the smoothing would be figured in a manner similar to this:

New Average = 10% (150) + 90% (120) = 15 + 108 = 123

The new average of 123 then becomes a 12-month weighted moving average ($\overline{X}$)–differing from the "$\overline{X}$" developed by the manual system using a simple average technique, by the smoothing factors only.

The MAD function is also smoothed by the computer in the same manner as average demand. For economy reasons, the computer allows an order point calculation to be made using only three composite periods of demand instead of the actual 12 periods within a 12-month moving average. Because the individual 12 months are not retained as history, the deviation cannot be calculated per month. It must also be retained and smoothed in a similar set of three composite periods, namely: the *old* MAD, the *current* obsolete deviation and the *new* MAD forecasts.

Selecting a Demand Period

The period used to record demand (i.e., days, weeks, months, etc.) will depend on the product being sold, normal lead times established, inventory limits, and personal preference. An appropriate demand period would be a time interval equal to lead time; however, all merchandise handled doesn't carry the same lead time, lead times change, and a fast reaction time is generally required on unusual demand. One thing is certain, though, the demand period selected must remain consistent.

An even increment demand period (such as a 1-week or a 4-week period) should be used with computer systems; or a method should be developed to adjust monthly or irregular periods by work days existing within each period. Manual systems, through design, normally use only the calendar month period. Work day adjustments should not be ignored here either.

Demand Averaging

Once a demand period has been selected, a decision must be made concerning the number of demand periods to use for averaging demand. A 12-month period of time is normally required to identify most trend patterns, and is normally used for demand averaging. A 12-month moving average method, with smoothing factors, is recommended where computer assistance is available, and irregular demand items (those without demand patterns) don't exist with regularity or in large volumes. A similar system can also be used in manual systems. As long as cyclic or trend movements are identified and coded, a lead time period for demand averaging can be adequate. Averaging of demand will be more responsive where smaller increments of time are used, and could reduce stock-outs marginally, but there is an inherent trade-off of increasing the average inventory investment.

Varying Forecast Strategy

An important factor to consider is that a single forecast method won't work for every situation. A computer's 12-month moving average, with smoothing factors, will build inventories greatly–where the majority of stocked items don't have any existing demand patterns. Automated forecasting can not allow for human judgment, and will create an excess inventory condition where judgment is completely ignored. A method should be selected, therefore, which is simple to understand, easy to work with, flexible in use and highly responsive to customer needs.

Varying the forecast strategy is important. Strategy coding assigned to accomplish this will describe alternate processing flow to bypass order point calculation. An ordering system should not be limited to a single method of order point (or order quantity) calculation, but should be flexible to handle different movement items differently—or not at all.

Forecast Restrictions

An inventory classification, based on sales activity and demand patterns, will help define different forecast strategies for items carried in inventory. Some conditions that would alter normal order point calculation would include:

- Unusual demand situations caused by fads, promotional sales, warranty and other returns, seasonal sales and national disasters.
- Planned obsolescence.
- Consignment inventory.
- Special build items and other non-stockable material.
- New model parts.

Many different coding methods can be adopted for restricting an item forecast. Assigning a fixed order point to an item within a computer file, with the computer unable to override the fixed forecast, or assigning a low order point to an item within a computer file, with the computer able to override the fixed forecast at a later date, are two ways to adjust order point strategy in a simple manner.

Manual record systems can carry a color coding method where demand fields can be circled. Manual systems are not as critical to control as computer-based systems, though, as history activity is visible and activity problems are pronounced.

Fixed Order Point Forecasting

The best way to prevent a new computer forecast from being made on an item is to code the order point so that it is fixed and can't be machine changed. The fixed order point desired must be assigned to the item within the computer file when its order point is fixed. Special listings can be printed, upon request, which will contain all items with fixed order points, and the necessary data to determine if the fixed code should be removed.

A date code, or counter, could be programmed to allow machine erasing of the fixed order point code. (I.e., a field can be designated in each item record, within a computer file, for assigning a variable number relating to time periods. During each forecast period, this field would be reduced by one—but not to go below zero. As long as the field is zero, the computer forecast order point would be used. If not yet zero, the fixed order point assigned would take priority. If a date code is used, the code would be matched to the current computer date index, to determine when its change-over date would be.)

Low Order Point Forecast

New model merchandise cannot be machine forecast until enough demand history occurs to allow a forecast to be calculated. An order point can be entered when new model parts are placed in inventory, to signal for any sales made on initial lay-in stock. In this manner, a forecast can be planned before any of the lay-in stock is sold. The order point code assigned could cause the computer to erase the fixed order point as soon as a machine demand forecast becomes greater than the fixed forecast entered.

Item Forecast Variables

An item forecast is calculated similarly for both manual record card and computer-based systems. The order point formula used can be expanded upon (made more sophisticated), but will remain with three basic variable needs: average demand, lead time and safety stock requirements. (The number of periods used for averaging demand can vary as will lead times. Safety stock is sometimes arbitrarily set as a percentage of average demand, in fixed period quantities, in terms of mean absolute deviation, or by other statistical methods (only the latter two are recommended)–and can even vary on each item being forecast.)

Order Point Symbols:

OP = Order Point
$\overline{X}$ = Averaged Demand
LT = Lead Time
MAD = Safety Stock Requirements (computed by measuring Mean Absolute Deviation)

Order Point Calculation

The basic order point formula (OP = $\overline{X}_{LT}$ + $2MAD_{LT}$) is shown calculated below. The needed variables are:

Last 12 Months Demand   : 3,6,8,7,4,4,4,6,7,6,4 and 5
Demand This Month   : 8
Item Lead Time   : Two (2) months
Smoothing Factor   : 10%
Safety Stock   : 95% desired service level (2MAD)

The following steps will guide you in the calculation of an item's order point:

1. Average demand $(\overline{X})$ is calculated first, by dividing the sum of the last 12 month's demand quantities by 12:

$$\overline{X} = \frac{3+6+8+7+4+4+4+6+7+6+4+5}{12} = \frac{64}{12} = 5.33$$

2. $\overline{X}_{LT}$ requires X being extended over a lead time. Since both $\overline{X}$ and lead time are in the same measurements (months), no adjustment is necessary: $\overline{X}_{LT}$ = 5.33 (2) = 10.66.

3. $MAD_{\overline{X}}$ is required to be calculated before $2MAD_{LT}$ is obtained.

   $MAD_{\overline{X}}$ consists of the absolute differences of $\overline{X}$, and the last 12 month's demand quantities, divided by 12:

MAD = |3 - 5.33| = 2.33 |4 - 5.33| = 1.33
          |6 - 5.33| = .67 |6 - 5.33| = .67
          |8 - 5.33| = 2.67 |7 - 5.33| = 1.67
          |7 - 5.33| = 1.67 |6 - 5.33| = .67
          |4 - 5.33| = 1.33 |4 - 5.33| = 1.33
          |4 - 5.33| = 1.33 |5 - 5.33| = .33

$$MAD_{\overline{X}} = \frac{\begin{array}{l}(2.33 + .67 + 2.67 + 1.67 + 1.33 + 1.33 \\ + 1.33 + .67 + 1.67 + .67 + 1.33 + .33\end{array}}{12} = \frac{16}{12} = 1.33$$

$2MAD_{\overline{X}}$ = 2 (1.33) = 2.66

$2MAD_{LT}$ = $2MAD_{\overline{X}}$ adjusted to lead time. Since smoothing is accomplished on MAD each demand period, the need to adjust to individual lead time is discouraged. The service level factor of 2 can be changed to adjust the service level percent desired.

4. Placing the above calculations together, without the use of "smoothing" factors, we have the following item forecast: OP = $\overline{X}_{LT}$ + 2MAD$_{LT}$ = 10.66 + 2.66 = 13.32, or 13 (rounded).

Exhibit 9-1 shows the steps necessary (using these variables) to smooth average demand and safety stock, once demand averaging is established. The following steps are involved:

Step 1. Smooth $\overline{X}$: 8 (10%) + 5.33 (90%) = .80 + 4.80 = 5.60
Step 2. Calculate $\overline{X}_{LT}$: 5.60 x 2 (months) = 11.20
Step 3. Smooth MAD$_{LT}$: 2.67 (10%) + 1.33 (90%) = .27 + 1.20 = 1.47
Step 4. Calculate 2MAD$_{LT}$: 2 (1.47) = 2.94
Step 5. Calculate order point : $\overline{X}_{LT}$ + 2MAD$_{LT}$ = 11.20 + 2.94 = 14.14

Increasing the "smoothing" percentage will bring about a more rapid response to changes in demand. (CAD stands for Current Absolute Deviation, and is the absolute difference between "Current Demand" and "$\overline{X}$.")

(10%)	(90%)	(Smoothed)	FORECAST	(10%)	(90%)	(Smoothed)	FORECAST	ORDER POINTS
Current Demand	$\overline{X}$	$\overline{X}$	$\overline{X}_{LT}$	CAD	MAD$_{LT}$	MAD$_{LT}$	2MAD$_{LT}$	$\overline{X}_{LT}$ 2MAD$_{LT}$
8	5.33	(5.60)	10.66	2.67	1.33	(1.47)	2.66	13 (13.32)
	(5.60)		(11.20)		(1.47)		(2.94)	14 (14.12)
		(1)	(2)			(3)	(4)	(5)

EXHIBIT 9-1:   Order Point Calculation with "Smoothing" Added

Case in point: An air conditioning/heating manufacturer uses computerized marketing forecasts for determining replenishment stock purchases. The order point technique is the trigger for ordering. "Safety stock" quantity is figured in terms of mean absolute deviation. Average demand is calculated on a 15-month time period, using a weighted moving average method. Demand is smoothed with a 10% weight factor used. (Items with extremely rapid movements up or down, in prior recent months, are tracked and given a larger weight factor of 50%—to provide quicker response action.) The same basic forecast method is used for all inventory items, with lead time changes the prime mechanism to control unusual demand for altering the order quantity strategy. Order release is controlled by manual order form input.

Order Point Reviewed

An order point forecast quantity is compared to an item's available stock balance quantity each time demand occurs (continuous order review), or at a specified reoccurring time period (intermittent order review). A combination of the two methods can exist, as continuous order review might be desired on critical need items, with other items placed on an intermittent review basis. The time span for the order review period is considered as administrative lead time, and is included in an item's overall lead time requirement.

"Available" Quantity Guide

Replacement inventory should be ordered when an item's available stock balance reaches a quantity equal to or below the order point forecast. The available stock balance, for an individual item, is made up of both its quantity "on order" (but not yet received) and its current "on hand" quantity balances. If the available quantity balance is below the order point when reviewed, a quantity equal to the difference between the available balance *and* order point should be added to the normal replacement order quantity.

Automated Requirements Estimating Systems

In an automated system, requirements-estimating is accomplished on a continuous order review basis–via computer forecast and ordering. For all practical purposes, human judgment is ignored, and is normally related "after the fact" as an audit or corrective measure.

The Suggested Order Guide

A suggested order print-out is normally provided in most requirements ordering systems. This type of print-out gives the benefits of automated ordering, without order quantities automatically being released for procurement. The order review period is planned to match the time span required to manually review inventory needs. The suggested order guide presents the facts used by the computer in estimating an order quantity, so that judgment can be exercised on machine results prior to actual release of replacement order quantities. Information that should be printed on such a listing would include:

- item number and/or description (material code, etc.).
- unit of measure.
- current replacement cost information.
- current quantity on hand (and not allocated).
- total quantity on order (not yet received), in due date sequence.
- sales demand by demand period. To include the last 12 months and the current month's activity. (This is not available where "composite" data are used such as a 12-month moving average, demand this month and the new average; or where a full year's demand is not kept on file.)
- averaged demand quantity.
- lead time stated in increments of demand periods.
- safety stock quantity.
- order point forecast.
- order quantity (EOQ) and due date.
- special coding information such as vendor code, buyer code, order restrictions, etc.
- suggested order sequence number.

Manual Systems Bypass the Suggested Order Guide

A suggested order guide is necessary in computer-oriented systems because the inventory record cards are not visible to sight. It's impossible to see what values the order points are, or if order points have been reached. On the other hand, continuous order review is easily capable with manual systems, as all information is available to sight when a transaction posting is made. In manual systems, the suggested order guide is usually replaced by removable colored tabs or similar methods; while the suggested order guide tear strip is replaced by an actual purchase order request (or purchase order) form.

Manual Order Release

Manual order release causes a hesitation in an otherwise automated order release system. This is necessary where judgment is exercised, or for control where remote service bureau inventory control processing occurs. Three methods of such manual control are offered:

1. *Control by an "on-line" computer order release file.* (See Exhibit 9-2.) An order release file is created by the computer when order review is accomplished, and is established as an "on-line" file. This file would contain ordering data exactly as shown on the suggested order guide. Such data would include an item's order sequence number, unit of measure, item number and/or description (material code, etc.), order quantity, due date, and special coding information such as vendor code and manufacturing status.

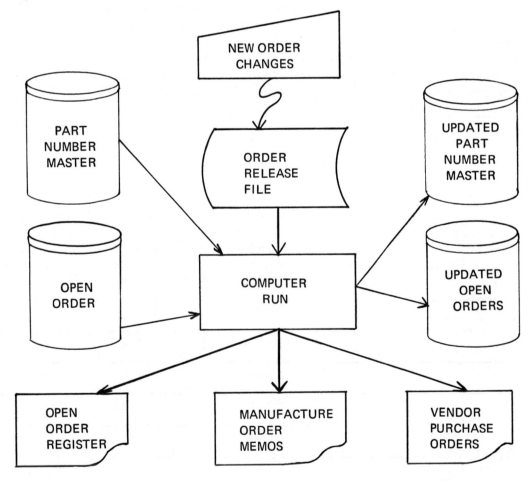

EXHIBIT 9-2: **"On-Line" Order Release**

In Exhibit 9-2, manual order release is keyed through data entry input. Order sequence numbers (from the suggested order guide) are used to match item information on the order release file. Change information is processed, and uncancelled orders are released for manufacturing or purchasing procurement. (A purchase order is released on vendor procured parts.) An "open order" register is printed which lists all open order items, quantities and due dates (either manufacturd or purchased), and has accumulative activity since order date.

The suggested order guide would be reviewed, with an "exception" list of order sequence numbers inputed to the computer on-line order release file, where immediate order data correction or order cancellation would occur. The unchanged order information, on the on-line order release file, is immediately released for manufacturing breakdown and order release processing, or for preparing machine-printed purchase orders on vendor procured items.

2. *Control by a "batch processing" computer order release file.* (See Exhibit 9-3.) A file, identical to the on-line file, is created during computer order review but is not recognized as an on-line file. Similar machine release action would take place, except processing would occur in a batch processing environment. A tear strip (on the right hand side of the suggested order guide listing pages) is separated from the guide and used for the batch processing activity. The tear strip contains a control number (a duplicate order sequence number), a code to indicate a change in quantity or due date, and space for adding corrective data. Properly marked for corrective action, this tear strip is sent to data processing for preparing machine input data to correct the order release file during batch processing of data. The order sequence numbers are used as the "match" information, as in the on-line order release file.

	TEAR STRIP (CODES): (1) CANCEL (2) QUANTITY INCREASE (3) QUANTITY DECREASE (4) DUE DATE		
	Order Sequence Number	(CIRCLE) Change Code	Write-in Change Data
	000001	1 2 3 4	
	000002	1 2 3 4	
	000003	1 2 ③ 4	50
	000004	1 ② 3 4	100
	000005	1 2 3 4	
	000006	1 2 3 4	
	000007	1 2 3 4	
	000008	1 2 3 4	

EXHIBIT 9-3:   Suggested Order Guide "Tear Strip" for "On-Line" or "Batch" Processing

In Exhibit 9-3, the tear strip shown is normally printed to support manual order release, controlled by on-line or batch processing files. Exception data would be processed against on-line order release files (via source data entry), but only where changes were being made. The order sequence number, the change code and change data—in that sequence—would be entered. Where batch processing files are concerned, the tear strip is forwarded to EDP. Input data is prepared, identical (in procedure) to input for source data entry.

Exhibit 9-4 shows how manual order release is accomplished through suggested order tear strips being inputed via punched cards, magnetic tape, etc. Order sequence numbers from the suggested order guide are used to match item information on the order release file. Change information is processed, and uncancelled orders are released for manufacturing or purchasing procurement. (A purchase order is released on vendor procured parts.) An open order register is printed which lists all open order items, quantities and due dates (either manufactured or purchased), and shows accumulative activity since order date.

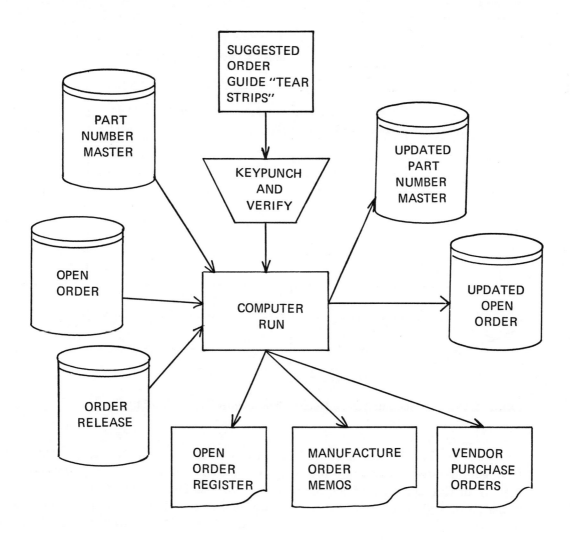

EXHIBIT 9-4:   **"Batch Processing" Order Release**

Exhibit 9-5 illustrates how a tear strip is normally printed to support manual order release, where order release files are not created during order review. Computer generated order release data is printed on the tear strip of the suggested order guide. (The order sequence number is not needed with this tear strip.) Order corrections are made directly to the tear strip before sending to EDP to key as machine input data. Cancellations can be made by lining through an item.

3. *Control by manual order form input.* An order release file is not created by the computer during order review. The suggested order guide tear strip (modified to include all necessary order-requirements information) is submitted to data processing for preparing machine input data to generate order release action. A manual order form can be used, in which case all necessary order-requirements data must be entered as handwritten. This form would replace the tear strip mentioned, and is used where forecast and ordering system data results require a lot of changing. (This manual order form must be used to enter requirements-estimating data for new model item stocking, and all other items that have restrictive order point and/or quantity coding.)

	Item/Part Number (Material Code)	Item Description	Model and S/N	Order Quantity	U/M	Due Date

SUGGESTED ORDER GUIDE
(Manual Order Form Tear Strip)

EXHIBIT 9-5:   **Suggested Order Guide—Manual Order Form "Tear Strip"**

See Exhibit 9-6 for manual order forms. Manual order release is controlled through suggested order guide tear strips (modified to include all order data requirements), or through handwritten manual order forms. The manual order form *must* be prepared on certain categories of parts (such as new model parts, or parts coded with restrictive order point or order quantity information). The order release file is created from this input data. Otherwise, similar action takes place as with the on-line or batch processing order release procedures.

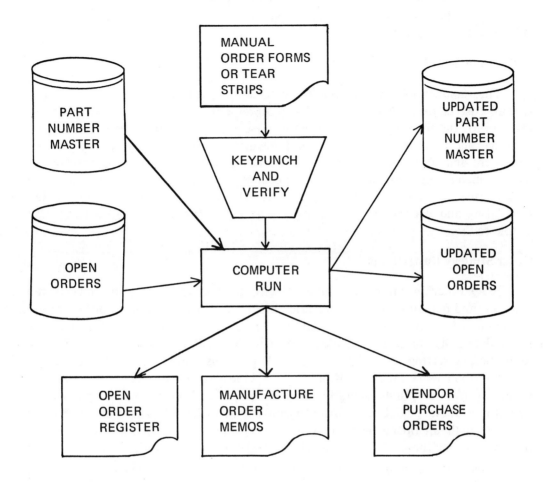

EXHIBIT 9-6:   Manual Order Forms

RELATING "WHAT TO ORDER" TO EXPECTED DEMANDS, AND THE PROCUREMENT AND STORAGE ACTIVITY COSTS

Order quantities on items being purchased for the first time are usually arrived at subjectively by planning personnel, as the order quantity decision can't be swayed by any past sales activity characteristics. Chapter 5 explains two methods (return on investment, and breakeven point) which can aid in making such subjective decisions. The need for accurate ordering points out the indispensibility of item records and the record keeping function. Proper ordering activity cannot occur without maintenance and knowledge of such prior, and present, factual sales support.

Replacement Order Variables

The replacement order quantity must be based on prior and current sales activity. It should include consideration for when the item is needed, present and past sales levels, demand patterns and deviations, lead time, size and type of item, its damageability and obsolescence factors, its unit cost, the set-up cost (if a manufactured part), quantity price breaks or minimum quantity buy (if a purchased part), and any additional order processing, receipts and storage costs that can be attributed to buying and storing inventory items.

EOQ Order Strategy

The standard EOQ (Economic Order Quantity) formula balances the buying and storing cost factors made available for requirements estimating. These data must be realistic for the formula to give correct results. With the use of realistic costs, the EOQ formula allows a quick, uniform and accurate order strategy—where demand is consistent and cost remains constant. EOQ has often been considered unfavorable for use in manual systems in the past, because of the lengthy manual square root calculation required in using the formula. However, EOQ nomograms, slide rule calculators and even desk calculators are available for quick EOQ solving. Each is simple to use.

Order Strategy Restrictions

EOQ ordering must be tempered with judgment. Costs don't always remain constant and demand seldom does. Price break information should not be overlooked on purchased items, even though EOQ use might be time consuming. It is necessary to recalculate EOQ for each available price break on an item to determine the effects of each, before setting an order quantity. A previous statement made ". . . . a single forecast won't work for every situation . . .," holds true for a single order strategy also, because certain corporate operating goals must be followed in managing an inventory. Sometimes these guidelines provide a conflict in ordering. Where an order strategy conflicts with an operating goal, order strategy restrictions should be developed to permit honoring the goal. EOQ restrictions might include the following:

- Items manufactured or purchased to-order, and items subject to rapid product improvement will be restricted from EOQ use.
- Shelf life items (those good only for a specific length of time), should be restricted to a quantity not greater than one-fourth of their age limitation.
- Items with unusual sales will be identified, with annual sales reduced by appropriate quantities, prior to calculating EOQ.
- Critical supply items (those having the most effect on customer service), will be ordered in greater than normal quantities. The time supply quantities selected will override EOQ.
- If EOQ is less than the current month's quantity needs, on all items not restricted on EOQ, a minimum of one month's supply is ordered.
- A minimum supply of three months (or another quantity correlated to manufacturing's lot release period), will be ordered for nonrestricted inactive items. EOQ is to be raised to this minimum.
- If EOQ is greater than a year's quantity supply, on all items not restricted on EOQ, the order quantity will be reduced to a maximum of a year's quantity supply.

The EOQ Formula: $EOQ = \dfrac{\sqrt{2CF/I}}{V}$, where:

C —is the acquisition or procurement cost.
F —is the annual item dollar sales at cost (or forecast).
I —is maintenance or carrying cost.
V —is the item's unit cost value.

Acquisition Costs. The average dollars spent in purchasing (or building) an item, are referred to as acquisition costs, and are expressed as dollars. These costs include materials to issue a purchase order such as purchase order forms, envelopes, checks, receiving forms, and stamps; tooling set-up costs; material for expediting such as telephone, telegraph, telex; and personnel costs for salaries, equipment, space used, automobile expense, etc. Acquisition cost could vary depending on whether an item is manufactured or purchased, or if it is active or inactive to current production models.

Maintenance Costs. The costs required to carry inventory are referred to as maintenance costs, and are expressed as a percentage of the inventory value. These costs include taxes, insurance, storage, obsolescence and depreciation, special handling, and cost of capital. Maintenance cost will vary depending on the type, size and obsolescence factors of a particular item. (Type relates to vendor, activity, and functional use of an item. Size relates to physical measurement and weight of the item in relation to awkwardness of handling. Obsolescence relates to product improvement, damageability characteristics, and shelf life restrictions.)

Controlling Order Quantity (EOQ) in a Manual System

The order quantity (EOQ) is usually figured only once per year with manual systems. However, increasing company operating costs and/or frequent vendor price increases can require periodic appraisals on the order quantity in use. EOQ should be reviewed and/or refigured whenever order point quantities are revised, also.

CONTROLLING ORDERS AFTER "WHAT" AND "WHEN" TO ORDER HAVE BEEN DECIDED

The two questions of "when to order" and "what to order" are the key elements in requirements estimating. But deciding when to order an item, determining what quantity is needed, and releasing orders for an item do not satisfy the total action required. Controlling orders, once they are released, becomes a vital activity. A good computer method for controlling orders is by due date need—and picking priority based on this need. Manual control will be more difficult, but can be guided by the same concept.

Order Release Pick Tags

Pick tag documents are dual purpose inventory tools. First, they provide a document for item location within a factory or stockroom, and control the movement of these items within the company. Secondly, they provide a ready-made receipt document when items are physically received into the finished goods inventory storage area.

The Pick Tag Concept

The feasibility of using pick tags becomes apparent where multi-divisions exist for a given company. The pick tag concept makes the (finished goods inventory) open order file the central control file, as it is the most current file at any point in time. This control open order file contains original order requirements data, as released; plus accumulated receipts since an order's release, the date of last receipts, a change or cancellation code (where change information is pending), and a date when the last pick tag document was released. Using the inventory file as the control file, other divisional files must relate to it, and the need for reconciliation of many files theoretically disappears. Pick tag logic would include the following ideas:

1. The manufacturing memos, or vendor purchase orders, created from order release, would still provide the authority for divisional procurement of items ordered.

2. Pick tag "sets" would be machine created a selected number of days (or weeks, or other time periods) prior to the due date of each order. Inventory items would be classified so that this selected time period could vary, realistically, to division need.

3. Stock-out situations, occurring in the finished goods inventory prior to pick tag release date, would override the logic and release pick tags immediately. (This, in effect, authorizes a due date change to the divisions on the item concerned—for the stock-out quantity, or for the complete quantity on order.)

4. Partial quantities would be acceptable against a pick tag, and would release another pick tag document for the quantity balance due, based on original pick tag logic.

5. A request would be issued covering a cancellation or reschedule of open order quantities, where drastic reductions in sales or similar reasons occur. The change form would note whether a pick tag set was released. (If a pick tag set had previously been released, immediate action would be necessary to handle the request before the item is picked.) The open order file would be flagged by the change request date. This flag would prevent any future pick tags from being released. Change request answers would remove the flag; and where cancellation was approved, would remove the order information from the file and print a control listing for audit purposes, to control open order changes after order release occurs.

6. 10% (or a different selected percent) quantity overages and shortages could be recognized as automatically being cancelled by the machine, providing customer backorders did not exist, or total quantity ordered was not for a made-to-order situation.

Pick Tag Results

The use of machine-created pick tag documents offers many benefits:

— Handwritten tags become almost nonexistent, creating a time savings on manual preparation of such documents.
— Document errors are reduced to nothing, and immediate and accurate close-out of open order quantities is permitted.
— Picking priority is assigned by the computer, releasing pick tags only after ordered items are supposedly available for picking, or to flag an early stock-out situation. Less time is required, overall, in the picking process.
— Item movement is controlled while change information is being processed. This prevents needless transfer of material and reduces overall expenses.

MATCHING SYSTEM SOPHISTICATION TO PEOPLE CAPABILITY

No attempt was given in this chapter to demonstrate the many advanced mathematical techniques associated with inventory item forecasts and/or ordering systems. Several library reference books are available which expound sophistication in the systems approach, or the use of deterministic or simulative inventory management techniques. Instead, a simple time-proven technique was discussed which can provide inexpensive, rapid and accurate (enough) answers for managing inventories–providing that inventory management judgment is also exercised.

The mathematical expertise of those individuals doing the work, the electronic computing equipment available for their use in inventory management, and the maintenance capability to maintain the forecast and ordering system implemented–are all important and necessary to consider, and contribute to the decision of what inventory management technique to use.

Too many computer-based inventory management systems have failed to produce desired results, mainly due to ignorance (of inventory and EDP operating personnel) of the techniques employed; individual inability, confusion or misunderstanding of system flow or decision methods because of extreme system sophistication; a lack of exactness in maintenance of data base requirements; and numerous other reasons.

The "when to order" and "what to order" questions can be answered by a simple (order point–EOQ) technique. Inventory-requirements estimating should be simple, understandable, and have data requirements that are easily maintained. Future sophistication can be applied as operating knowledge increases, but must not exceed the capability of the personnel or support equipment concerned.

10

Utilizing Purchasing Skills and Resources to Beat the Competition

The importance of the purchasing agent, or buyer, can best be witnessed in inventory cost results, and in the current level of customer service being offered. This chapter proposes some working tools which are useful to the buyer, with information on how they can be used to help keep costs down, service up and still maintain a proper product quality. Various types of purchase order forms are described; yet a method is presented which allows the use of a single purchase order form—by permitting an image change to fit the vendor, the product or the necessary support requirements.

SELECTING THE RIGHT VENDOR[1]

The purchasing agent should look upon a vendor as an employee applicant. The vendor's past production performances to other companies, its product acceptance, and its references should all be thoroughly checked. A visit to the vendor's manufacturing facility should be planned. Other company management representatives should make the trip, also, to help the purchasing agent appraise the vendor's management and production features for:

- management depth and expertise
- management involvement with community
- community acceptance of vendor
- condition of vendor's facility
- equipment variety
- condition of equipment
- product line (or work) flow
- manufacturing capacity
- shipping capacity
- business growth rate
- financial position

---

[1]From Somerby Dowst, *Basics for Buyers,* by permission of Cahners Publishing Company, Inc. Copyright © 1971 by Cahners Publishing Company, Inc.

Much of this information can be obtained by solicitations from other vendor customers, or by an analysis of such sources as industry trade directories, Dun and Bradstreet and trade journals, but should be compiled first hand if possible. A sample of the vendor's product should be obtained for detailed inspection by company inspection and engineering personnel. Permission should be obtained to select product samples from the fabrication or assembly areas, instead of taking samples pre-selected by the vendor. A review of the vendor's source inspection procedures should be made. The vendor's inspection policy should be known. (See Exhibit 10-1.)

Vendor Rating

The initial vendor rating will be a consensus of the vendor appraisal made, opinions from other customers, common trade information and the information furnished by the vendor. A true rating will be developed, after awards are made based on delivery compliance, product equality, price stability, cost reduction suggestions offered and timeliness of catalog information. The purchasing agent should establish vendor ratings and keep them timely and accurate. A formal rating system is recommended. If a formal rating system cannot be maintained, one should be kept for at least the first two or three buys from a new vendor. This will take away pure subjective judgment of a vendor by the purchasing agent, and might possibly prevent a disastrous buying decision. Formal vendor ratings are recommended because they provide management with reasons why purchasing made vendor changes—whether because of price, quality or delivery. They show justification for an arbitrary purchase from another vendor at higher than present prices. (See Exhibit 10-2.)

Developing Multi-Vendor Sources

The need to have multi-sources available is easy to understand. Corporations can be shut down for many different reasons, and for varying lengths of time, as witnessed by acts of God, bankruptcy, law suits, union strikes, expansion of plant facilities, retooling needs, lack of raw material support and physical inventory taking. A vendor plant shutdown, or an increase in material needs beyond a vendor's manufacturing capability, would probably require an alternate vendor source to handle either existing or additional anticipated product support needed.

Alternate vendor sources must be developed to handle such unexpected business fluctuations or demand increases. The alternate vendor's product quality must at least be equal to the original vendor's quality. Buying blindly from an unknown vendor, to satisfy immediate requirements, might be worse than purposely creating a backlog in production or in repair support.

Quotes should be obtained, as well as vendor product samples. The samples should be tested before an emergency source is needed. If tests on the product prove satisfactory, small percentages of the total quantity needs should be awarded the new vendor source to accumulate reliability in the other rating qualities.

Vendor File Prepared. Multi-sources should be developed when the initial search for new product needs is made. A vendor file should be set up by company or product line at that time. A formal vendor rating form should be prepared when new vendors (and their customers) are interviewed. Information should be added from interviews with businesses in the same community. The vendor's financial position should not be overlooked. Obtain financial information to question the company's profit margin and business trends. Add this information to the vendor's file.

VENDOR NAME AND ADDRESS:

PHONE_____

VENDOR APPRAISAL VISIT: (Date)	TOPS	GOOD	AVRG	FAIR	POOR
Management depth and expertise-------------------------					
Management involvement with community-----------------					
Community acceptance of vendor------------------------					
Condition of vendor's facility-----------------------					
Equipment variety------------------------------------					
Condition of equipment-------------------------------					
Production line (or work) flow-----------------------					
Manufacturing capacity-------------------------------					
Shipping capacity------------------------------------					
Business growth rate---------------------------------					
Financial position-----------------------------------					
Was product sample tested? ___NO ___YES (If yes:)					
What was the product's appearance----------------					
How was the product's workmanship----------------					
What were results of functional test------------					
How did specified tolerances test---------------					

QUOTED COSTS   (Effective from   to   ):

```
   1-   24 $_____      25-   49 $_____      50-   99 $_____

 100-  249 $_____     250-  499 $_____     500-  999 $_____

1000- 2499 $_____    2500- 4999 $_____    5000- 9999 $_____

                                                   10000- & on $_____
```

VENDOR RATING:	TOPS	GOOD	AVRG	FAIR	POOR
Delivery compliance----------------------------------					
Product quality--------------------------------------					
Price stability--------------------------------------					
Cost reduction participation (suggestions)-----------					
Timeliness of vendor catalog information-------------					

EXHIBIT 10-1   Vendor Appraisal Form

VENDOR NAME AND ADDRESS:

PHONE_____

QUOTED COSTS   (Effective from   to   ):

   1-   24 $_____   25-   49 $_____   50-   99 $_____

 100- 249 $_____   250- 499 $_____   500- 999 $_____

1000- 2499 $_____ 2500- 4999 $_____ 5000- 9999 $_____

                                         10000- & on $_____

VENDOR RATING:	TOPS	GOOD	AVRG	FAIR	POOR
Delivery compliance					
Product quality					
Price stability					
Cost reduction participation (suggestions)					
Timeliness of vendor catalog information					

QUOTED COSTS   (Effective from   to   ):

   1-   24 $_____   25-   49 $_____   50-   99 $_____

 100- 249 $_____   250- 499 $_____   500- 999 $_____

1000- 2499 $_____ 2500- 4999 $_____ 5000- 9999 $_____

                                         10000- & on $_____

VENDOR RATING:	TOPS	GOOD	AVRG	FAIR	POOR
Delivery compliance					
Product quality					
Price stability					
Cost reduction participation (suggestions)					
Timeliness of vendor catalog information					

REMARKS:

EXHIBIT 10-2   Vendor Rating Form

Vendor Contact Made. Friendly relations should be established with all vendors who can provide the needed products. Interviews should be held with new vendor salesmen who call at the company. The interviews should be summarized to describe sincerity of salesmen in their product. Their attitudes, product suggestions and ability to present a good showing of items offered should also be recorded, and placed in the vendor's file.

Periodically Review Vendor Files. The vendor file can be reviewed, when a new vendor source is needed, without additional effort. The file should be used before then, whenever practical, to spread current quantity needs among several vendors, even if only small buys are made—providing the costs remain competitive. This will allow a good relationship to develop before the time a new vendor might be depended upon for total support.

Case in point: A large company, manufacturing refrigerated dough and poultry products, reviews and updates their vendor files twice a year. Vendor ratings are based on delivery compliance, product quality, price stability, and cost reduction suggestions offered. Quality is heavily weighted. New vendors are selected on the basis of management depth and expertise, facility condition, equipment variety, condition of equipment, product line (or work) flow, manufacturing capacity, shipping capacity and financial condition. Visits are made to prospective vendors before approving them as a buying source.

CONTROLLING PURCHASES WITH PURCHASE ORDER REQUEST

The purchase order request (POR) initiates action in the purchasing department, to buy requested material needs. (See Exhibit 10-3.) Outside of vendor name and address, price quotes, and contractual information, the POR contains the same information found on a purchase order form. Today, with the lowering cost of computers, and their growing use in inventory control systems, the vendor source and pricing information can be coded and kept updated within the computer and the purchase order can be printed by the computer—eliminating the need for a POR. (Actually, the source document to the computer will be a single-part facsimile of a POR, but will not be treated or filed as a POR.) The POR is still commonly used for supplies and capital equipment purchases, and also for materials requisition in manual ordering systems or less sophisticated computer ordering systems. Two copies of the POR are prepared. One copy should be retained by the originator. The second copy should be forwarded to the purchasing department as a "buy" action notice.

Request for Cost Quotation

A POR (or a computer output purchase order form) will cause the purchasing agent to review the vendor files. If the cost quote information is still valid, and the vendor rating is still acceptable, the purchase order can be released. New cost information will be needed if the previous cost quote is no longer valid. A new vendor (or several) will be sought if the current vendor's rating is unacceptable, with new vendor data incorporated in the computer's data base files.

A request for cost quotation is issued by the purchasing agent to vendors, requesting new cost quotes based on quantity breaks, and the period of time the new

SHADED AREAS FOR PURCHASING DEPT. USE ONLY

UARCO BUSINESS FORMS CHICAGO

PURCHASE REQUISITION

ORDER FOR DEPT.	DATE	PURCHASE REQUISITION
FOR USE ON	CHARGE ACCOUNT	03651
DELIVER TO - NOTIFY	DATE WANTED	PURCHASE ORDER NO.
VENDOR		SHIP VIA - F.O.B.
ADDRESS		TERMS

QUANTITY	DESCRIPTION	MO. USAGE	ON HAND	UNIT PRICE	EXTENSION
1					
2					
3					
4					
5					
6					
7					
8					
9					
10					
11					

REQUISITIONED BY	APPROVED BY	DATE	PURCHASING APPROVAL	DATE

ORIGINAL

FORM ES 111-ID

EXHIBIT 10-3: **A Purchase Order Request Form. (By courtesy of Uarco Incorporated Business Forms, Barrington, Illinois.)**

cost quote will be valid. Three copies of the request should be prepared. One copy should be retained by the purchasing agent. Two copies are forwarded to the vendor. (If more than one vendor is being queried, a ditto master or other alternate method should be used.) The vendors are to fill in requested cost information and return a copy to the purchasing agent. The vendor retains one copy for his record. Exhibit 10-4 is a typical request for quotation form. This specially designed form allows four vendors to be queried for price quotes on the same material. Carbon leaves are cut to permit only one vendor name and address per copy, except for the original copy which will contain all vendors queried. The back side of the original copy (retained in Purchasing) contains a quotation analysis and vendor selection chart.

DOCUMENTING THE PURCHASE AUTHORIZATION

The vendor's acknowledged cost quotation, if competitive, will cause the purchase order to be approved. Control information (such as POR number, originating department or person, vendor selected, date) should be entered into a purchase order log opposite the next unassigned purchase order number. This PO number should then be assigned to the approved POR and PO form. Before the PO is released for mailing, this control information and the ordering data covering quantity, schedule dates and cost quotes are posted to a purchasing record card (or file book "page") for the materials being ordered.

REQUEST FOR QUOTATION

NO. _____

VENDOR

1.

2.

3.

4.

THE   COMPANY assumes no obligation to purchase items covered by this inquiry. When such a form is available, quotations should be made on vendor's form on which the basis of quotation is specially stated.

THE   COMPANY agrees to exercise due care in handling parts, drawings, or samples submitted by the prospective vendor, but assumes no additional responsibility.

Drawing information furnished by Company is confidential, and is not to be used for other than quotation purposes.

Quotations will be handled in a confidential manner.

It is requested that a quotation be furnished by _____ on all items in quantities shown.

ITEM	QUANTITY	UNIT	DESCRIPTION	APPROX. DEL. SCHEDULE

A copy or Vendor's Warranty to be supplied with quotation

Your suggestions for lower costs are solicited.

By _____

Title _____

EXHIBIT 10-4:   Request for Quotation Form

Quotation Analysis — Vendor Selection Chart

ITEM NO.	VENDOR	REASON NO.	F.O.B.	TERMS	DELIVERY	COMMENTS
1.						
2.						
3.						
4.						
5.						
6.						
7.						
8.						
9.						
10.						
11.						
12.						

REASON FOR VENDOR CHOICE

1. Contacted Only One Source: _____ Standard Price: Non-Competitive
    Patented Materials

2. Most Prompt Delivery.
3. Better Quality and Service Anticipated on Basis of Past Performance.
4. Difference in Quality and Service Outweighs Price Consideration.
5. Consideration of Terms and/or F.O.B. Points Shows Net Savings in Total Cost.
6. Facilities of Vendor Chosen Indicate Greater Ability to perform contract.
7. The Products Chosen is Preferable for Economy, Quality and Operation.
8. All conditions Equal; "fielders choice".
9. Best Available Price, Taking All Factors into Consideration.
10. Order Placed on Basis of Previous Competitive Bidding on Purchase Order No. _____ Dated _____
11. "No Substitution" Requested by Using Department and/or Requisition,

    Reason: _____

    _____

Other Reasons or Remarks: _____

_____
Buyer

For Purchases of $100 and over on initial purchase of new items and multiple source items.

EXHIBIT 10-4:   **(continued): Request for Quotation Form—Reverse Side**

In the purchase order log presented in Exhibit 10-5, the approved P.O.R. must have control information entered on the line beside the next unused P.O. number. The P.O. number is then assigned to the P.O.R. and/or the actual P.O. form. (The first two digits of the P.O. number are for year. The dash number -XX is for account coding.)

PURCHASE ORDER NUMBER:	Date	Purchase Order Request Number	Dept.	Originator	Vendor Selected
73-044501-XX	11-29	376,443	103	Jones	Office Equip. Co.
73-044502-XX					
73-044503-XX					
73-044504-XX					
73-044505-XX					
73-044506-XX					
73-044507-XX					
73-044508-XX					
73-044509-XX					
73-044510-XX					
73-044511-XX					
73-044512-XX					
73-044520-XX					
73-044521-XX					
73-044522-XX					
73-044523-XX					
73-044524-XX					

EXHIBIT 10-5:   **Purchase Order Log**

Exhibit 10-6 illustrates a purchasing record card. A card similar to this one, or a file book "page," is used to record control information from the Purchase Order Log and order quantity, schedule dates and price, after the purchase order is approved. Date received, quantity received and rejection quantity help to rate vendors. A check mark closes a P.O. quantity.

The computer written purchase order form can be mailed immediately, after being approved. However, the POR must be routed to "order writing," after approval, for preparation of the purchase order. Office typewriters are quite proficient where purchase order writing volume is low, but semi-automated document equipment, by application of magnetic tapes selected by vendor code, can pre-print the form's heading information mechanically, with only variable information having to be keyed. This equipment is becoming more popular today—partly because of the advent of "word processing" techniques—and should be utilized where a high volume of purchase orders are written.

ADDING CONTRACTUAL INFORMATION TO THE PURCHASE ORDER

Certain information must be contained on all purchase orders. This data would include the issuance date, vendor name and address, POR number and/or PO number, shipment method, F.O.B. point, material part number and/or description, quantities being ordered, unit of measure being ordered, scheduled shipment dates, cost information, special notes for overriding contractual wording and the contractual information. Other information can be contained on a purchase order, but its presence is by company preference only.

Prepaid Freight Can Be Costly

Product cost figures can include prepaid transportation by the vendor for a set method of transportation, with deviating shipment directions to be at the expense of the buyer. Freight bills should continually be checked, even if unit cost includes prepaid transportation, to insure that they *are* prepaid. Many dollars are lost by businesses each year to transportation expense—where the vendor used a collect bill of lading which goes by unnoticed.

Multi-Part Number Reference

The vendor might require the industry standard part number, or his part number, to be identified on the purchase order form, where proprietary part numbers are being assigned to purchased vendor parts. It is best to show both part numbers with the company part number in parenthesis, to prevent received parts from being stocked wrong, and to aid receiving personnel in identifying the correct stocking part numbers.

Contractual Data Requirements

Contractual data is normally pre-printed on the back side of the purchase order form. It is important that this contractual information is known and confirmed by the vendor on each purchase order released. A personal typed copy of the contractual information, with assigned space for signature approval, can be a part of the original agreement established with a vendor. The personal copy can be annotated to compel

Description: Typewriter ribbon—black, 5/16" x 40'   **U/M** EA   **Part No.** 2015—B—5/16

V E N D O R		
1	J.B. Jones & Company	
2	Office Equipment Company	
3	Swazukis Office Supplies	
4	Smith Typewriter Repair & Sales	
5		
6		

P.O. Number	Date	P.O.R. Number	Dept.	Originator	V	Order Qty.	Due Date	Date Recv'd.	Qty. Recv'd.	Reject Qty.	Close	Vendor Cost
73-044501-XX	11-29	376,443	103	Jones	4	12	12-21-3	12-20-3	12	- - - -	✓	1.05
											✓	

EXHIBIT 10-6:   A Purchasing Record Card

contractual information to be binding until new issuance of contractual information is made and acknowledged. In the event temporary changes are desired, notes could be applied to the face of a purchase order. The notes would be significant only to the purchase order upon which they appeared.

Normal procedure is to have the vendors return a copy of the purchase order as an acknowledgment that acceptance is given, or altered changes are to be noted. One manufacturing company in the Midwest, to increase productivity, had all purchase orders imprinted with information saying that PO approval was taken for granted, and was binding, unless change information was received within 15 days from the issuance date. Vendor acknowledgement of purchase orders became an unnecessary step for that company, and relieved them of extra follow-up duties.

The contractual agreement must state company positions on pricing stability, quality control compliance, delinquency charges, expediting charges, early shipments, shipment shortages, shipment overages, shipment methods utilized, F.O.B. charges, etc. Notes must be added to the purchase order for special conditions or restrictions, if not contained in the contractual information printed on the back of the form, or for overriding information which is a part of the printed agreement. Examples of special notes:

"Ship in one shipment only. All material short at shipment date is to be automatically cancelled."
"No overages acceptable on this shipment."
"Ship complete. No shortages accepted."

CLASSIFYING PURCHASE ORDERS FOR COMPANY USE

The types of purchase order forms used could be identified by one of the following categories. Pick those that best meet company requirements:

1. Single shipment purchase orders.
2. Standard purchase orders with multi-shipment capability.
3. Specific material–time limit purchase orders.
4. Open material–time limit purchase orders.
5. Special contract, or blanket, purchase orders.

Single Shipment Orders

One-shot, or single shipment, purchase orders are designed for special one-time buys, or where multi-shipment dates are not required. This form prevents the need for preparing a receiving report when the material is received, as enough copies of the purchase order are retained to receive material. This form has no advantages where more than one shipment is to be made.

Standard Purchase Orders

Standard purchase orders are most commom. They apply to a set quantity and type of material being ordered, but they allow more than one shipment to be made.

Time Limitation Orders for Specific Material

"Specific material" time limit purchase orders allow the quantity ordered to be revised or added to. This type of purchase order is used to restrict ordering to specific material, usually a single part number or kind of material, and covers a specified length of time. The quantity may be restricted to a maximum amount, but usually is open ended so that any quantity may be ordered, at any time, during the purchase order life.

Time Limitation Orders with Material Open

"Open material" time limit purchase orders are used in ordering material relating to a product line, and are not limited to a single part number or type of material. This normally covers a vendor's full line of products or can be restricted to just a portion of products offered. The original purchase order lists all materials or part numbers the purchase order will cover. Any quantity for any of the materials or part numbers specified may be ordered at any time.

Special Purchase Orders

"Special contract or blanket" purchase orders might be thought of as one kind of open material—time limit purchase order. However, this type has additional flexibility. It usually is restricted by an attached "special" contractual agreement. For instance, this form might cover a drop-shipment proposal where the vendor ships to a number of addresses specified in the contract, upon request, and with or without direct billing provisions.

One Form with Many Functions

The various purchase orders described perform different functions, but the form itself does not have to change—only the contractual information or special notes added to the form must change. The flexibility achieved? New purchase order paperwork is not required where addendums can be made. The POR can be routed through the purchasing department for approval and mailing to the vendor; or such information can (in some cases) be mailed direct to the vendor—bypassing purchasing altogether. Control should not be abdicated, but savings in time and form preparation are significant, and should be considered.

A purchase order form is presented in Exhibit 10-7. This form can assume many different functions, by the addition of special notes to alter or replace normal contractual data. These special notes can be a few words added to the front of the form, or a special multi-page contract addendum. Standard company contractual information is usually printed on the reverse side of the copy sent to the vendor.

The accounts payable copy (Exhibit 10-8) of the purchase order form is usually the back copy, in manual systems, as it is heavier in weight for hand-posting and filing use. This manual data posting is not needed in computer supported systems, as computer output listings contain this information as a by-product of invoice payments processing.

PURCHASE ORDER
ORIGINAL

TO

PURCHASE
ORDER NO.

DATE

CONTRACT OR
MODEL NO.

INVOICE IN DUPLICATE TO·

PACKING LIST MUST BE IN DUPLICATE

TERMS: SHIP VIA:

F.O.B.

SHPMT'S FOR   CHARGE N⊕

REQ.
BY   ↑ SHIP TO ↑

ITEM NO.	MATERIAL CODE	UNIT OF MEASURE	DESCRIPTION	REQUISITION NUMBER	PRICE

THE MATERIAL CODE AND DESCRIPTION OF THE ITEMS ORDERED ABOVE MUST APPEAR ON ALL PACKING SHEETS AND INVOICES

THE DELIVERY DATES SHOWN ARE FOR DELIVERY AT _____

CHANGE NO.	DATE	ITEM NO.	QUANTITY ORDERED	MO.	DAY	YR	MO.	DAY	YR	MO.	DAY	YR	MO.	DAY	YR	MO.	DAY	YR	MO.	DAY	YR	MO.	DAY	YR	MO.	DAY	YR	MO.	DAY	YR	MO.	DAY	YR	MO.	DAY	YR

WE SHALL CONSIDER THIS ORDER ACCEPTED ON THE TERMS AND CONDITIONS HEREIN SET FORTH AND WILL RELY THEREON UNLESS WE HEAR FROM YOU TO THE CONTRARY WITHIN 15 DAYS OF THE PURCHASE ORDER DATE.

BY _____

EXHIBIT 10-7:   The Purchase Order Form

PURCHASE ORDER

ACCOUNTS PAYABLE

TO:

PURCHASE ORDER NO.

DATE

CONTRACT OR MODEL NO.

INVOICE IN DUPLICATE TO:
_____ COMPANY

TERMS: SHIP VIA:

PACKING LIST MUST BE IN DUPLICATE

F.O.B.

REQ. BY	↑ SHIP TO ↑	SHPMT'S FOR		CHANGE NO
ITEM NO.	MATERIAL CODE	UNIT OF MEASURE	DESCRIPTION	REQUISITION NUMBER	PRICE

THE MATERIAL CODE AND DESCRIPTION OF THE ITEMS ORDERED ABOVE MUST APPEAR ON ALL PACKING SHEETS AND INVOICES

THE DELIVERY DATES SHOWN ARE FOR DELIVERY AT _____

CHANGE		ITEM NO.	QUANTITY ORDERED	MO.	DAY	YR	MO	DAY	YR	MO.	DAY	YR	MO	DAY	YR	MO	DAY	YR	MO	DAY	YR	MO	DAY	YR	MO	DAY	YR	MO	DAY	YR	MO	DAY	YR
NO.	DATE																																

WE SHALL CONSIDER THIS ORDER ACCEPTED ON THE TERMS AND CONDITIONS HEREIN SET FORTH AND WILL RELY THEREON UNLESS WE HEAR FROM YOU TO THE CONTRARY WITHIN 15 DAYS OF THE PURCHASE ORDER DATE.

BY _____

EXHIBIT 10-8:   The Accounts Payable Copy of the Purchase Order Form

CONTROLLING PRODUCT SPECIFICATIONS

The engineering department establishes product specifications such as dimensions, tolerances, stress, hardness, operating limits, etc. Any vendor's product meeting these specifications is technically approved by such engineering paperwork. Determining the right vendor is a great responsibility. Once selected, the vendor must maintain quality compliance. The purchasing agent is responsible for controlling this vendor quality in the least expensive manner, and poor quality must not be regarded as a trade-off for lower cost.

The purchasing agent controls quality uniformity by keeping a watchful eye on the receiving report rejections, engineering reports on field failures and on the volume of returned goods credit issued. Inferior vendor quality should result in cancellation of open purchase order commitments with the vendor—or immediate product improvement. Cancellation of purchase orders can present problems, where the only other acceptable vendors are operating at full capacity and can't handle any new business. Negotiation must be a practical and continuing thing between purchasing agents and vendors, because teamwork becomes essential in the control of product specifications.

ANTICIPATING VENDOR LEAD TIME PROBLEMS

Lead time changes make a big difference where inventory replenishment is based on an order point formula. A significant increase in vendor lead time can precipitate a future period of stock-outs until ordering is again in tune with lead time requirements. Lead times increase, because abnormal increases in demand build temporary backlogs, until increase in vendor production capacity can again balance supply and demand. Where plant capacity cannot be increased, and demand still increases, then lead times must be permanently lengthened. The purchasing agent must work closely with the vendor and develop a good foresight for anticipated lead time changes.

INCREASING THE INVENTORY SERVICE SUPPORT

Consignment inventory is described generally as merchandise which changes hands without ownership to the merchandise changing. Today, a new concept of consignment merchandise is seen, and has come about due to a method of advance inventory ordering known as vendor capacity planning. Inventory requirements for a product can be planned in advance with the vendor. This usually involves a yearly advance planning schedule, by month, showing quantity requirements for materials needed. The planning schedule is adjusted to current demand trends each month, and submitted to the vendor. Some vendors will commit an allocation of plant capacity to handle such requirements, as they benefit from a constant manpower level, and will build schedule quantities without a signed firm purchase order agreement. (Some vendors deviate from this and require the signing of a binding purchase order to cover demand droppage which might occur, to relieve the vendor of liability for the already completed material held in vendor storage.) Merchandise built up ahead of delivery is retained and stored by the vendor. Shipment is not usually made by the vendor until order "ship" commitments are received. This merchandise is considered consigned by the vendor—with the merchandise not changing hands but the ownership to the merchandise technically changing hands. Inventory replenishment ordering under the vendor capacity planning technique, for finished goods inventory items, should be restricted to critical need situations or to constant demand items where monthly sales will vary but remain fairly constant over a long period of time.

Case in point: A manufacturer of flour and prepared mixes relies on vendors to inventory a "protection stock" (of raw material) for them. Most of their vendors will stock from two to three months' supply in advance, for which there is an additional charge in unit costs. However, even with additional charges, from $25,000 to $50,000 is estimated saved in annual inventory expenses, as nearly 25% of their purchases are immediately available from their vendors.

Pipeline Stocking

Tied in with the new consignment inventory concept is what is called pipeline stocking. Vendors agree to keep built up, in advance, a set period worth of product support, without contract. A yearly schedule, by month, is requested here also, with demand revisions made periodically. The vendor also relies on his past sales records. This works well where lead times could fluctuate greatly, as a high degree of service is permissible. In most cases, the vendor does this to obtain all of the product business. Overnight delivery is usually available. Emergency situations are easily handled.

Vendor Drop-Shipments

As an add-on to the consignment and pipeline stocking ideas, vendors agree to provide a set availability of stock and also to ship any portion or all of it to any destination within the sales distribution network. This is covered by a special purchase order agreement which spells out the length of the contract, the pricing information, procedures covering the release of orders, and shipping and invoicing operations. The vendor may agree to invoice for and/or to the company. Items that are manufactured by a subsidiary of the company, or necessary service items that are an insignificant part of the business and contribute little to profit, would work well with a vendor drop-shipment agreement.

PRE-PACKAGING FOR IMPROVED PROFITS

Items are pre-packaged in incremental quantities where low unit cost and high volume sales exist. Pre-packaging merchandise reduces order pick time and aids in physical inventory counting. Special packaging machines are available which can count, sack, seal and label packages for small size items. Shrink film wrapping machines are available for sealing larger items on a fiberboard backing, or for sealing complete skids of many cartons together as a unit.

The purchasing agent should work closely with receiving personnel to anticipate pre-packaging bottlenecks in the receiving area, and to keep costs down. Bottlenecks will occur where an increase is found in the number of total items to be packaged, without an offsetting increase in equipment or manpower being made. A review of pre-packaging expenses should be made to determine if the vendor can provide the packaging more economically. In many cases, some form of pre-packaging can be done by the vendor without any additional cost. In other cases, making packaged quantities compatible with pre-pack quantities available from the vendor will also prevent added costs.

RATING VENDORS TO KEEP COSTS CONSTANT

The purchasing agent is the man with the whip when it comes to minimizing product cost. This is a main reason for maintaining formal vendor rating files. The purchasing agent is not a clerk, but is a dedicated administrator controlling the company's money and its competitive edge over the products sold. The company's buying power should, on purpose, be used as a leverage to keep vendor costs down and quality up. The purchasing agent must approve all vendor cost changes in advance of buying. Formal rating of vendors will reflect frequencies of cost changes, and will permit discovery of vendors who purposely quote low prices on initial bids to win a contract, and then raise prices on a renewal buy, knowing the company's service position might be jeopardized and that the cost increase will be approved.

A nickel added to a $1 item doesn't seem like very much. But, with annual sales of 5000 units, a total of $250 is lost if retail prices can't be raised and sales remain the same. An additional $12,500 in sales will need to occur—above normal—just to offset this nickel increase in unit cost (if a company is operating on a 2% net profit basis). This example is an increase of 2½ times the present sales rate and quite an ambitious goal!

REDUCING COSTS THROUGH VALUE ANALYSIS

The value analysis approach requires, first of all, that valid and complete answers be developed for the following five questions:

1. What is the item or service?
2. What does it cost?
3. What does it do?
4. What else would do the job?
5. What would that alternative cost?

These basic questions serve the end of uncovering needed pertinent facts. With the establishment of answers to them, the foundation is laid for developing objective data for presentation to the decision makers. Hence the importance of understanding and effectively using these questions cannot be overemphasized.[2]

A manufacturer in Minnesota is a firm believer in value analysis. Its purchasing department is estimated to have saved the company from *two* to *three million* dollars average per year since the inception of their value analysis program.

The value analysis function is performed by the purchasing agent, because he has the biggest group of engineering talent available—the vendors—working for him. Each vendor wants to increase his product sales position with the company, and because of this, vendor representatives continually contribute product improvement and cost reduction ideas. The purchasing agent should bring the company engineers and the vendor representatives together. Frequent brainstorming sessions over current design or production problems can normally provide the needed solutions.

---

[2]Lawrence D. Miles, *Techniques of Value Analysis and Engineering,* (New York: copyright © 1972, 1961 by McGraw-Hill, Inc.), p. 18.

USING SHARED ADVERTISING

Vendors frequently share or donate advertising space and costs with associated companies. Advertising is a big business expense. Shared (or reduced price) advertising won't hurt any budget. The vendor's advertising policy should be investigated by the purchasing agent and his findings forwarded to the company's advertising director.

OBTAINING VENDOR WARRANTY AND RETURN AGREEMENTS

The vendor's product warranty and the company's warranty period must be equal, or added warranty liability expense could raise the overall cost of the article. The purchasing agent should seek a cost reduction from the vendor where the warranty programs remain incompatible. However, management approval should be required before any new order contracts are released. The desired quality of the product might be above the present vendor's product quality, and the engineering design might allow additional warranty to be offered by the vendor. Where a vendor's quality is superior to the quality desired, a cost reduction might be found by using the vendor's existing product, rather than designing one that has never been proven.

Procedural steps for processing warranty claims must be worked out—after the warranty period has been agreed upon by the vendor. Specific instructions and policy information on warranty should be included in the purchasing agreement with the vendor. Other return goods procedures should also be contained in the agreement, and would include vendor-company disposition on errors, rejected merchandise, overages and shortages.

11

Warranty and Returned Goods Administration Qualifies Sales

This chapter separates warranty administration from other merchandise return programs. Itemized steps are given for formulating a product's warranty policy, with ideas included for controlling program costs. Other merchandise return programs are fully detailed with a decision table illustrated for assistance in their program administration. Methods are included for controlling inventory expenses while still providing good sales support. A policy and procedures manual is described, with specific uses offered. And finally, seven suggestions are listed which can provide company good will, and which should keep the customer who comes back with warranty problems coming back for additional purchases.

ALLOW FOR LIBERAL BUT POSITIVE INTERPRETATION

The real key to effectiveness is how the return goods policy is communicated and administered. The man selected for this job should possess the attributes of a lawyer, the finesse of a bridge-playing champion and the salesmanship of a public relations man. A blank check policy interpretation on returned goods will corrode gross profits, cause a loss or price a product out of competition. But too strict a policy could create a sense of poor product support, undermine good will and decrease sales.

The return goods manager might help keep expenses down by keeping merchandise from being returned, or by denying company liability, but he might also be keeping the consumer from returning. This must be constantly evaluated in all decisions where judgment is exercised.

SEPARATE WARRANTY FROM MERCHANDISE RETURN POLICY

Better control of inventory expense can be accomplished if separate publication and processing are made between warranty and non-warranty policy. Inventory planning and control is affected by both of these policies, but inventory expense is increased mostly by the non-warranty policies. Policy decisions must be reached on most warranty return items because of product misuse or misuse of warranty privileges. Non-warranty returns can be processed with warranty items, but should be done only on a paperwork basis. The physical processing duties should be assumed by inventory control, and warehouse functions, for:

- receiving.
- inspection.
- inventory disposition.
- remarking (or scrapping).
- stocking.

Warranty Policy Formulation

Provide the consumer with good warranty coverage but don't overextend company liability for the product. Steps to follow:

1. *Determine the warranty period.* The product's expected life, its estimated market value and known market competition can restrict replacement or repair coverage, and thus help determine the length of the warranty period. Planned obsolescence—based on yearly or frequent styling changes or product modification—can create an almost nonexistent sales saturation point for any product. The planned obsolescence period is an important factor in formulating the warranty period.

2. *Keep warranty wording simple, short and understandable.* Do away with "fine print." The consumer must know what is covered and under what conditions, but in terms that can be understood—by both himself and company employees—and without a lawyer. Notice the short warranty wording of a large cookware manufacturer:

> With proper care, this applicance is guaranteed for one year from date of purchase. The Company agrees to repair or replace any defective parts free, if the appliance is returned to the factory.

3. *Use the warranty policy as a sales tool and not as a sales approach.* Look at the turn-around in the warranty period for automobiles. In 1967, all four major U.S. car makers extended their general warranty to 24 months or 24,000 miles, with the power train, steering and suspension systems extended to five years or 50,000 miles warranty. This warranty was developed as an approach to stimulate sales. In 1971, these warranties were reduced back to a 12-month or 12,000 mile warranty. The apparent reaction is better acceptance for a simple one-year warranty period, with a well-supported "complete coverage" policy, than for a long warranty period with restrictive clauses which are difficult to interpret or understand. Today the one-year warranty policy of one of these companies is a better sales tool than was the previous five-year warranty.

4. *Warn the customer of himself.* The going thing today is consumer protection. Warranty has long been a legal safeguard for the manufacturer, as well as a sales tool. But, due to the rising popularity of consumer protection, product liability is becoming increasingly more comprehensive. The philosophy of planned obsolescence has tended to make consumers more wasteful in product use. Because of this, emphasis seems to have been placed by manufacturers on salability of product—without necessarily looking at increasing its durability, quality or safety potential. The customer should be made fully aware of the nature and characteristic of the product, its purpose and how to use it and the hazards that the product presents. A warning clause in the warranty affords good protection to the consumer—and also to the manufacturer where it is not feasible to improve a product's performance or to provide for safety devices for certain conditions or situations.

HELPFUL NOTE

A short power supply cord is provided with this appliance to reduce the hazards resulting from becoming entangled in or tripping over a longer cord. Extension cords may be used if care is exercised in their use.

If an extension cord is used, the following must apply:

1. The market electrical rating should be at least as great as the electrical rating of the applicance.
2. The extension cord should not drop over the counter top or tabletop where it can be pulled on by children or tripped over accidently.

EXHIBIT 11-1:   **Warning the Customer of Himself**

The helpful note shown in Exhibit 11-1 is included in each popcorn popper sold by a leading small appliance manufacturer. This is an example where the manufacturer is assuming the responsibilities of consumer protection, and at the same time, limiting company liability for hazards possible in the use of the product.

Review the warranty policy periodically, at least yearly, or based on the planned obsolescence period. Historical data showing warranty performance will give you guidelines for changes in your warranty policy.

Keep Warranty Records. Record and keep warranty information to show the current actual warranty costs, and how profits for any prior period were affected. Warranty claim tickets should be prepared for each separate merchandise return to control merchandise replacement or dollar refunds, and to permit accumulation of warranty data by product, type, color, etc. The warranty claim ticket should allow space for:

1. Customer information.
2. Verification of proof of purchase.
3. Type, identification or description of merchandise.
4. Length of time in use.
5. Serial or model number.
6. Cause of defect or reason for return.
7. Disposition of claim.
8. Date warranty claim is prepared.
9. Claim adjuster's signature.
10. Customer's signature.

Keep Tabs on Warranty Costs. A weekly or monthly warranty credit analysis report should be published to summarize warranty action from the credit claim tickets. This report should contain:

1. Kinds or types of merchandise returned.
2. Volume of returns.
3. Individual serial or model numbers.
4. Reasons for defects.
5. Dollar repair or replacement allowance.
6. Labor dollar expense.

This report will show what items in a product line are failing. It will reveal the severity of the problem. It can pinpoint when the problem began. It can help determine if the problem is related to a general lack of quality control, or to a specific manufacturing operation. But most important of all, this report will reflect current warranty costs and what their trends are.

Protect the Customer Against Poor Warranty Support. The best warranty written is worthless without service. And it's not much better off if service is available—but the parts aren't. Parts shortages, or nonexistent replacement merchandise, can ruin the sales value of any warranty. This is where a return goods manager needs to be a public relations man. The customer must be kept waiting until parts or repair are available, without losing any "good attitude" previously held towards the company. This means being courteous and tactful to the customer in approach, and realistic in commitments.

Two things can help make this job easier. *First,* always look for ways to reduce or eliminate customer dissatisfaction. A leading car manufacturer offers a "loaner" car, if an extensive waiting period is necessary on repair work. *Second,* keep abreast of new or sudden increases in warranty repair or replacement needs, and know the reasons why. (Customers will generally go along with a valid reason.) Report abnormal returns immediately to sales, service and inventory management, so proper replacement support is provided to lessen stock-outs.

The question of consumer safety might become important, and an oversight in manufacturing, quality control or packaging could result in a disaster on profits if not caught in time.

Warranty Effect on Inventory Planning and Control. Warranty claims are of vital interest to inventory management. The sales demand accumulated due to defective merchandise must remain a special consideration of inventory planning and control. Warranty expense is normally considered as a reduction to sales, and will cause a lower inventory turnover and a reduction in normal profits. Inventory management must be aware of this activity. To help inventory management, follow these four steps:

1. Review total returns periodically (at least monthly).
2. Break returns down into various categories such as true warranty, wrong merchandise purchased, gift returns, etc.
3. Forecast future return volume for each category.
4. Support forecasts which look out of line with documentation or personal observations.

The weekly or monthly credit analysis reports should support most of the forecasts. Individual credit claim tickets should be researched where detailed information is required.

Development and Organization of Merchandise Return Policy

The return goods policy for non-warranty returns must satisfy good product support, permit adequate inventory control and allow for good and fair customer relations. Obviously, one return goods policy cannot be broad enough to handle all returns and still be clear and simple in language. Therefore, merchandise adjustments need to be defined and organized into definite types of returns. Most non-warranty returns would be included in one of the following categories:

1. Shipment errors.
2. Customer buying errors.
3. Unclaimed C.O.D. shipments.
4. Periodic surplus or obsolescence return.
5. Termination of distribution (or franchise) contract.

Each of these categories will be looked at separately. A policy decision summary table will be presented after the various types of non-warranty returns have been discussed.

Shipment Errors. Shipment errors are the responsibility of the supplier or the carrier and not of the buyer. Such errors might be caused by merchandise being marked wrong, catalogs wrongly identifying merchandise, service or sales representatives giving out wrong information, wrong substitutions made, wrong merchandise packaged, too much or too little picked, duplicate shipments made on mail orders, or merchandise misrouted in shipment.

Transportation charges incurred through shipment errors should be the responsibility of the supplier and/or the carrier. This includes both outgoing and incoming freight where such expense is definable, easily obtained, and verifiable through bills of lading or receipted freight bills.

Freight claims arising through lost shipments should be initiated by the supplier to the originating carrier, upon receipt of a lost shipment "trace" request from the buyer. Freight claims arising from partial loss or damage of original shipment should be initiated by the buyer. Full credit should be allowed the buyer upon receipt of returned merchandise.

Customer Buying Errors. Ordering, or buying, errors as discussed here pertain only to those that are the responsibility of the customer. Buying errors might occur because repair items were ordered that weren't needed, wrong merchandise was ordered by using outdated catalogs, or merchandise purchased was a wrong color, size, style, brand, or just a wrong selection.

Transportation charges incurred in returning such merchandise, if any, should be the responsibility of the buyer.

Freight claims arising from partial loss or damage of original shipment should be initiated by the buyer. Freight claims due to non-delivery of merchandise should be initiated by the supplier to the originating carrier upon receipt of a lost shipment "trace" request from the buyer.

Full credit should be allowed upon proof of purchase, subject to the condition of merchandise being returned, length of time taken to return items and conditions under which the sale was made. Certain merchandise should be unacceptable for return. A list of items not normally accepted back would include:

1. Marked-down items such as surplus, special buy, out-of-season, loss leaders or other sale priced items.
2. Sealed items where the package or seal has been broken, such as special multi-pack items or drugs.
3. Merchandise that has been used, damaged or altered in any way.
4. Items of a perishable or shelf-life nature, such as dairy or bakery goods, rubber goods and sealants.
5. Made-to-order items such as upholstery articles cut to length, prescription medicine or items specially procured.
6. Intimate apparel such as undergarments, bathing suits, etc.
7. Personal items such as toiletries, perfumes and hairgoods.
8. Mattresses, bedding and upholstered furniture.
9. Gifts, unless in resalable condition, not used, and returned for exchange.
10. Sanitary goods.

Restock, handling or exchange charges should be made to offset inventory expenses incurred in placing returned material into a resalable condition. Charges will vary within the same industry due to the level of distribution involved, resalability value of the article, type of customer returning merchandise or value of customer, etc. The closer to the retail customer, the less restrictive this return policy will be.

Unclaimed C.O.D. Shipments. C.O.D. shipments remain the property of the supplier shipping the merchandise until delivery is made and payment is received by the carrier. The carrier will notify the supplier in cases where shipments are refused. The supplier should contact the buyer, or consignee, to determine why shipment was refused. If an agreement can't be reached for accepting the C.O.D. shipment, the supplier should authorize the carrier to make immediate return. Sometimes return approval is given in advance to the carrier before delivery is made. If advance approval is not given, prompt action in approving a return might prevent damage while stored, and could reduce further expenses for storage charges.

Transportation charges for outgoing and incoming freight expense are the responsibility of the supplier. Freight charges as well as reasonable handling charges should, however, be billed to the C.O.D. account, even though it may never be collected. A company is money ahead if it is collected; but if it isn't, the billing records will be available to prevent future expenses from reoccurring unnecessarily by the same customer. Stopping shipments to customers who have refused prior C.O.D. shipments, or requiring an advance payment made prior to shipment of merchandise, should be company policy where a C.O.D. refusal has occurred.

All freight claims arising on unclaimed C.O.D. shipments are the responsibility of the supplier.

Periodic Surplus or Obsolescence Return. Some manufacturers and supply houses will offer some type of periodic or annual return program to cover inventory obsolescence or surplus stock conditions. This type of return privilege is often considered a part of a special stock purchase incentive plan, and allows a fixed percent of net purchases to be returned. Except in the case of consignment inventory agreements, such periodic returns are selective in nature. Return conditions are known in advance of purchase. Types of merchandise returnable under this agreement are often limited to industry standard items, or commonly used merchandise with high demand, which have little if any obsolescence potential.

Transportation charges incurred in these return shipments should be at the expense of the participating buyer.

Restock or handling charges might be deducted from allowable credit.

Termination of Distribution Contract. Most contracts for distributing specific product lines allow for unexpected business shutdowns and disposition of remaining inventory investment. The termination return clause is more liberal for standard product lines. Proof of purchase may or not be required, depending on whether the merchandise is specialized or proprietary in nature. Condition of the merchandise being returned, its age, original purchase price, and resalability value will usually determine whether inventory may be returned and what amount of credit will be given. Credit is generally based on present selling prices. However, if a recent price increase is made prior to a termination return, processing expenses involved in using older prices should be compared against the anticipated loss in credit dollars (due to the price increase).

Exhibit 11-2 lists five steps to potential savings on terminations. Manual pricing should be followed if potential savings are indicated. The following variables were arbitrarily used here:

Termination return value   : $31,800
Termination line item total   : 1,200
Hourly rate estimate for manual pricing :   60
Current labor rate average   : $3.00
Amount of recent price increase   :   6%

PRICING GUIDELINE FOR TERMINATION RETURNS

1. Establish the current dollar value, and total line items, for a termination return:
$31,800 for 1,200 total line items.

2. Calculate manpower requirements by dividing the total line items by the number of items that can be looked up, hand priced, extended and typed (manually) per hour: 1,200 line items÷60 per hour =20 hours.

3. Calculate manpower cost by extending manpower requirements by the current labor rate: 20 hours x $3.00 per hour labor rate = $60.00 .

4. Determine the potential dollar value that will be lost due to the general price increase, by dividing the current dollar value of the termination return by 106% and subtracting the result from the current dollar value of the termination:
$31,800 − ($31,800÷106%) = $1,800

5. Compare manpower costs (to manually price the termination return) against the potential dollars lost (because of the price increase) to determine if a savings potential exists:

$1,800.00	Potential dollar loss
- 60.00	Manpower cost to manually price
$1,740.00	Potential savings if manually priced

EXHIBIT 11-2:   Five Steps to Potential Savings on Terminations

Transportation charges incurred for the return shipment would normally be the responsibility of the original buyer. Exhibit 11-3 summarizes general policy decisions concerning most returned goods programs offered. Decision tables such as this are easy to follow and aid in new employee training. Corporate policy approval will be required in setting up restriction guidelines, or as to the amount of handling charges to be made. Handling charges will vary from nothing to 20%, or more, depending on the type of merchandise manufactured or distributed, and at what distribution level the charge is to be made.

Effect of Non-Warranty Returns on Inventory Planning and Control. Falsely posted sales exist on all merchandise returned. Inventory planning and control are difficult if the kinds and quantity of merchandise being returned are not known in advance. And if demand records aren't corrected to wipe out the prior sales, additional purchases for such merchandise can be made in error. Such errors will contribute to any already excessive inventory picture. Of biggest help here is utilization of a history of demand correction method. In manual systems, this method is simply an erasure and rewrite of quantities on the inventory record card. With computers, it's different. A supportive program is required which will recognize demand correction quantities;

POLICY DECISIONS	MERCHANDISE RETURN PROGRAMS AVAILABLE				
	SHIPMENT ERROR *1	ORDERING ERROR	UNCLAIMED C.O.D. *2	SURPLUS OBS.	TERMI-NATION
Purchase proof needed?	Yes	Yes	No	Yes	Yes
Restrictions made?	No	Yes	Yes	Yes	Yes
Return Charges made?	No	Yes	Yes	Yes	Yes
Who pays freight charges?	Supplier	Buyer	Supplier	Buyer	Buyer
Who initiates freight claim:					
Non-delivery	Supplier	Supplier	Supplier	Supplier	Supplier
Missing parcels	Buyer	Buyer	Supplier	Buyer	Buyer
Concealed loss	Buyer	Buyer	Supplier	Buyer	Buyer
Obvious damage	Buyer	Buyer	Supplier	Buyer	Buyer
Concealed damage	Buyer	Buyer	Supplier	Buyer	Buyer

*1 -- Where mis-routing or lost shipment is the liability of the carrier, full transportation expense should be charged to the carrier as well as repair costs on damages occuring or return charges applying to shipping error returns.

*2 -- Transportation expense and return charges should be billed to the original consignee, with future shipments stopped until payment is made.

EXHIBIT 11-3   **Policy Decision Table for Merchandise Returns**

associate them with the right demand periods; make the proper adjustment; and provide an audit trail of the corrections made. A note of caution: fix responsibility for correction of demand with a single person. Wiping out the past can be easy. Regaining it is more difficult.

Effect of Non-Warranty Returns on Inventory Expense. All merchandise returned for credit must undergo an inspection prior to being restocked for another sale. Items not able to be sold as new or for full price must be marked down or thrown away. Return of perishables or shelf-life items will most often become a total loss. Back up the return policy where it makes sense:

1. Don't accept material back which is not resalable. Normal inspection results show that special handling such as cleaning, repackaging and remarking (or retagging) of such merchandise is necessary to make it resalable. Reduce allowable credit if expenses will be incurred.

2. Don't accept collect returns. If permitted, deduct from allowable credit. Additional expenses can be incurred on return freight costs.

3. Be restrictive on return of specially procured or seasonal merchandise. It's easy to end up with a long storage need for inventory not normally stocked.

A SELECTIVE RETURN POLICY IS NEEDED

To limit non-warranty merchandise return, a company's return allowance must necessarily become selective in nature. One of the leading automotive manufacturers limits dealer returns to only those items found on a prepublished list. Other such manufacturers in the transportation field have found it necessary to offer a similar program, or to publish a policy which requires prior company approval before any return is authorized. Both of these policies discourage the return of a large percentage of merchandise. Although the second type of policy is not accompanied by a published list of nonreturnables by individual number or description, it does qualify such merchandise so as to achieve the same effect. Selective policies help keep expenses and consumer prices down, and permit more room for price competition. This can benefit the consumer and strengthen the attributed profits for the distribution system.

RETURNED GOODS MANAGEMENT IS A POLICY-MAKING POSITION

The returned goods manager, at least in the eyes of the customer, is doing and saying what the company's management supports, when disposition is made on customer returns and adjustments. In many cases he has the last word with the customer. It is understandable, then, that he is in a policy-making position. He is required to be well conversant on all of the merchandise offered for sale. He is required to know his customers. He feels the customer's heartbeat probably better than anyone else, and is therefore well qualified to determine a customer return and adjustments policy—a policy good for the customer and good for the company.

SUPPORT A WRITTEN COMPANY POLICY ON ADJUSTMENTS

A policy must be known if it is to be followed. A published, written company policy permits responsible action. The retail customer receives his warranty and product information when he purchases an article. Usually this is a brochure included in a mail shipment, or a tag attached to the article itself. But what about the retail and wholesale distribution levels?

Ordinarily, the distribution levels receive information from each vendor they do business with, but the format and content of this information may vary by vendor (sometimes even within a same product line). Variance in manufacturer's policy and information, coupled with the multitude of manufacturers involved, constitutes the need to list and index all manufacturer's warranty and return policies into a company returned-goods policy and procedures manual.

An Operating Manual

The policy and procedures manual for returns and adjustments should be organized into sections, by product or type of merchandise, with each section having:

1. A lead sheet, which would contain a general statement of company policy concerning warranty replacement, adjustments or returns for the merchandise covered.
2. A listing of all vendors, from which such merchandise is procured. (This listing should follow the company policy statement sheet of each section.)
3. Vendor statements filed, showing exact warranty replacement, adjustments or return policy.
4. Individual pages of typical complaints concerning applicable merchandise. These pages would complete the remaining portion of each section. Pages would be filed in description sequence

so they could be indexed for easy use. (Each "complaint" page would explain the complaint, describe the merchandise affected, list all extenuating circumstances surrounding the complaint, give disposition, and summarize the customer's attitude and response to the disposition made. The complaint page should be given to the returned goods manager for review and approval, if he didn't prepare it, before being entered into the manual. A routing to sales and returned goods personnel should be made before filing. This makes these personnel aware of new complaints and the disposition made to take care of the customer. Additional advice or revised comments by the returned goods manager should be noted.)

OFFER AN ADJUSTMENTS TRAINING PROGRAM

The returned goods policy and procedures manual permits the same set of rules to be used by everyone in the company, and is a good starting point for the adjustments training program. The training program should contain in-depth handling of the following subjects:

1. Manufacturer's warranty policy.
2. Information on purpose, nature of use, expected hazards existing in its use, and any necessary precautions to be taken in maintenance of the product.
3. Company customer service philosophy.
4. Case histories on most common customer complaints.
5. Causes of customer complaints, differentiating between internal company policy, manufacturer, service or customer oriented causes.
6. General disposition guidelines for complaints.
7. Company policy and information on nonreturnable merchandise.

Merchandise is not always labeled with adequate or accurate information by some manufacturers. Sales personnel, as well as claims personnel, are expected to know all facts asked for by the customer on merchandise offered. Such personnel, unaware of a products limitation or warranty, can either lose a customer through lack of product knowledge, or sell something not suited for the purpose the purchaser intended—and create a return problem.

GOOD WILL–A MOST VALUABLE POSSESSION

The primary intent when selling merchandise is to satisfy the customer, for customer satisfaction results in good will. Good will precipitates new business as well as repeat business. The need for good will is apparent, and is listed as an asset by many companies today on their financial balance sheet. The president of a group of New York department stores tells his employees not only to lean backwards to permit the customers to have any benefit of any doubt, but also to "bounce."

How do you give the customer the benefit of any doubt?

1. Offer courtesy, diplomacy and honesty.
2. Notify the customer of unforeseen delays on shipments; don't make him ask.
3. Keep the customer alerted on price increases of special made or procured items.
4. Offer substitutes for out-of-stock items, but let the customer make the decision for substitution.
5. Segregate or allocate a supply of merchandise to support mail-in or phone-in orders for special sales promotions to prevent backorders, if lay-away is permitted. (Some companies offer a special reduced price on an article of merchandise before manufacturing them. This replaces the need for pre-market research, but it can delay shipments for several months if heavy sales result. If this is practiced, the item must be priced low enough to prevent

cancellations which would result in an inventory over-stock condition. Otherwise, backorders should be avoided to prevent lost sales.)

6. Offer a company service contract for company namebrand items; or, where vendor warranty is coordinated by the company, offer a "loaner" item where applicable. Provide emergency service.

7. Alert the customer immediately if a special factory order was "shorted," cancelled or received damaged. (Acquire his decision to wait for another shipment or substitute another selection.)

12

Controlling Parts Movement into Inventory

Six "receiving function" duties are emphasized in this chapter for controlling inventory investment dollars. Several valid points are stressed to aid receiving personnel in stopping those conditions which materially contribute to inventory expenses. Ideas are offered which will result in both time and money savings in the receiving function. Packing-sheet/receiver flowcharts are illustrated to depict paper movement requirements; and an overall receiving system flowchart is outlined (Exhibit 12-6) which compares the functional breakdown control differences for manually operated, EDP batch and EDP on-line processing systems.

PLAN FOR PARTS RECEIVING

The physical function of receiving merchandise can be quite costly. Can the merchandise be easily unloaded into the storage receiving facility space? Does the merchandise have to be unloaded from one form of container or skid onto another? Do union contracts prohibit a conveyor from being extended into the incoming truck, or other form of transportation? Is material handling equipment available to efficiently perform the job? Is there adequate room for temporary unloading or storage of new receipts until the receiving function is completed? Is sufficient manpower available to prevent jamming up of incoming trucks, for example? Scheduling of manpower, equipment and space for incoming receipts can save lots of money, time and worry.

Don't Pay for Damaged Merchandise

It is considered mandatory, before and during the unloading operation, to check incoming merchandise for any type of apparent visual damage to the containers or packages which contain the merchandise. External package or container damage should be brought to the attention of the carrier so that he can note this fact on the freight bill to permit quicker claim processing, in case merchandise is found damaged when unpacked. Frequently, concealed damage occurs where the package does not appear damaged but the contents of the package are broken or damaged enough to prevent sale of merchandise. Unpackaging of new merchandise should be accomplished immediately, at least within three days after receipt, in order to locate any concealed damage, and still have the carrier representative assume liability as to the damage claim. The carrier will determine fault for the damage. If packaging was inadequate, then a statement to this effect will be prepared by the carrier, and is usually necessary in order to return damaged merchandise to the vendor and still receive full credit. A little extra time in receiving merchandise can sometimes be more than justified in return credit received instead of lost dollars.

Verify the Packing Sheet-Receiver Before Signing

Obtain the packing sheets which accompany the incoming receipts. Make sure all cartons recorded on the packing sheet are received. Make sure that none of the cartons are damaged. If damage is apparent, the cartons should be opened in front of the carrier, so he can witness the condition of the contents and note any exceptions on the packing sheet before the packing sheet is signed. Once the merchandise has been signed for, the carrier's liability has technically ended—unless concealed damage is found within a reasonable amount of time (usually within 10 days) after receipt of goods. Sometimes extra merchandise is delivered which should be given back to the carrier. Receiving mistakes can happen, but they are less likely to happen if the packing sheets are checked immediately before signing.

Case in point: A manufacturer of steam generating equipment counts and checks incoming merchandise prior to signing the delivery ticket, with multi-counts deemed necessary on high value items in small packages. This receiving control provides almost full recovery for defective and damaged material, or shorted quantity orders. Over 10% of the company's total purchases are received either damaged, defective or as a "shorted" quantity, so the control is amply justified.

Verify Open Order Status and Date Due

A record check will ascertain that all merchandise received was actually on order from the vendor who shipped it. The quantities on order should be checked to determine if an overage or shortage of merchandise was shipped. Most industries accept a 10% overage (maximum) as common business practice, and will also allow a vendor to ship and close orders 10% short. If a percentage overage is not approved by corporate decision, the purchase orders should state this fact. Anything over the exact quantity ordered should then be returned to the vendor for full credit. Shortages should also be communicated with the vendor to make sure the shipment was a complete shipment and not a split or partial shipment. Any 10% shortage that is not to be shipped should be confirmed by the vendor as a "closed short" quantity. It must then be closed out of the open order balance so dependence is not made on merchandise on order which is really not on order. (This can provide an early stock-out situation and prevent adequate lead time given on a new order shipment quantity.) When business is booming, overages are generally kept and paid for (even for quantities above the 10%), while shortages are not permitted to be closed because of the need for such merchandise. Likewise, when business starts to drop or fall off, overages are less likely to be popular, because the sales support need does not exist.

Early Shipments Can Be Costly. The scheduled due date of material on order can be quite significant to the average inventory dollar balance. It is common, in some types of industries—especially in aerospace and transportation, to find excessively long lead times for material procurement. Many items require from six to 12 months, or more, for manufacture. Assuming normal investment turn is four times a year, and annual sales are 12 million dollars, a three-month supply of material could cause several things to happen if it came in two months early:

1. A backlog of receipts would occur in the receiving area, causing an abnormal receiving situation which would tax the manpower, material handling and space requirements allowed for incoming merchandise.
2. Restocking of much merchandise might be required (due to the larger quantities being received into inventory), or surplus stock locations would need to be assigned.
3. The average dollar inventory would immediately increase dramatically, and could prevent achievement of the annual turnover goal.

If all receipts were received on time except for this one occurrence illustrated, the average inventory dollars would be doubled for the months in which the extra three-month supply was received early. Although the increase in average inventory for the year would amount to about 16%, the immediate effect would be to increase average inventory for the immediate two months by 100%. Three million dollars tied up for three months at 10% lost interest per month would amount to $75,000. For a business operating on a 2% net margin, $3.75 million of extra sales will be required to offset this interest loss and regain a proper cash flow balance.

It is unlikely that a full three-months' supply of merchandise would be shipped early by all vendors. This example is an extreme in early shipments. However, it does stress the necessity for controlling early receipt of merchandise. Vendors should know how far in advance they can ship merchandise, and they must be held to this condition to prevent any unnecessary loss of money tied up in early shipments.

Note Lead Time Discrepancies

Unexpected early shipments result, in most cases, because false lead times are published by the vendor and are being used. Vendor delivery performance should be recorded on the purchase order copy and/or the inventory record card. Repeated early shipments from vendors should be acknowledged and an appropriate reduction in lead time figures made. The fluctuations in business cycles can cause random lead time variations. By continually adjusting the lead times used, a more accurate receipts time can be anticipated. In doing this, it is best to have good communications with the vendor so that any unexpected increases in lead time are brought to light as soon as possible to prevent customer shortages from occurring due to lead time being expanded without notice. In more sophisticated computer ordering systems, lead times are even forecasted and smoothed, just as monthly or weekly demand figures are when they are calculated. The same thing can be achieved manually, simply by recording and knowing the trends in lead time variation and allowing for them.

Inspect Merchandise Received

A thorough look at goods received, with the knowledge of what should be received, will prevent buying defective merchandise or items that won't sell. This can be a simple inspection check, or it can require hiring qualified technical people specifically trained in the manufacture and operation of the type of merchandise being purchased. Wrong sizes received in wearing apparel can be disastrous, in terms of money losses, if not found before they are accepted. Merchandise received in oddball colors might become shelf warmers because no one wants them. Some items of a technical nature have certain tolerances and "adhered to" specifications which must be met in their manufacture. Certain data facts must be labeled on articles when sold.

Sampling Shortcuts Inspection. Time and cost factors might make it impossible for all merchandise to be individually inspected. Sampling of merchandise (inspecting a few of a large quantity), can be quite effective in achieving and maintaining quality standards for purchased vendor products, without requiring all merchandise received to be individually checked. It is probable that any particular item among a large quantity would reflect the average characteristics of the product; detailed inspection of several pieces will either confirm or deny this fact. If deviations are found, larger selections (at some point which is statistically proved) will eventually conclude the types and proportional percentages of deviations which exist among the entire quantity of the item received. If certain percentage results are beyond company desired limits for quality, the entire quantity might be rejected. In this manner, the time savings is in determining the entire lot quality by a small percentage of the parts. Most manufacturers accept the results of statistical sampling methods and will allow return of such merchandise on the basis of the sample taken.

Sampling Guidelines. The number of samples to take and the accuracy level of such samples can be found in published form for most product sampling, and make sampling easy to use.

Exhibit 12-1 illustrates a sampling table used by one manufacturing company. Sampling results provide a clear-cut yes or no decision, when sampling tables are used. The decision to accept or reject is made on an impartial basis. Limited inspection on large item quantities can save time and money and still insure quality.

LOT SIZE	SAMPLE	SAMPLE SIZE	COMBINED SAMPLES	
			ACCEPTANCE	REJECTION
Under- 25	First	All		
26- 75	First	25	0	1
76- 500	First	25	0	3
	Second	50	2	3
501- 5000	First	50	1	4
	Second	100	3	4
5001- 20000	First	75	1	6
	Second	150	5	6
Over- 20000	First	100	2	6
	Second	200	5	6

EXHIBIT 12-1:   An Inspection "Sampling Table"

Three guidelines are offered for using sampling techniques:

1. Know what items should be sampled and what inspection is to be needed. (Time limitation, cost, item function, dollar value and perishability—age of life, seasonality and style—will help determine this.)
2. Select a predetermined sample quantity for different classes of merchandise to be inspected, and confirm that these recommended quantity checks are being taken. (Recording and filing of inspection forms, adequate spot-checks taken on the receiving inspection function—itself a management sampling method—or future analysis of inventory returns and obsolescence will show inspection conformance to the sampling policy established.)
3. Know in advance what disposition to take in regard to bad sample results. (Inspection sampling tables are handy and easily referenced for making such disposition. The various sample size tables will list rejection points where the pre-established number of bad occurrences exist.)

The accuracy of sampling results depends on the quantity (sample size) inspected. Greater confidence in quality, vendor, etc., can be obtained as the sample size grows, until 100% sampling is accomplished (all items are individually checked).

Count Merchandise Quantity Received

All companies do not inspect merchandise received, but a manual count is arbitrarily made. If you're going to pay for something, make sure you get all you pay for. This makes good sense. You will be able to record and know what is available for use or resale. Inventory management depends on this. Accurate recorded counts will also let you calculate what is attributable to losses. Space allocation and/or proper material handling needs can be mechanically figured at point of receipt for computer assignment of storage area, parts movement control, etc., if correct counts are known at time of receipt.

Record Shortages and/or Rejections

The vendor's packing sheet (receipts document) should have all shortages and rejection information noted on it to prevent a company from paying for more than is due for what was actually received; to prevent closing out a total quantity ordered when only a portion of the total quantity was received; and to record vendor performance information. The permanent file copy of the purchase order should also have this information recorded. A high rejection rate should indicate the need for an alternate vendor source, a change in the manufacturing technique, or both. Rejection data on vendors should be recorded and kept current to justify those purchases made from a new source at a higher than current price. Count errors, if consistent, will lower vendor's dependability rating and is important data for decisions in procuring replenishment stock.

Sign Packing Sheet-Receiver, as Corrected, for Payment

Signing of a receipt document is a simple task, but one with significant ramifications. Once it is signed, both vendor and carrier liability is discharged. Because of this, it is necessary that a preceding count and inspection be made, and that it is accurate. In many large companies, where large volumes of receipts are handled, it is not unusual to find two counts of certain merchandise being made with two signatures. These of course are preliminary, as a designated supervision signature is also required before the carrier's packing sheet is signed. Signing of the packing sheet-receiver certifies that such quantities, as corrected on the document, were actually received. (Count corrections or rejections noted on the packing sheet-receiver should be initialed.) Payment is authorized once the required signature is placed on the receipts document. Processing of this packing sheet-receiver will cause record balances to be updated.

Identify Customer Backorder Items

The receipts processing area is an ideal point to catch new merchandise which was ordered for present customer backorders. Detecting backordered merchandise at this point will enable processing such parts for a customer shipment instead of placing parts into stock and then rehandling merchandise later. Quick reference to a computer-connected inquiry terminal, a current printed customer backorder listing or the material's inventory record card will show what backorder quantities exist.

In smaller companies, backorder processing occurs at the time material is being received. The customer's backorder form set is already prepared and waiting for receipt of merchandise, so that incoming parts may be routed direct from receiving into the shipping area. Where pre-printed customer packing sheets are not available, the vendor's packing sheet-receiver is noted for customer backorder allocation. The oldest customer backorders are allocated to first, unless extenuating circumstances place priority on a more recent backorder. Aircraft manufacturers assign high priority to A.O.G. orders (Aircraft on the Ground), while the automobile manufacturers assign a "Car Down" order priority. Sometimes personal judgment dominates in regard to a valued customer, or to prevent a new customer lost sales, etc.

Direct Allocate Backorder Items

In manual order processing systems, allocation of customer backorders is initiated by placing the customer backorder number and merchandise item number on the packing sheet-receiver at the time it is determined that a customer backorder exists. If packing sheets for customer backorders are pre-printed, the respective backorder form set is pulled from the backorder file and placed with parts forwarded to shipping. If backorders are not pre-printed, the packing sheet-receiver (with backorder notation) is forwarded to the order processing section where a backorder form set is prepared.

Computerized systems provide mechanical preparation of the backorder form set. Batch processing systems would require the same order/item information written on the input document (packing sheet-receiver) to provide data necessary to machine allocate. When receipts updating occurs, the backorder data contained on the receipts input document are compared electronically to the customer backorder file to permit flagging of the allocated backorder quantities and to signal the need for customer backorder-packing sheet printing when order processing takes place. On-line "real time" systems would permit information to be entered when merchandise is received, via a remote terminal entry unit located in or near the receiving area. Customer order numbers and merchandise item numbers would be entered, via the terminal unit, to flag backorder-packing sheet printing. A printer connected to the terminal unit would be activated to print-out the necessary backorder form set and picking tags.

Direct allocation of incoming merchandise, to backorders, overrides normal manual or computer priorities established by policy on existing backorders. Flexibility is allowed for in handling changing customer needs. Emergency needed backorder items can be processed more competently and accurately by a direct allocation method.

Identify Merchandise Before Stocking

Labeling of merchandise, whether as part of the product or temporarily attached when merchandise is distributed, is necessary to facilitate better management control over dollar investment and parts movement. Merchandise identification is necessary to show warranty information; provide technical and service information; create sales motivation; establish a means to capture sales data; or to provide age limitations. Information (to distinguish the vendor source, department or account for assigning merchandise sales, product classification, type, sizes, colors, weights, shelf-life restrictions, prices, etc.) can be placed on tags or labels and attached directly to merchandise.

Size identity on clothing articles limits try-on need before buying, and permits pre-packaging to prevent excessive soiling. Material content and/or special cleaning instructions, if not mandatory, will help sell some merchandise, due to customer preferences. Lead grading is needed on pencils to identify softness. Dairy products require date markings to avoid selling spoiled products. These illustrate the need for identification.

Source record punches, mechanical label machines or electronic computers prepare such labels or perforated tags quickly and accurately. Sales can be processed faster with less assistance when merchandise is correctly and adequately identified. Fewer returns occur. Detailed sales information is easily and quickly obtained from tag stubs retained, for control over investment and discovery of sales trends.

Find and Assign Storage Locations

The assigned storage location must be known, if incoming merchandise is to be stocked with present on-hand inventory. A storage location will exist if the merchandise received is considered a restockable item. Otherwise, a new storage location assignment will be necessary. Storage locations are found on the inventory item record card, an annual physical inventory listing, a computer-printed stock status listing or a computer inquiry terminal unit.

The storage location is written on the packing sheet prior to stocking. In a manual system, this directs the stock clerk to the correct location for storing merchandise. (Backorder quantities will be removed prior to stocking. All other quantities would be placed in inventory.)

Computer oriented systems force packing sheet-receiver information to be immediately processed for timely inventory update and backorder processing, and therefore, require a different procedure for stocking merchandise than do manual systems. Some companies prepare receiving report documents called "receivers," from information on the vendor's packing sheet and the purchase order copy filed in receiving. This creates extra copies to work with, and permits prompt data processing. This also allows simultaneous action on receiving, computer update and stocking to occur. Other companies prepare a stocking sheet or use individual stocking labels to record merchandise identification and bin location.

Pre-Package Multi-Quantity "Pack" Items

Requirements for multi-packaging of merchandise must be determined when receipts occur. The record card, stock status report or inquiry terminal unit will identify those items which need to be stocked in packages. Normally, merchandise is purchased in pre-selected package quantities. If vendors refuse, or if costs are too great, the merchandise must be routed to a "pre-pack" area to have counting, bagging and labeling accomplished. After pre-pack, parts are placed back into the stocking procedure flow.

Stocking Sheets Help Move Receipts

The vendor packing sheet-receiver is normally used as the stocking sheet in manual systems. Where computers are used, machine printed stocking sheets, or labels, are created—or a standard form is manually prepared and used. The stocking sheet is limited to a set number of material items per sheet, and thus per stocking cart. As material is received, inspected, counted and assigned existing storage locations, the material number (or description), quantity received and storage location are written on the stocking sheet.

Exhibit 12-2 presents a typical stocking sheet. A cart number is assigned to this sheet. Item number and quantity are added. Parts are placed on an assigned cart after inspection, counting and marking. One copy is placed in the warehouse receipts stocking logbook. The original has storage assignments added and is then placed on the assigned cart to locate merchandise. Material that is relocated has the new location entered on the second storage location line for later updating.

CART NO. _____

PART NUMBER	QUANTITY	STORAGE LOCATION	REMARKS:

EXHIBIT 12-2:   **Stocking Sheet**

A pre-sort of merchandise should be required before preparing the stock sheet assignments. This allows merchandise in close storeroom locations to be placed on the same stocking cart, instead of having articles with locations all over the storeroom on the same cart. The extent of the pre-sort required depends upon the volume of receipts and the size of the storage areas. The stocking sheet is prepared in duplicate. The carbon copy is placed in a control book before storeroom locations are assigned. At the time the stocking sheet is prepared, merchandise is placed on the cart whose number is assigned to the stocking sheet. A scrap sheet of paper with the same cart number written on it (3"x 5" is sufficient) is taped to the cart until the stocking sheet has locations assigned. The completed original copy of the stocking sheet is then matched and taped to the cart. The stocking sheet is used for locating and storing those parts on the cart. Some manual judgment is required for saving steps if the stocking sheets are not arranged in storeroom location sequence.

The duplicate copy of the stocking sheet is needed only if emergency information is required on incoming receipts (for special customer order processing, inventory discrepancies and/or direct allocation reference needs). Location of a new receipt is made by reference to the control book copy to discover the cart the part is on. If merchandise is removed from a cart prior to stocking, a note is placed on the stocking sheet. If the stocking sheet is not completed, and can't be immediately found, a note is placed on the duplicate copy in the control book.

Process Receiving Paperwork

The vendor furnishes at least one copy of a packing sheet with material shipped. Additional copies are sometimes available from a vendor, but the vendor must be told this when material is purchased. The need for more copies of the packing sheet than the vendor will furnish requires the preparation of additional copies when merchandise is received—either handwritten, by typewriter, source record punch or computer printing of an in-house receiving report document. Facsimile copying of extra copies is a fast method and doesn't require adding handwritten information on all copies. A single copy should be used, whenever possible, and should normally suffice. (Normal business requirements can be handled as shown on the packing sheet form flowcharts in Exhibits 12-3, 12-4 and 12-5.)

A New Receipts Idea Saved Time and Money

One multi-divisional company having high volume receipts from several divisions, to support after-market distribution activities, designed and implemented a combination material transfer-receiver form set. The form set, called a "picking tag," is computer generated. Picking tags are printed and routed to the proper division and department based on order "due date" information. While some tags are printed when order memos are released for procurement of material, most tags are released a set number of picking days prior to due date. Unanticipated stock-outs cause an early tag printing, with back order quantity data added to the picking tag. Item location, within the finished goods inventory warehouse, is also printed on each tag released.

Merchandise is not shipped without computer printed tags, except for emergency demand requirements which can be transferred, upon request, on handwritten tags. This permits a "hold" to be entered in the computer open order requirements file, where a change or cancellation becomes urgent, so that material movement is

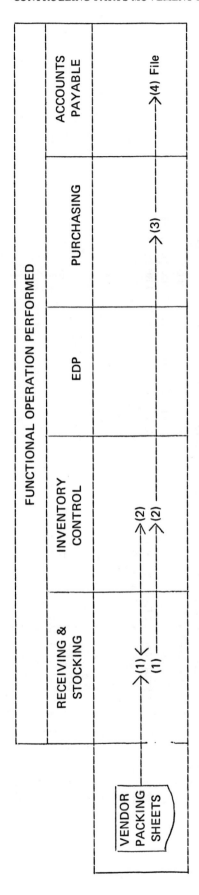

EXHIBIT 12-3: Flowchart for a Packing Sheet in a Manual Receipts System

Exhibit 12-3 presents a flowchart for a packing sheet in a manual receipts system. Merchandise and accompanying packing sheets are received in receiving (1). A manual system requires Inventory Control assistance (2) for referencing stock-keeping records in checking open order status, due dates, backorder status, packaging requirements, and storeroom locations of material received. Once stocked (1), the packing sheet is forwarded to Purchasing (3). Purchasing notes on the purchase order—the vendor packing sheet number on which merchandise was received; quantity received—to close out open order quantities; rejected quantity—to provide information for shipping authorization on return of defective merchandise, and to adjust open order quantities and vendor's rating; vendor lead time discrepancies—to correct future purchase order scheduling; and to initial the packing sheet when completed. The packing sheet then flows to Accounts Payable (4) for payment of a soon-to-be-received invoice.

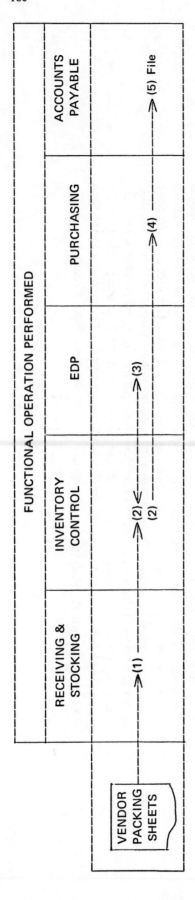

FUNCTIONAL OPERATION PERFORMED

RECEIVING & STOCKING	INVENTORY CONTROL	EDP	PURCHASING	ACCOUNTS PAYABLE
➤(1)	➤(2) ◄ (2)	➤(3)	➤(4)	➤ (5) File

EXHIBIT 12-4:   Flowchart for a Packing Sheet in a "Batch" Processing Computer System

In Exhibit 12-4 we see a flowchart for a packing sheet in a batch processing computer system. Merchandise and accompanying packing sheets are received in receiving (1). A batch processing system requires the use of a stocking sheet concept so the vendor packing sheets can be immediately monitored by Inventory Control personnel (2) to provide receipts updating data to EDP (3). A key-to-tape, key-to-disk or key-to-card operation is completed. If source data entry is not used, the packing sheet flows to EDP for capturing data requirements, with return of the packing sheet to Inventory Control personnel for verification of accurate update. The packing sheet then flows to Purchasing (4), and on to Accounts Payable (5) as it does in a manual system.

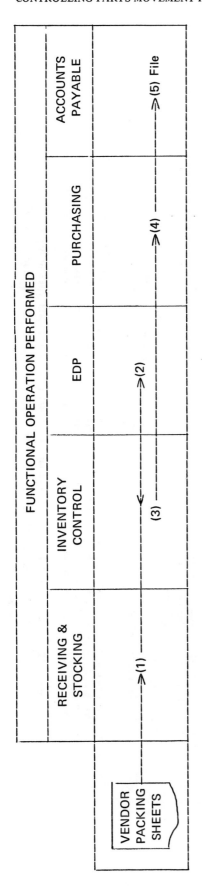

FUNCTIONAL OPERATION PERFORMED

RECEIVING & STOCKING	INVENTORY CONTROL	EDP	PURCHASING	ACCOUNTS PAYABLE
→(1)	(3) →(2)		→(4)	→(5) File

VENDOR PACKING SHEETS

EXHIBIT 12-5: Flowchart for a Packing Sheet in an "On-Line" Processing Computer System

The flowchart in Exhibit 12-5 is for a packing sheet in an on-line processing computer system. Merchandise and accompanying packing sheets are received in receiving (1). An on-line processing system requires source data entry at point of receipt (1). Key-to-tape or key-to-disk entry of receipts updating data is made to EDP (2) with immediate print-out of a receipts/open order errors listing in receiving. A computer-printed stocking sheet and/or labels (for stocking purposes) are also printed. The packing sheet and receipts/open order errors listing flows to Inventory Control personnel (3) for receipts/open order errors verification and/or correction procedure. The packing sheet then flows to Purchasing (4), and on to Accounts Payable (5) as it does in a manual system.

RECEIVING SYSTEM FLOWCHART
Comparison of Functional Breakdown
For Manually Operated/EDP-"Batch"/EDP-"On-Line" Processing Systems

Functional Description	Manual System	EDP-"Batch" System	EDP-"On-Line" System
Receive Parts	•	•	•
Check for External/Concealed Damage	•	•	•
Find and Pull Packing Sheet-Receiver	•	•	•
Verify Open Order Status and Date Due	Purchase Order or Record Card	Open Order Listing	Computer Terminal Inquiry
Note Lead Time Discrepancies	Purchase Order or Record Card	Computer Listing	Computer Listing
Inspect Merchandise Received	•	•	•
Count Merchandise Quantity Received			
Record Shortages and/or Rejections	Purchase Order and Packing Sheet-Rcvr	Packing Sheet-Rcvr	Packing Sheet-Rcvr
Parts Mark Merchandise Received and Date Code	Ink Pen, Crayon, etc., or labels	Ink Pen, Crayon, etc., or labels	Computer Labels via Terminal
Sign Packing Sheet-Receiver, as Corrected, for Payment	•	•	•
Identify Customer Backorder Items	On Packing Sheet-Rcvr from Record Card	On Stocking Sheet from Backorder List	Computer Listing via Terminal
Direct Allocate Customer Backorder Items	•	•	•
Determine and Assign Storage Locations	Packing Sheet-Rcvr	Stocking Sheet from Stock Status List or Computer Inquiry	Computer Listing via Terminal
Pre-Package Multi-Quantity "Pack" Items	•	•	•
Place Receipts on Stocking Carts with Stocking Sheet	•	•	•
Forward Packing Sheet-Receivers to Purchasing Dept.	•	•	•
Prepare Return Paperwork on Rejections	•	•	•
Reinstate Vendor "Reject" Quantity or "Close Short"	Disposition Sheet	Computer Listing	Computer Listing
Forward Packing Sheet-Receivers to EDP Dept.	Not Applicable	***	***
Forward Packing Sheet-Receiving to Accounts Payable	*	*****	*****
Prepare Formal Receiving Report Document	*****	*******	*******
Prepare Informal Receiving Report Document	*******	Stocking Sheet & Computer Listing	Computer Listing
Prepare Daily Receipts Register	Packing Sheet-Recvr	Computer Listing	Computer Listing
Open Orders Closed Out By Receipts	Purchase Order or Record Card	Computer Listing	Computer Listing

* Functions are performed the same in all systems.
*** Methods vary—mark-sensing cards, keypunched cards, key-to-tape, key-to-disk, perforated tags, etc.
***** Required where receiving function is centralized for multi-plant activity, and/or where additional packing sheet-receiver copies are needed.
******* Useful where keypunch source document standardization is desired for the variety of vendor packing sheets or receiving documents in use.

EXHIBIT 12-6: An Overall Receiving Flowchart, Comparing the Functional Breakdown Control Differences for Manually Operated, EDP Batch and EDP On-line Processing Systems

temporarily halted and controlled. Tag printing cannot occur on any item assigned a "hold." The "hold" is automatically removed during processing of the change disposition.

This material transfer-receiver tag concept reduced this company's average receipts processing time by 24 hours, with a better than 90% reduction in processing errors. Added benefits accrued from the pre-printed bin locations, allowing manual or carrousel conveyor sorting of receipts by storage location for speeding up the receiving and stocking operations. Stocking sheets were eliminated.

13

A "Stocking" System Considers Both Storage and Retrieval Needs

Filing something in storage requires that some system exist which will permit fast efficient retrieval of it whenever needed, whether it be in a file drawer, an office storage room or a finished goods inventory area. The system requires a formal storage procedure, however, when supporting a finished goods inventory, because of the monetary value involved. This chapter discusses the important elements of such a storage system: assignment of warehouse locations, preparation of merchandise for storage, need for pre-sorting, stocking methods, and the paperwork support to provide back-up information; and offers some common-sense guidelines to observe during the stocking process.

ASSIGNING ITEM LOCATIONS

A numerical sequence is often used on items in the storage area, but becomes limited in storage efficiency as the volume of inventory items increases. Product line sequencing is also used frequently, and is also limited in value for the same reason: the activity of an item is not compatible with the part number or product line of an item in stock. Randomly assigned methods should, therefore, be used where larger inventories are found.

Random Location Assignment

Random assignment of storage locations permits full utilization of available warehouse space and allows rearrangement of stock to keep a highly efficient flow going. Each stocking area can be separated into fast and slow moving sections. (Use of the "ABC" classification formula is recommended.) Faster moving items can be placed closest to the main picking aisle at good picking heights; slower moving items furthest from the main picking aisle. New items can be stored in any available storage location based on:

1. Size and weight of part or awkwardness to handle.
2. Activity code based on similar item movement.

190

3. Product line identity.

4. Special item characteristics such as shelf life.

PREPARING RECEIPTS FOR STOCK

Receiving personnel will position new item receipts on stocking carts (or equipment) based on the locator system developed. The stocking clerk does not usually load the stocking carts, but he must be able to know logically when errors occur (i.e., when an item is designated for a location it should not be placed in). Stocking equipment is normally loaded in such a way that ease in stocking is present. For instance, mixing of items to be stocked in two distant separated areas, out of sequence, on the same stocking cart can create more steps to be taken than is necessary—and thus create more processing time than needed. This should be prevented, or caught before stocking occurs.

The diagram in Exhibit 13-1 shows the distance to the various zones of a warehouse storage area, considering each area to be 100 feet in length. If the new items required five carts, and were sorted by storage area before stocking, then the maximum amount of distance traveled (to and fro) would be 200' plus 400' plus 600' plus 800' plus 1000' or a total of 3000'. If the same five trips were made without sorting, and some area "E" items were on each trip, the maximum distance would be 5000' when five trips at 1000' per trip are made (or two-thirds more walking than necessary). If the example were two trips to "A" area and two trips to "E" area vs. four trips to "E" area, twice as much walking as necessary would be done. If new items aren't sorted prior to stocking, there's a good chance that time (and money) is being wasted. Walking at 2¼ miles per hour and making 30 trips per day to "E" area, a minimum of 2½ hours are spent in to-and-fro walk time alone.

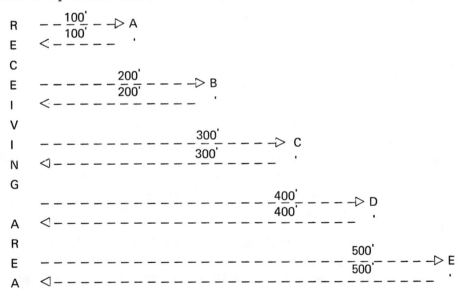

EXHIBIT 13-1:   Sorting Received Items Prior to Stocking Can Save Steps

DECIDING THE STOCKING METHOD

Manual stocking of inventory items can be accomplished in two general ways:

1. Open stocking, where items are stocked by any available stock clerk, regardless of where the item is to be located in storage.

2. Zone stocking of inventory items where an individual is responsible for a given defined storage area.

Open Stocking

In the open stocking method, it is usually found that received items are loaded on a cart in the same sequence they are checked and counted in, and not necessarily in the sequence they should be stocked. Thus a stock clerk will usually take more steps to put away merchandise than really required. In Exhibit 13-1, we considered a warehouse storage area having five separate stocking areas located in storage, with these areas (A, B, C, D and E) numbered from the front of the storage area to the back. A stocking cart may be loaded with items to be stocked in each of the five areas. Of course, a stocking sheet may be prepared for the cart showing the exact locations of each of the items to be stocked, and the clerk will probably have to use some "sort sequence" thinking to minimize walking from areas "A" to "E" and back. This can be a good stocking plan, providing that the total items received each day could be loaded on a single cart, and that "sort sequence" thinking could be done rapidly. If more than this minimum volume of items are received, then more than one cart will be loaded for the stock clerk, and he might be walking to area "E" (at the extreme end of the storage area) several times each day—when only once would be necessary.

Sorting Eliminates Extra Walking. Extra walking can be prevented by prior sorting of receipts before loading the stocking carts. In this manner, all area "A" items will be placed on the same cart, all area "B" items will be placed on another cart, and so forth. The size of the storage area, the number of receipts to be stocked and the number of stock clerks available will determine the sophistication of this system.

This sort method works best where a pre-assigned stocking location is given to all items being received and is shown on the receipts document. Where pre-assigned locations are not given, then the location system parameters will be used to fix the general area for stocking, with an appropriate random location later assigned by the stocking clerk.

Importance of Location Assignment. Open stocking of inventory items, by any available stock clerk, works well for a small storage area with relatively few parts (up to 500 or so items), but does require an assigned storage location system which is easy to follow. When a stock clerk is absent or on vacation, someone else will be doing his stocking. Instant training has to be given, and it's difficult to memorize placements of various product lines within the storage warehouse without some master plan. A location system which permits an exact location for an item gives flexibility to the stocking procedure.

Each warehouse employee is expected to know how to find any given storage location number with the fewest steps. A row-bin-shelf system of locating parts was described in Chapter 1. Any similar coordinate system will offer the same type of benefits. The item's location number has to be known before the item can be stocked. A method to determine random storage locations was covered in Chapter 3. Only new items, which are not for a customer's backorder, would require a storage location assignment when using this method. This reduces an item's location "look-up" to new items only.

Zone Stocking

The zone stocking method offers decided advantages—where it can be used. Zone stocking confines a stock clerk to a defined area of responsibility. Where the zone method is used, the stock clerk generally assumes the order picking responsibilities too. Sorting is made mandatory—at least for each zone within the storage area. Receiving personnel deliver incoming items to a zone and leave them in a designated staging area. The carts can either be returned to the receiving area for reuse in processing other items if desired, or can be left in a zone area (loaded) for more efficient use in stocking.

Case in point: A company manufacturing, processing and distributing foods and grocery products uses the zone stocking method with their 20 warehouses situated across the United States. Continued use of zone stocking has resulted in a 10% reduction in picking and stocking discrepancies and errors. This reduction was restricted due to the low number (800) of stock-keeping units stored in each warehouse, and the highly efficient operation in existence prior to employing the zone stocking method. But, with each warehouse averaging 300 daily stock trips of multiple items, the 10% reduction was a significant benefit.

This method should be considered only where many stock clerks are required to handle large volumes of received merchandise and large order picking quantities, with many stock-keeping items being inventoried and large areas to be covered. Under these conditions, the following advantages exist:

1. Consistency in stocking merchandise.
2. Consistency in picking merchandise.
3. Performance rating of stocking clerks is made easier, and more accurate.
4. Responsibility is assumed for given location areas.
5. Inventory discrepancies and picking errors can be corrected with less investigation of who is responsible.
6. Housekeeping improvements usually result where responsibility is assumed.
7. Inventory count accuracy is improved.
8. Inventory group leaders are already assigned when physical inventory time arrives.
9. Pride is more evident in work performance.
10. Conveyor equipment is more suited for a zone stocking arrangement.(A complete conveyor system is not initially required to improve the stocking function, but what is installed is adaptable to an overall warehouse conveyor system where the zone areas flow into a main warehouse aisle.)

Case in point: A large warehouse area (200,000 square feet), and a large volume of merchandise required to be stored each day, prompted one manufacturer in Michigan to install a zone stocking method, and to sort incoming merchandise prior to stocking. The company's goal for speed, accuracy and consistency in item picking and stocking was achieved. Inventory discrepancies were literally cut in half; and a 60% drop in picking errors resulted.

Case in point: A pharmaceutical company claimed zone stocking was responsible for "over 90%" reduction in their inventory discrepancies.

ASSIGNING A NEW STORAGE LOCATION

New storage locations are randomly assigned by the stocking clerk when an item is stocked for the first time. Storage locations are also assigned when the previously assigned location will no longer hold the quantity being received, or when items are rearranged in storage to permit more efficient order processing. Some method is required to control the issuing of a storage assignment so that an item will not be lost in inventory storage. The information requirement will be the same, regardless of whether a manual or computer inventory control system is used.

Manual Systems

In manual systems, a single line item form is used for assigning storage locations. This permits one copy (usually a hardcopy) to be filed in a central warehouse tub file, with a second copy retained in the stocking zone, if the zone concept is used.

Exhibit 13-2 presents an example of a single line item "location assignment card set." This card set is used to assign a storage location to a newly received inventory item, or can be used to restock an item already having a storage location. Restocking (or rearranging) occurs where an item is originally assigned a wrong area location; when increased usage demands a larger storage area need; or through "ABC" analysis to improve warehouse productivity. Where computer resources (batch processing mode) are available, the #1 copy is routed for location update; the #3 hardcopy is placed in a central warehouse mini-tub file (until verification is made that the computer file location has been changed); and copy #2 is kept in the zone stocking area (for a limited time period) to cover potential customer pick tags released without a storage location. In manual systems, or where on-line computer files exist, only two copies of this form will be required.

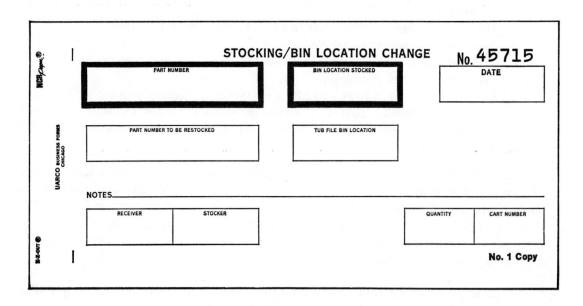

EXHIBIT 13-2:   A Single Line Item "Location Assignment" Card Set

Batch Processing Computer Systems

The same system works well with a computer system, especially where a batch processing environment exists. In this manner, one copy is forwarded for update within the computer file while the other is retained and filed in a central warehouse mini-tub file, until verification that the newly assigned location is properly updated in the computer file.

On-Line Computer Systems

Where on-line computer systems exist, a terminal unit becomes the mini-tub file, if a location is questioned. In this case, only one copy of a bin location assignment is necessary for keying into the computer file. It then could be returned to the originating zone area for retention for a specified period of time to prevent picking discrepancies.

PREVENTING DISCREPANCIES FROM LOCATION REASSIGNMENT

In warehouses with high volumes of activity, many customer order line items might be printed awaiting picking at the time an item's location is being reassigned. The bin location assignment card should be retained in the zone area long enough to cover a maximum customer order backlog period, which usually would be within a 24- to 48-hour period.

Location Assignment Card Is Cross-Reference

The location assignment card serves an additional purpose when an item is relocated in storage. The copy normally retained in the zone area is not filed, but is taped to the old location to serve as a cross-reference to where the new location is to be found. The copy should be taken down after the retention time period has elasped (48 hours, for example).

Purging Cross-Reference Cards

Since all location forms carry a date, the location cards in the zone area could be searched during a slack period each day, and all cards beyond a set time period thrown away—or at least verified (that the location is recorded) by inquiry into the central warehouse tub file or the computer's terminal unit, before being thrown away.

USING RECEIVERS FOR ASSIGNING LOCATIONS

Where a receiver form is used showing pre-printed storage locations, and if the form is in card form (to facilitate easy filing), then a three-part form could be used for receiving, stocking and bin location control. The original copy would be forwarded to data processing for receipts quantity update. The remaining two copies of the form become the stocking sheet and would accompany the items into storage. Where bin location assignment appears on the receiver, both copies can be thrown away after proper stocking of the item's quantity. If, however, item location is not present on the receiver form, space on the form is allocated to new location assignment. After assignment of a storage location to the item, the location number is handwritten on the receiving form in the allocated space. The two remaining receiver copies are then used as a bin location assignment form.

The stocking sheet (used to place many items on a single sheet of paper per cart), can also be used for updating locations within a computer file, but is unhandy to file because of larger size. Since many items are contained on the same sheet, they will be out of "sort sequence" and will also be difficult for finding new locations fast. To counteract these disadvantages, a separate location assignment card set can be prepared from information on the stock sheet—if the receiver form is not in service.

REARRANGING SPACE FOR BETTER USE

Warehouse space requires constant monitoring to insure that a proper stock density is being maintained. Warehouse rearrangement is the tool for controlling storage space and to guarantee it is reused whenever and whereever possible. Rearrangement becomes necessary for various reasons. It will occur due to a stocking error (in which case a restock sheet will be prepared). It is necessary when too much quantity is received to fit the present location assigned (in which case a location assignment card set will be prepared). It will also come about, as a result of "ABC" analysis, to improve warehouse productivity (in which case a location assignment card set would be prepared).

Make Use of Empty Containers

Retaining locations permanently (once they have been assigned) will tend to use up existing warehouse space unnecessarily. A manual method of control can correct for long-standing vacant areas in the warehouse, and permit immediate reuse of space. As stock is exhausted, the item's container is placed upside down in its storage location. During slack periods of time, the zone clerk, or other stock clerk, reviews the upside-down containers to determine if the item is still to be stocked, if the inventory quantity level is to be reduced with smaller containers used, or if the container may be removed and the location assigned to another item. If the container is removed from storage, the item's location card would be removed from the central warehouse tub file, or blanked out of the computer file.

Empty Container Listing. This is one miscellaneous area where the extra advantages of a computer can be proven. The computer can periodically review all inventory items (based on the inventory classification system in use) and prepare a sequenced listing, by location, of each item's containers which can be removed. At the time the listing is prepared, all item locations can be automatically blanked out.

A second listing can be prepared for those items classified as true slow movers. This listing can be sequenced also, by item location, and can show the maximum expected quantity that will be stocked on an item in the future. This permits the item's containers to be replaced by smaller size containers, and frees more space for new inventory items, or rearrangement of other items into better picking locations. Manually placing the empty bin boxes upside-down should be done, even with a computer system, and especially where the zone concept is not in force.

Discrepancy Prevention. A periodical check can be made by the stock clerk, during slack periods, to make sure that inventory record balances are zero for the empty containers placed upside-down. An early correction on stock variances could prevent a future costly discrepancy audit.

INVENTORY STOCKING GUIDELINES

A common-sense approach, in servicing the inventory storage facility, should include the following guidelines:

1. *Provide adequate storage space for each item stocked.* The inventory classification system is extremely helpful here. The item's class will describe activity volume. Minimum stock quantities will be defined. Allowance should be made for minimum quantity where less than this quantity is initially received. Containers should be checked whenever new quantities are received, and the class marked on the container. A simple coding like this can allow an easy way to spot those items which need to be relocated.

2. *Practice safety.* Items should be stocked so that no overhang occurs (out of the storage area assigned). Flammable or explosive materials should be stored in a separate warehouse area by themselves. Assistance should be obtained when storing large, heavy or awkward-to-handle items. Handling equipment should be used whenever applicable. Proper protective clothing should be worn to suit the storage environment.

3. *Insure adequate item protection.* All items should be wrapped, if they are subject to becoming soiled, scratched or otherwise adversely affected by not being so protected.

4. *Rotate stock properly.* Items that carry an assigned shelf life require shelf rotation so that the first in—first out picking practice is followed, without the picking clerk having to sort through the entire stock quantity to select the oldest dated items.

5. *Visually check new merchandise before stocking.* Prevent stocking errors by comparing the merchandise in the container with the new quantity, before placing new stock in a container. If they don't match or look alike, don't stock them until both the old and the new items have been inspected.

6. *Check for obvious damage when stocking merchandise.* Damaged merchandise occasionally gets past receiving personnel. If no damage is apparent, then proceed with stocking. Don't cause damage, however, by throwing merchandise in a storage location. Handle the merchandise as though you were paying for it.

7. *Keep multi-quantity packaged items in proper size packages.* Recommend that the package size be increased where large volume picking continually occurs on a specific item. Pre-packaging is done much more efficiently in the receiving area when an item is received than during the order-picking process.

8. *Check empty storage containers.* Items having an empty storage container may be no longer available, could be superseded, or may have just stopped selling. Valuable picking space may be wasted or misused if empty bin boxes aren't checked periodically. Placing the empty containers upside-down helps you to keep an eye on them.

9. *Keep an updated listing of available storage locations.* The computer can generate a listing of open storage areas, and even assign a storage area location to an item when it is ordered for inventory. Automated warehouse operations use this technique where standardization is possible, but they operate on fixed size storage openings and depths. Sizes, weights or other important coordinate characteristics are required to be assigned to each item so that computer control is permitted. Maintaining up-to-date records of storage space on computer can be quite expensive where large warehouse areas are controlled.

A manual method can be used which is helpful in locating a new item in storage—and which can be a step saver. A list of storage locations with openings can be placed on the front end of each storage row, showing the width and shelf height for the available openings. When open locations are taken, the location would simply be lined off. (A slotted hardboard holder could be used with locations and dimensions placed on uniform size paper and inserted in the holder in location sequence. New locations could be added as a result of rearrangement of items in storage, and used locations could be deleted, by rearranging the slips of paper.) With this manual method in use, the procedural steps for stocking a new item could be as follows:

1. Select the item that needs the assignment of a new storage location.
2. Select a general position (close to, half-way or far away) from the main picking aisle—in relation to the item's inventory classification.
3. Proceed to the front of the selected row to check for location openings. (If none exist, select another adjacent row that has such openings.)
4. Locate, store parts and update the listing of location openings.

A manual method for recording empty bin locations is illustrated in Exhibit 13-3, in which three simple inexpensive methods are shown for recording empty storage bin locations: (A) A hanging slotted hardboard holder has a supply of paper strips on which to record bin locations and width-height dimensions before inserting in slot. This method permits sequenced arrangements either by location or by dimensions, by moving paper strips in the slots when adding new locations. (B) A tablet sheet is taped to the end of a storage bin. Empty locations are simply written on the sheet of paper. (C) An envelope with a self-sticking back contains blank cards on which to write available locations. Empty storage information is placed on the forward-facing end of respective storage bins, to aid in locating available stocking places for new items. (A) offers a sequencing option, but each serves a useful purpose by saving steps in searching for storage room.

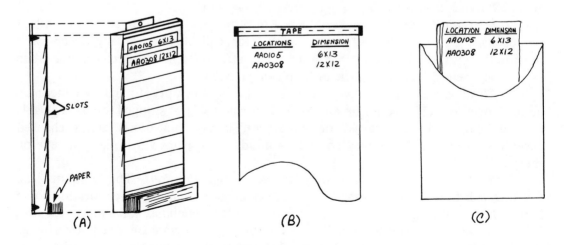

EXHIBIT 13-3:   A Manual Method for Recording Empty Bin Locations

14

How Surplus
and Obsolescence Administration
Controls Unwanted Inventory

This chapter proposes a workable four-step remedial action plan for the reduction and control of unwanted merchandise. Several easily applied checking tools are described and suggested for preventing surplus inventory build-up, regardless of current sales trends. A special computer-supported program is also offered for use, and is designed to minimize the costs involved in a surplus and obsolescence program.

PINPOINTING CAUSES OF OBSOLESCENCE

The causes of inventory obsolescence are listed by order of importance:

— Lack of coordination and communication on product improvement or design changes.
— Lack of regard for components standardization.
— Lack of corporate obsolescence guidelines.
— Lack of sound inventory management techniques.
— Lack of positive attitudes among inventory personnel.
— Carelessness.

While most of the *causes* of inventory obsolescence might be attributed to the last five factors, most of the *dollars* are usually caused by the first factor. The desire to continually improve a product, or to change a product to prevent market saturation, leads to planned obsolescence. The degree of company obsolescence in supporting such action largely depends on the coordination and communication exercised internally by the company.

ESTABLISHING A REMEDIAL ACTION PLAN

A four-step remedial action plan can effectively reduce future obsolescence in the finished goods inventory. Time involvement and salesmanship are the two main criteria for success, and should furnish a return proportionate to the investment made. This plan is:

1. Promote common parts usage to limit the total number of probable inventory items, or urge

a limitation of the quantity (or variety) of manufactured models, styles, colors, etc., that the company offers.

2. Urge development and establishment of corporate guidelines for controlling inventory obsolescence.

3. Classify stock-keeping units for activity status and inventory worth, and conduct timely appraisals.

4. Recommend, obtain approval for and implement an inventory write-off and disposal program.

Promote Common Parts Usage

An analysis of all proprietary inventory items will provide data for common parts usage. Determine and list item categories which would qualify for common parts usage (interchangeable in use among more than one model; a universal part).

Review Questions. Review a category of items at a time, with the following questions in mind:

1. *Are several items being stocked where only one item would suffice?* (It may not be necessary to stock both the detail item as well as sub-assemblies and assemblies that contain the detail item. Difficulty of replacement by customers, and cost, can help determine some of these decisions. Other items, especially in the repair parts category, can be stocked in bulk and cut to size, rather than encouraging different lengths or sizes of a same item to be stocked. Some items, however, *must* be carried in bulk. Yard goods in a fabric store cannot possibly be carried in cut lengths and still meet customer demands.)

2. *Can modification of an item make it interchangeable with other items?* (Lamp assemblies usable for different voltages, which include bulbs, should be stocked without the bulbs—with the bulbs stocked separately.)

3. *Are right and left hand parts stocked where both are interchangeable?* (An exhaust inlet tube which contained a loose flange clamp on the assembly was stocked in both a right hand and left hand configuration by a Midwest parts distributor. This was because the flange clamp could not be used for both of the installations. A different clamp was required. A manufacturing change was made to have both flange clamps placed on the inlet tube, prior to being completed, to permit stocking only one part. Larger volume build quantities lowered the cost enough to stock and sell only one item without an increase in price. The user simply snips off the clamp that is not needed. Lower inventory needs provided an additional expense reduction which increased overall profits.)

4. *Does stock duplication exist on identical parts, unknowingly, under different vendor numbers?* (This can occur quite readily with electronic and electrical parts where a common part may have as many identification numbers as it has manufacturing users.)

Report Findings. Document results by reporting the volume of items that can be reduced, total sales activity for all items involved, cumulative inventory dollar levels for items studied, and potential inventory savings through reduction in number of items stocked. (Carry out a plan to reduce inventory respectively.)

Obtain Corporate Guidelines

Corporate guidelines can offer the one item that is usually missing in most inventory management areas: specific *measurable* goals. With measurable goals defined and approved, more time can be spent in creative activity. How much easier it is to work for a "95% service level" (fill rate), than to achieve "adequate stock availability." Or, not having to worry about inventory dollars being limited to "a minimum value," when the dollar limit is approved as a set value related to the service level goal.

A Positive Approach. Guidelines, submitted for corporate approval, should set forth positive stocking criteria for:

1. When to stock;
2. How much to stock;
3. How long to stock;
4. When to discontinue support.

When to stock should be predicated on actual sales frequency of a new item, anticipated lost sales if not stocked, or prior sales frequency of a similar item. Many companies simply restrict stocking of new merchandise until the second or third sale occurs. Breakeven point, or ROI, should, however, be considered.

How much should be supported by a customer service level established as a measured percent of fill rate, which rates the entire inventory activity and not just individual items alone. This generally permits EOQ to be followed and results in individual items having different turnover rates. (Some items will have limited inventory, and others may have upwards to a year's supply or more.)

How long can be regulated on the basis of frequency and quantity of demand, current model status, function of item and market availability. A trend to stop stocking slowest moving items (less than three per year) is gaining in use, with made-to-order status increasing on more kinds of inactive (out-of-production) merchandise.

When to discontinue support will ordinarily be determined by the competitive market position, demand frequency and profitability. As long as made-to-order items can be acceptably priced, without creating a loss of profits, support can be extended indefinitely. Made-to-order permits support without increasing potential obsolescence.

Classify—Then Appraise Inventory Regularly

Several methods can be employed to classify and appraise an inventory. Chapter 3 furnished several classification methods, and Chapter 5 describes inventory appraisal based on its working value. Frequent inventory appraisals will identify potential surplus conditions before they become real, by acknowledging the trend towards a slow or "no sales activity" status, or a general increase in inventory. The classification system will identify the selling characteristics of an item. Items reaching an excess stock situation can be selected and valued by the classification code assigned. Other methods exist, besides the needed inventory classification, which can provide an edge against surplus conditions that are caused by other than sales reduction.

A High Value Inventory Listing. A monthly listing can be printed which contains information on all items having an inventory dollar value greater than a pre-selected amount (i.e., $500). The listing can be arranged in descending dollar sequence, by item, with the item having the largest inventory dollar value first. In this way, the item with a greater dollar value will be given review priority—as it should be.

A complete review of the listing should be made with the following questions in mind: Has the dollar value increased? What caused the increase? Is the inventory value justified? Should any action be taken? What can be done to effectively reduce any excess dollars?

An extracted report should be compiled from the listing, showing those items which have either increased in inventory dollar value, or which have (abruptly) stopped in sales activity. A disposition decision should be given for each item on the report, with follow-up action taken. Data shown on the extracted report should include:

1. Part number and/or description.
2. Current on-hand quantity.
3. Quantity on hand at end of previous month.
4. Current extended on-hand dollar value.
5. Current on-order quantity.
6. Quantity on order at end of previous month.
7. Receipts quantity for the current month (including inventory adjustments and returned goods).
8. Last 12 months' sales.
9. Number of months item has been on report. (Should stay on the report until adequate disposition is made.)
10. Reason for appearing on report.
11. Disposition decisions and/or follow-up action taken.

An Open Order Summary Sheet. An open order dollar value summary sheet can be printed each time the current open order listing is printed. This summary sheet can show the number of items, and total dollar value relating to these items, that are currently on order with the company's manufacturing facilities (or with outside vendors). Dollar values (and items) can be listed as past due (due prior to current month), due this month, and due by month for each of the next 12 months. All dollars (and items) due beyond the next 12-month period can be grouped in a 13th period total. An overall dollar value (and item) total can also be shown.

The summary data can be split by inventory classification, by purchased and manufactured responsibility, or by other desired breakdown methods. Summary dollars should be compared to the current 30-60-90 day sales forecasts to analyze potential effects on inventory worth, with the following questions in mind: Are enough dollars open to support the normal monthly, or 30-60-90 day, sales forecasts? Will the total dollars open result in a general inventory increase next month? Will the increase be significant, so that open order dollars should be reviewed for justification or supportive reasons? A monthly management report should be issued disclosing the open order dollar values, and schedules, for the next 30-60-90 days.

A High Value Receipts Listing. A daily itemized listing can be made of those items received, where total receipts dollars (per item) are greater than a pre-selected amount (i.e., $500). This is an after-the-fact method for spotting an inventory dollar build-up, but can depict drastic changes in vendor delivery, in ordering strategy, or in error shipments. Even though dollars and items have already been received, it's still not too late to dispose of unnecessary items and initiate remedial action steps.

An Order Review Listing. An order review listing can be printed at each order review period to recommend rescheduling or cancellation of open order quantities which appear in excess of need. A simple guide can be established to look objectively at all quantities on order. Since an order quantity is not placed until an order point is reached, then:

$$\underline{\text{Potential Excess} = \text{Available Quantity} - \text{Order Point Quantity} - \text{EOQ} - \overline{X}}$$

Where a greater than zero quantity remains, anything on order should be analyzed. This guide can be lengthened to suit any specific company, by multiplying a desired factor times $\overline{X}$. (See Chapter 9 for description of variables.)

A Dust Check. A periodic dust check can be made by means of a walk through the storage area—looking at those parts actually collecting dust, taking down part numbers, having the items reviewed. Answers can show action being taken at present, or action that is recommended to be taken. A reason why no action has been taken, when items evidently aren't moving, should also be noted. This method is not recommended as the *only* method to use, but it can stimulate immediate concern.

An Inventory Write-Off and Disposal Program

What should be done with unwanted inventory? The dollar value conditions the decision, because we're really speaking of limiting company profit. Unwanted inventory must be disposed of, but it can't just be thrown away. It must be recognized, first, as an inventory loss.

Case in point: A chemical and plastics manufacturer has practiced a surplus and obsolescence write-off policy for more than ten years. Most of the company's products have an average shelf life of about six months, and overages can be (or are) normally recycled. However, write-off appraisal is still made annually. Write-off criteria are based on the average sales demand rate, inventory quantity balances, engineering/design change information, and the company's product discontinuance policy. Disposition of write-off is accomplished by returning to vendor, bid sales, scrap or as donations to trade schools. (Disposition is generally by sales in a secondary market through the effort of a special personnel group.) Write-off items are kept in normal storage until disposition is made. This company's obsolescence and write-off policies have lowered total company investment requirements by an average of 5% per year over the last four years.

Write-Off Reserve. A write-off reserve should be created to recognize the liability of unwanted merchandise. It is usually established as a percent of net sales, and is allocated to absorb the dollar losses of unwanted inventory. The reserve reduces profit as it increases in value. Disposal action should not normally exceed the dollar accumulation in the write-off reserve. Reserve dollars must be controlled, so that the greatest benefit is obtained from its use.

Selecting Write-Off Items. The first step in any write-off action is selection of material to write off. The inventory classification system should offer guidance in this selection. The two most influencial factors (in the classification system), which would acknowledge an unwanted status, are sales frequency/quantity *and* production/non-production status.

A measurement is made on the continuous length of time where no sales have occurred. Items are placed in descending sequence by monthly time increments of no sales. A time qualifier is needed (i.e., all *non-production* items must have a minimum of

12 months' "no sales" to print on the listing, with *production* items requiring a minimum of 24 months' "no sales"). This listing is separated by production/non-production status. Items still used in the manufacturing of currently sold material (production items) are listed separately from others. Extended dollars, by item and by monthly age, should be assigned to all listings to help determine write-off dollar amount.

The listing of *production* use items should be reviewed by the company's (or vendor's) production-planning personnel to pick those items (and quantities) that can be returned for use. Non-usable *production* items will be candidates for write-off consideration, after all *non-production* items have been selected for the same time period. (Items with a non-production status will be automatic write-off candidates.) Write-off items are selected by descending time periods, adding dollar totals until the maximum (write-off reserve) dollar value is reached, or no more unwanted merchandise is left.

A final write-off listing is prepared and forwarded for corporate write-off approval. A summary sheet should be attached to this listing, which shows the allowable dollar value existing in the current write-off reserve, the total dollars classified as unwanted inventory, the total dollars selected for write-off, and any remaining unwanted inventory value existing—after write-off determination is completed.

Write-Off Approval. The write-off reserve should not signify automatic capability to write off inventory items, without control being exercised. Approval from the corporate Controller should be mandatory before write-off is definite, or any action can be taken towards inventory disposal. The write-off amount might be reduced, increased or not even allowed by the Controller. If write-off does not occur at fiscal year-end, the reserve must be added back into operating profits.

Write-Off Removal from Active Inventory. Items that are approved for write-off must be removed from active inventory, and disposed of; or if retained, must be placed in a separate area with adequate inventory control administered so that full profit (no cost of sales) is reported if later sales are made. It's possible that IRS (Internal Revenue Service) will permit write-off material to remain in active inventory. IRS approval is, however, a prime consideration of any write-off method used.

With IRS approval, and the development of a corporate-approved classification/appraisal system, it is conceivable that a company's write-off value can be computer determined at the end of each fiscal operating period. The computer would need to calculate the following five-dollar figures:

1. The ending dollar value of unwanted inventory for the previous fiscal year (FY) period, at cost.
2. The *total* inventory dollar value for the current FY period, at cost. (This figure includes the current unwanted inventory.)
3. The ending dollar value of unwanted inventory for the current FY period, at cost. (This value is obtained through a consistent classification/appraisal technique.)
4. The inventory dollar book value for the current FY period, at cost. (This value is obtained by subtracting the ending dollar value of unwanted inventory for the current FY period *from* the *total* inventory dollar value for the current FY period.)
5. Write-off dollars would be generated if the ending dollar value of unwanted inventory for the current FY period *is greater than* the ending dollar value of unwanted inventory for the

previous FY period. (If the reverse occurs, then an add-on to operating profit would have to be considered.)

When physical disposal of write-off material is accomplished, both years' unwanted inventory values would be decreased by the original cost values used in prior calculations *less* the total revenue obtained. A "full profit" report would be prepared showing specific material disposed of, the total cost dollars for such material, the total revenue dollars received for such material, and, the remaining cost dollars to be deducted from the (both years) unwanted inventory value. It might be advisable to consider using an estimated salvage value for write-off material. Experience indicates that if retained, a certain percent of unwanted material will eventually sell, and recycling also permits a residual scrap value. (An estimated across-the-board percentage could be established for this purpose.)

IRS approval of a machine write-off method could prevent:

1. Removing write-off material from active inventory.
2. Setting up a separate inventory area and control.
3. Reporting profits differently each month.

The intent of write-off, however, is to get rid of unwanted merchandise, not to keep it for potential future sales. Sometimes, though, it is not practical to physically dispose of material written off due to the corporate policy on product support. And product support must be considered in the disposal procedure.

Write-Off Disposal. Disposal action should begin after write-off approval is received, and before items are physically removed from active inventory (if a separate area must be assigned). This can prevent multiple handling of write-off items. Common items, easily procured or made, which have a total dollar value of less than the value to move them into another area, should be placed in a large container. A listing of these items should be made for soliciting bids, or the items should cumulatively be scrapped. Other write-off items should be placed on a special reduced price list, and offered through the distribution system for quick sale prior to relocation. Additional price reductions can be made until a time deadline is reached, or until items are sold.

When a time deadline is reached, and all items are not yet sold, they should be categorized into lots of similar items and offered on a bid basis. Upon expiration of the bid closing period, items would be subject to physical scrap. Where corporate policy demands a required number of years' support, retention of some quantity is recommended—or the item must be placed on an MTO (Made-to-Order) basis. Where vendors are out of business, or tooling has been destroyed, and support is still required, a quantity should be retained in write-off storage. However, the entire quantity written off need not be retained—only the potential sales quantity estimate. The remaining write-off quantity, not retained, should be physically scrapped, as flooding the market with these extra quantities will reduce any potential sales that do exist.

The methods of disposal of inventory write-off material shown in Exhibit 14-1 are listed in order of popularity, with the most often used method shown first. The "*" denotes an interesting fact. Less is being scrapped as the distribution flow gets closer to the end customer. Three methods of disposal are common among all distribution levels: *scrap, return-to-vendor* and *reduced price.* Another popular method, *bid sales,* is used primarily by manufacturing and wholesale-distribution. Retail outlets have their unique method of *door prize and promotions,* which is best suited for their type of operation. Other methods available (which include donations to trade schools and/or charitable institutions), are isolated in use, and contained under "other." (This information was compiled through questionnaires returned from 50 randomly selected businesses, varying in sales from $50,000 to over $2 billion annually.)

MANUFACTURING	WHOLESALE DISTRIBUTION	RETAILING
*Scrap	Return-to-Vendor	Return-to-Vendor
Return-to-Vendor	*Scrap	Reduced Price
Reduced Price	Reduced Price	*Scrap
Bid Sale	Bid Sale	Door Prize and Promotions
Other	Other	Other

EXHIBIT 14-1:   Disposal of Inventory Write-Off Material

15

Systematizing Physical Inventories and Audits

Physical inventory taking is necessary to verify what you have and where it is in inventory; to determine what must be ordered (if transactions are not recorded or kept for inventory control); and to confirm the accuracy of the paperwork system being used.

Physical inventory may appear as a simple task, but it can be a complex project where tens of thousands of items are controlled—especially where raw stock, work-in-process and finished parts inventory might all exist. The guidelines for taking physical inventory, however, can and should apply to all sizes and complexities of inventories.

This chapter presents an in-depth analysis of physical inventory taking, with flow sequences given for the most popularly used inventory methods. A complete detailed outline for establishing inventory procedures is an extra bonus. A physical inventory checklist of action steps, which follows, is covered in detail—another extra to guarantee successful inventory taking.

PHYSICAL INVENTORY ACTION STEPS

1. Establish a firm inventory date, and give customers, vendors, and employees advance notice.
2. Determine the inventory method to use.
3. Assign inventory responsibilities.
4. Decide on pre-inventory and inventory information requirements.
5. Assign operating cut-off dates.
6. Select auditing guidelines.
7. Develop inventory operational procedures.
8. Determine and schedule inventory requirements for manpower, supplies, training and equipment.
9. Provide adequate training instructions.
10. Count inventory.
11. Verify count.
12. Correct physical inventory errors.
13. Obtain an inventory "buy-off."
14. Analyze and discuss all inventory problems encountered.
15. Revise inventory procedures before corrections or suggestions are forgotten.
16. Prepare and submit the physical inventory report.

FREQUENCY OF INVENTORY

In many retail establishments, where point-of-sale terminals are not in use, it is difficult to determine what types of articles are sold over a given period of time without taking a physical inventory of the remaining merchandise. Because of this, many companies with small investments use physical inventory to substitute as an inventory control record system. They take physical inventory frequently.

Perpetual Inventory

Some companies use a perpetual inventory system, where the inventory records are kept current, and take inventory on an exception basis—similiar to the inventory classification system used. Some do this on a 100% item basis, with inventory taken continually throughout the year until all items are inventoried. If accurate inventories can be taken instantaneously on any item, this is an excellent way of controlling physical inventory taking with the least amount of time and cost.

Annual (or Periodical) Inventory

Outside accountants are required to substantiate corporation inventory investments periodically, to attest that records are properly kept in an acceptable accounting method. This creates the need for an annual or periodical physical inventory, if another approved method is not being used.

PHYSICAL INVENTORY PLANNING

Planning becomes increasingly important as inventory grows in size and complexity, but planning is necessary regardless of inventory characteristics. The inventory date must be established and approved well in advance of the proposed inventory. Cut-off times must be determined for all operating activities which have an effect on physical inventory. This would include interplant shipments and corresponding paperwork, outside sales and packing sheet documents, vendor shipments and receipts documents, and miscellaneous stock withdrawals and material movement paperwork. The method for taking inventory must be determined and agreed upon. Responsibilities must be assigned and delegated for inventory supervision, preparation of inventory procedures, training of inventory personnel, equipment and supplemental needs, auditing requirements, pricing and reconciliation of inventory.

Setting the Inventory Date

This may seem unnecessary for small retail businesses, but it is an essential part of any physical inventory planning. When to take an inventory will depend on things like the number of items in stock, the time needed to count these items, this time converted to estimated manhour requirements and the company's established business hours. The inventory taking should be done on non-business hours by company personnel. The time should be set in advance to prevent needed employees being on vacation. Operating cut-off times for business activities and paperwork, and desired inventory preparation, must be coordinated with the inventory date.

Cut-Off Requirements

Customers must be notified if the approaching physical inventory will affect normal business hours. Vendors should be notified to prevent needless shipments of merchandise being received the night before or the day of inventory taking. Employees must know what paperwork needs to be completed prior to inventory, and when to stop working new receipts, new customer orders, or other company needs. Establishing and publishing cut-off times in advance of inventory will foster a better relationship among customers, vendors and employees; will permit work-in-process items to be better controlled and even counted prior to inventory; and will limit the amount of inventory reconciliation otherwise demanded.

Choosing an Inventory Method

Many variables must be considered in selecting an inventory method. These variables would include the type of record-keeping system used, auditing guidelines assigned, the sizes and types of inventory to be counted, the storage location system in use, time and manpower availability for taking inventory, and personal preference. However, this decision can be arbitrarily simplified (as Exhibit 15-1 shows) to include only the first two variables: the record keeping system in use, and the auditing guidelines assigned.

RECORD KEEPING METHOD USED	AUDITING METHOD USED	
	USING SELECTED AUDIT GUIDELINES	WITHOUT SELECTED AUDIT GUIDELINES
Computer-based inventory control systems	Pre-printed listings	Pre-printed tags
Manual inventory control systems	Record cards (or) Handwritten	Record cards (or) Handwritten tags (or) Recording devices
No record system	(Not applicable)	Pre-printed forms

EXHIBIT 15-1:   Auditing as a Guide to the Inventory Method

Normal inventory auditing (without selected audit guidelines) will determine the accuracy of the actual stock count and verify that all parts are being counted. Using selected audit guidelines will permit an additional verification of the record-keeping function, especially on high value items. At least three methods can be used in selecting audit guidelines. The items to be audited can be selected *in advance* of inventory counting (on the basis of inventory dollar value or sales activity); *during* inventory counting (on a random basis); or *after* count is updated (on the basis of dollar variances from pre-inventory shelf balances).

Case in point: A large manufacturer of farm, construction and general industry machinery, located in the Northeast, audits both during and after physical inventory taking. 1% of total inventory items are audited during inventory counting, with recounts made on the basis of predetermined dollar limits. Audits during inventory are selected by the individual auditors, by a prior established random method. Recounts after inventory vary considerably, depending on the discrepancy rate experienced during the year. Since selected audit guidelines are not established for each item being inventoried, pre-printed tags are the most useful inventory-taking tool for this company.

The *advance* method used by many companies is to select a set percent of total inventory items (2% or 3%) based on inventory dollar value. All inventory items have their values extended and are arranged in descending dollar sequence. The top group of items equal to the percentage selected are coded for audit (recount) at inventory time. Some companies simply audit randomly, *during* inventory counting, by recounting a selected item on a selected shelf of each storage bin. Additional *after* audit selections can be made based on quantity or dollar count variance from pre-inventory shelf balance—usually based on the annual percent discrepancy rate.

Computers allow faster processing and more accuracy in inventory taking through the use of pre-printed tags or listings, and in machine updating of inventory count. Manual control systems require manual updating after physical inventory. Both computer-based and manual inventory control systems have one advantage over the absence of a record-keeping function. This advantage is in the physical inventory need being limited in frequency to a perpetual or periodical (in most cases annual) basis. More importance is placed on record keeping, and the physical inventory is complementary to it. Where records are not kept to control inventory, physical inventory taking becomes more important and must be done more frequently. Smaller shelf-life inventories might be counted as often as each day.

Many inventory methods are available today. However, those listed here are recommended as the generally accepted methods in use.

Pre-printed Inventory Tags. The decision to use pre-printed tags, or listings, with a computer-based record system, is a personal preference. However, tags appear to be a more favored method for the following reasons:

1. *Better control exists on missing items.* Each tag has an assigned number, while a single page number may contain as many as 20 to 40 separate items. A lost page from the listings affects more items.

2. *Tags can be pre-hung if desired.* Where the inventory shutdown time or manpower is limited, tags can be placed with respective parts ahead of the actual inventory shutdown, thus saving extra hours during the actual inventory.

3. *Easier computer updating is possible.* Less machine time for keypunch and verification of count is required when using tags, as only the count quantity is required to be punched. (Even when handwritten tags occur in a significant number, overall time should still be less.)

4. *Easier control of sales transactions during inventory shutdown.* Where emergency sales are allowed during inventory, accountability is easier when using tags. If a tag is not visible during picking, either the item has not yet been inventoried or it has already been inventoried and audited. Sales information given to accounting personnel is easily merged by them into actual inventory count.

Inventory Tag Flow Sequence. The following outline shows the inventory flow sequence which could be used when pre-printed inventory tags are used:

A. The master part number file shelf quantities can be zeroed, either during or after creation of an inventory tag file.

B. The tag file, prepared in tag number sequence, shows the tag numbers assigned, part number and/or description of items, storage locations, unit of measures, and shelf quantity prior to inventory cut-off. (NOTE: This tag file will be extended during inventory to include all other handwritten items.)

C. Inventory tags are printed when the tag file is created, and will show part number and/or description, storage location assigned, and unit of measure on the tag portion. Part number only will be printed on the stub. (NOTE: The inventory tags are pre-punched with tag numbers, by the vendor, for control.)

D. Tags are released for taking inventory.

  1. Inventory tags are matched to items in stock with count quantity for item entered on both the stub and tag.

  2. The complete tag is hung by or on the item counted. (NOTE: Steps one and two may be reversed if it is desired to pre-hang inventory tags.)

  3. Accounting personnel audits inventory tags by pre-defined storage areas, marking those tags which are audited. A good marking method is to circle quantity in red.

  4. Auditing personnel releases selected storage areas from inventory after auditing is complete.

  5. Inventory tags are removed from the released areas only, and forwarded to the data processing area, as release is given.

E. Tags are used to update inventory.

  1. Count quantities and audit codes are keypunched into the inventory tags and verified.

  2. Tag numbers of tags are machine matched to the tag numbers on the tag file, with inventory count quantities added to the tag file.

  3. The tag file part numbers and/or descriptions, for the tags processed, are machine matched to the master part number file with the master part number file updated by the inventory count quantity.

F. A missing tag listing is prepared after machine processing of each released area, and shows tag numbers missing, part number and/or description of items on missing tags, storage location of items, and unit of measure.

G. An optional "exception" listing can be printed on each released area to show all items which had counts falling out of auditing guideline ranges. (I.e., all counts with a variance under or over an assigned percentage of quantity or dollar value could be listed for recounting purposes. The presence of an audit code signals that an audit has previously been made, and the item can be overlooked.)

H. An error listing is printed on all part numbers and/or descriptions that are unmatched to the master part number file.

I. A listing of all handwritten inventory tags is printed, after being matched to the master part number file, to show all locations found on the same items, and to permit restocking of such merchandise into a single location.

J. A total inventory listing is printed in part number or description sequence, after inventory buy-off is given by the auditors. This listing can show all information in the created tag file, plus audit guidelines and pricing information. A summary page can define storage area densities (by number of different items, quantities and dollars), and the accumulated number of pre-printed tags, handwritten tags and duplicate stock locations found.

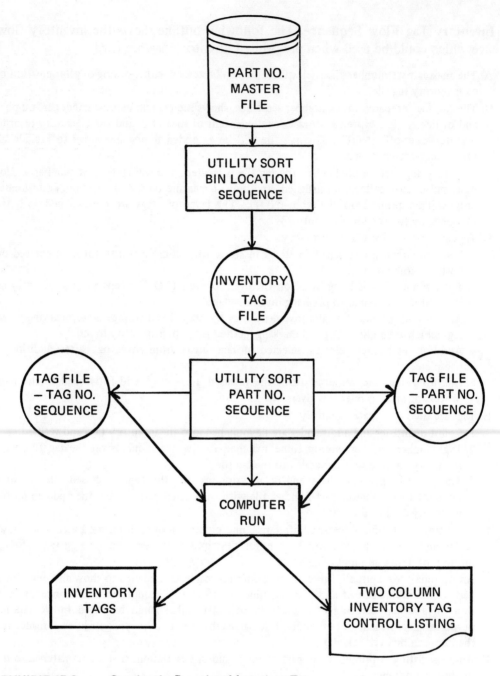

EXHIBIT 15-2:   **Creating the Pre-printed Inventory Tag**

Exhibit 15-2 illustrates how the part number file is sorted into bin location sequence to create the inventory tag file. An additional sort is accomplished to provide an optional part number sequence of the tag file. Quantity balances on the part number master file are zeroed as the inventory tags are printed. A tag control listing is printed in two parallel columns—the left hand column being in tag number sequence and the right hand column being in part number sequence. Each column contains inventory tag number, part number and bin location.

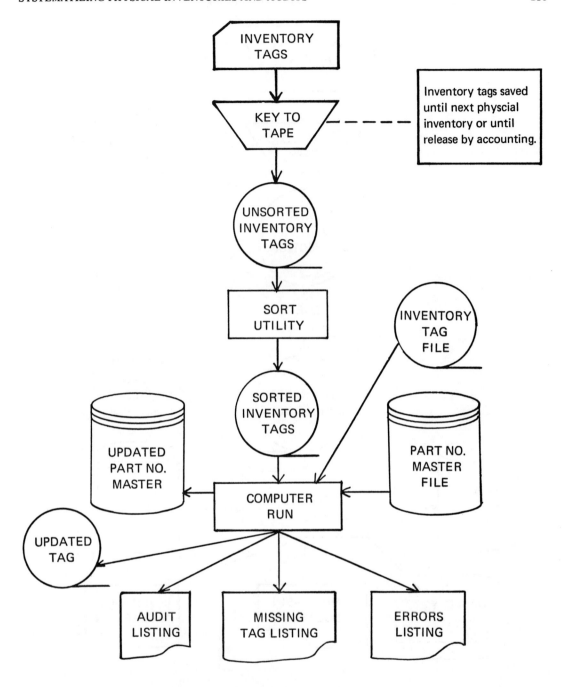

EXHIBIT 15-3: **Updating the Inventory Tags**

In Exhibit 15-3, released inventory tags, with count and audit code keypunched into them, are matched to the inventory tag file (in tag number sequence). Matching part numbers are selected, and both the tag file and the part number master file are updated by quantity. (Handwritten exception tags have complete tag information added to the tag file before being updated.) An audit listing is printed for all part numbers with quantity out of pre-established ranges. A missing tag listing is prepared. Unmatched part numbers are listed for correction.

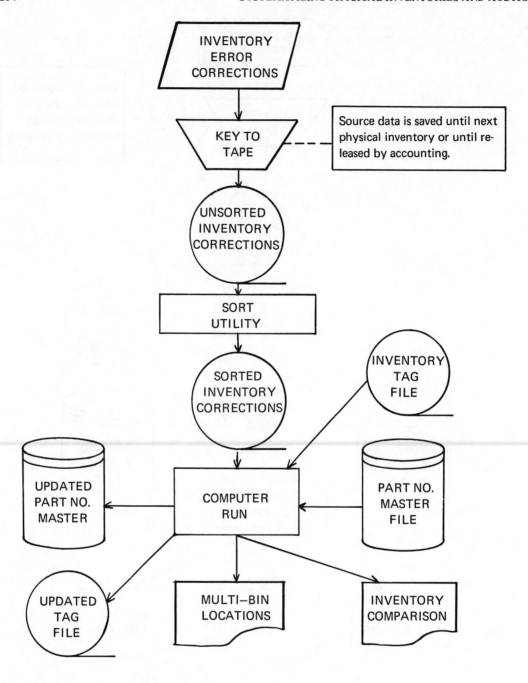

EXHIBIT 15-4:   **Completion of Inventory**

To complete the inventory (see Exhibit 15-4), missing tags, errors and audit corrections are updated—signalling preliminary inventory buy-off. A multi-bin location listing is prepared to allow gathering and restocking of like items into a common storage location. An inventory comparison listing is printed to show before and after inventory balances. This listing includes audit guidelines and identifies those part numbers actually audited. This listing is reviewed with final corrections made prior to final inventory buy-off, and before priced inventory listings are printed and approved.

Record Cards. All manual control systems require manual updating either during or after physical inventory. Duplicated effort can be eliminated if the record cards are updated during inventory. The record cards can be used as pre-printed inventory tags themselves. The preference between using record cards, inventory tags or recording devices to record inventory counts, will be greatly influenced by the size of the inventory to be counted. The use of record cards is urged with smaller inventories, while larger inventories favor the use of inventory tags or recording devices. Recording devices should not be considered, however, where preestablished audit guidelines are used, as duplicated effort will be involved in determining whether inventory quantities are above or below what they should be.

Flow Sequence for Record Card Use. If the record card is used as the method of taking inventory, inventory action might be as follows:

A. The count sequence is determined and the inventory starting point is selected.

B. The record card is found for the item inventoried.

C. The date and inventory count are recorded on the record card.

D. The on-hand quantity is corrected to match the inventory count, if necessary.

E. An inventory record card is prepared for items found on a storage shelf which do not have an inventory record card.

F. The record cards are coded where the inventory count is different from the current recorded on-hand quantity.

   1. If bottom triple-slotted cards are used, simply move the card to one direction where an increase or decrease in inventory exists—and in the opposite direction if the inventory count matches exactly.

   2. If visual record cards or non-slotted cards are used, use color coded tabs to achieve the same effect.

   3. Cards remaining in the center position (or not color coded) after inventory is completed, will be those with true zero balances. Correct the on-hand quantity to zero, if necessary, and then offset or color code for inventory variance.

   4. Prepare an exception variance report, after inventory, to show any overall gain or loss in investment.

G. The storage location is corrected, if items are counted in a location other than where the record card indicates. Restock merchandise where more than one location exists.

Handwritten Tags. Inventory tags can be pre-typed from inventory record cards prior to the start of inventory. However, unless storage locations are used for individual items, no real big savings in time or costs occur. The number of persons able to hang or use pre-typed tags is limited, when they are in part number, item number or description sequence. With storage location assignments made to individual items, tags can be typed (or sorted after typing) into storage location sequence. If this is possible, then tags can be distributed in groups by location areas for pre-hanging or for use in counting inventory. Otherwise, handwritten tag use is recommended.

Duplicated effort in the use of tags is apparent where a manual record card system exists, but in larger inventories, tags are recommended because many people will be required to assist in counting stock. Record cards would have to be split up for many counters to use them efficiently. Ideally, they would be pre-sorted into location sequences if the inventory itself is not in the same sequence as the record cards. Since the record card is the key to a manual inventory control system, loss, alteration or destruction to record cards must also be carefully considered.

Flow Sequence for Handwritten Tags. Inventory action for handwritten tags would be similar to that of record cards. The additional steps of handwriting and adding count to the tags, auditing them, and sorting them back into part number sequence (optional for easier card updating) is necessary before recording (as earlier outlined) onto the inventory record card.

Handwritten Lists. Handwritten lists using either pre-printed, ruled or plain unlined paper are appropriate for taking inventory on sufficiently small investments and should not be overlooked. Their use is not generally recommended over inventory tags due to the creation of more complex audit conditions, or lack of pre-hanging capabilities.

Flow Sequence for Handwritten Lists. Inventory action for handwritten lists would be similar to that of record cards. The additional steps of handwriting and adding count to the listings and auditing them is necessary before recording (as earlier outlined) onto the inventory record card. Auditing is more time consuming when using handwritten lists, as tags can be hung and immediately show what has been inventoried. Lists cannot. Verifying that all parts are counted is more complex. Spot auditing takes longer in searching for the entry on the handwritten list.

Recording Devices. Tape recorders, porta-punch machines or other recording devices can be used for taking inventory where auditing is not a critical requirement. It is difficult to see or easily find count information on a recording device to audit and determine if count is correct. Auditing must be accomplished after the fact, unless a pre-selected group of significant items is listed with on-hand quantity to allow checking of actual count when inventory is taken.

Flow Sequence for Recording Devices. Inventory action for recording devices would be similiar to that of record cards. The additional steps of voice or key entry into the recording device used; the transfer of this information into listings, punched cards, optical scanning input tapes or forms; and auditing requirements will be necessary. Information would then be recorded (as earlier outlined) onto the record cards.

Pre-printed Forms. Physical inventory taking becomes more important where records are not kept to control inventory investment, and must be taken more frequently—at least monthly—and more often will be on a weekly or daily basis. Pre-printed forms are normally used for inventory counting purposes. The forms list all merchandise stocked and are printed in the same storage sequence the stock is kept in. Inventory counts and retail values are recorded directly on the pre-printed form by the part number, item number or description of merchandise counted. Optional notations for age or classification can be made. Results of such inventory forms are used to price inventory, prepare an age analysis, order replenishment stock, and aid in preparing income accounting reports.

Inventory Supervision Assignment

The supervision responsibility for physical inventory should be delegated to the person with the functional duties of Purchasing Director, Production Control Manager, Materials Manager or Inventory Control Manager. "Who" is dependent upon whether the inventory is primarily raw stock, work-in-process or finished goods. The company Controller occasionally assumes total inventory responsibility in smaller companies, while in larger companies the Controller acts as chairman and retains final authority for inventory buy-off.

If a large number of items are stocked in inventory (thousands of items as compared to hundreds of items), the inventory responsibility should be split up into several separate areas. In retail department stores, such a separation already exists. Each department is considered a separate area with the department manager assuming the inventory responsibility. Otherwise, areas must be defined by location, with each area assigned a supervisor responsible for the inventory activities within that area. These responsibilities would include preparation of area for inventory, supervision and training of area counters, acknowledgement of a complete and accurate inventory count, a clean-up of area after inventory audit and buy-off, and preparation of an inventory activity report—with suggestions for improving company inventory procedures.

Inventory Procedures

The inventory procedure is an essential management tool. It illustrates step-by-step instructions for taking a physical inventory, and solicits consistency from year to year. It provides an inventory-planning checklist of easily forgotten information. A general outline for an inventory procedure should include:

A. Objective
B. Organization
C. Date of inventory
D. Operating cut-off needs
    1. Interplant movement
    2. Vendor receipts
    3. Returned goods or warranty items
    4. Outside sales
E. Pre-inventory planning
    1. Listing requirements
    2. Audit and clean-up guidelines
    3. Pre-packaging instructions
    4. Special equipment locations
    5. Inventory listing/tag requirements
F. Inventory operating procedure
    1. Training
    2. Supervision guidelines
    3. Counting instructions
    4. Identifying and correcting stocking errors
    5. Auditing guidelines
    6. Inventory update steps
    7. Inventory pricing method
G. Inventory reconciliation
    1. Packing sheet suspense (orders filled but not shipped)
    2. Invoice suspense (invoices released but not paid)
    3. Work-in-process (reductions from stock not yet allocated)
H. Manpower requirements and sources
    1. Supervision

      2. Counters
      3. Inspectors
      4. Auditors
      5. Coordinators
      6. Non-inventory personnel

I. Equipment requirements
    1. Communications equipment
    2. Recording devices
    3. Inventory tags/listings
    4. Check-sheets
    5. Count scales
    6. Step stools
    7. Clipboards
    8. Pencils
    9. Tape
    10. Etc.

J. Material movement procedure during inventory
    1. Logging requirements
    2. Order-processing method
    3. Paperwork control
    4. Auditing checks
    5. Invoicing steps

K. Advance inventory notification requirements
    1. Employee notification
    2. Vendor notification
    3. Customer notifications

L. Inventory guidelines (do's and don'ts)

Training of Inventory Personnel

Schedule inventory training dates, and provide advance notification to affected personnel. Conduct training with area supervision thoroughly, before having "working" personnel (counters, writers, inspectors, auditors, etc.) instructed. Although auditing personnel will be instructed with other working personnel, they will also have additional audit instructions from the auditing supervisor or company Controller.

Training Schedule. Inventory supervision should be instructed a minimum of a week prior to inventory, to allow them additional time to get familiar with their area of responsibility and make the area ready for inventory. It is best to wait and instruct working personnel as close to actual inventory as possible—such as the night before or the day of inventory—so that information will not be easily forgotten.

Supervision Training. Inventory schooling for supervision should cover the entire inventory program. The definitions of inventory areas (what parts to count or not to count), work assignments and accountability should be given. Accuracy should be stressed. An explanation and definition is required on the various types of items to be inventoried, such as raw material, work-in process or finished goods. Examples should be given on how to estimate the configuration status of partially fabricated or assembled parts. Instructions should be prepared in detail on how tags (listings, etc.) are to be prepared or used, collected, accounted for, and who they are to be given to.

Subordinate Training. Inventory schooling for working personnel would include detail information on why the inventory is necessary, how to count and write accurately, how to identify parts which have been inventoried and how to handle merchandise so as not to damage it. They must also be informed that auditing discovery of repeated bad counts will result in dismissal of the person concerned.

Hand-out Instructions. An instruction booklet or inventory information sheets should be printed and handed out to each person. Such information might contain the purpose of the inventory, but should illustrate and explain the method of taking inventory, reiterate certain key inventory steps to follow, list assignments and accountability, and point out certain inventory "do and don't" guidelines.

Inventory "Do and Don't" Items

Inventory guidelines can be presented as "do or don't" items. Information such as when and where break or lunch periods will be held, where smoking is permitted, the use of ladders in place of shelf climbing, and keeping inventory areas clean can be expressed in this manner. Specific "do and don't" items relating to inventory counting might include:

1. *Do* express count by the unit of measure assigned to the item being counted.
2. *Don't* count partial quantities of any items where the quantity would be less than an expressed unit of measure such as pounds, feet and gallons.
3. *Do* individually count the contents of all opened packages.
4. *Don't* open sealed packages to count. Use the count marked on the outside.
5. *Do* approximate bulk item lengths such as hoses, wires, etc., where lengths are extensive and too costly to count.
6. *Don't* sight-count merchandise. Take out of containers to count.
7. *Do* replace boxes or packages (of items counted) back in the original location after counting.
8. *Don't* disturb rotation sequence of items counted which carry an assigned shelf life.

Add any "do and don't" items not shown above which fit the inventory being taken, and delete those that have no relationship. "Do and don't" items answer many questions never asked, and provide answers that can't be ignored. They help insure a more accurate and meaningful inventory.

Equipment and Supplemental Needs

People head the list on inventory equipment needs. An adequate number of people is a must. If outside people can be used, then inventory can be taken over the weekend or on holidays. If union agreements prevent use of temporary personnel, then inventory might have to occur during working hours or evenings. Regular business might be interrupted, but manpower rates will be at straight time in place of time and a half for overtime pay.

People will need equipment to assist them in taking inventory. Listings, inventory tags, forms or recording devices must be decided on. Writing tools such as pencils, marking pens, etc., will be necessary. Masking tape, wire or string should be obtained if tags are used. A clipboard or something similar should be handed out to write on. Check-sheets or control sheets will permit recording actual count responsibilities. Small step stools should be obtained or constructed ahead of time, for easier counting of merchandise on upper shelves. Count scales could speed up small item counting, such as hardware. Communication equipment, such as walkie-talkies, is quite useful if the storage area is large in size. Otherwise, a PA or intercom systems will be satisfactory, and can save many footsteps. Don't forget about coffee breaks or lunch periods. Make sure the coffee and sandwich machines are stocked, or that they will be serviced during inventory. If such machines are not used, several vending companies have a lunch truck which can be scheduled for the lunch period. If a company cafeteria is available, make sure they're informed of the extra people that may be on hand. Adequate restroom facilities should be made available.

PRICING THE INVENTORY[1]

The inventory costing method used is clearly a subjective judgment decision made by accounting management. The concept selected does not necessarily have to reflect a true relationship to the actual movement of merchandise in inventory (such as first in–first out, average, or last in–first out). But because the costing method used can greatly affect taxes (either property, franchise or income), emphasis should be placed on consistency of use of whatever concept is selected. The Internal Revenue Service confirms this by requiring prior authorization before a change can be made in figuring income. They place greater weight on consistency of costing from year to year than on a business' particular method of costing.

The most popular business practice today is to cost inventories at either average cost, or average or current replacement cost, whichever is lower, on each item in inventory. (Average cost is updated as new receipts occur, or on a periodical basis such as monthly. If periodical updating of average cost occurs, the new average cost would usually apply to the next period's activity. Where a moving average or immediate updating occurs, the new average cost is used on all future transactions until a newer moving average cost occurs.)

Substantiating information should be retained to verify that all inventory items were accurately counted in a uniform manner, especially if the lower of average or current replacement cost is used for costing inventory. A copy of the inventory procedure would probably suffice, coupled with a statement as to how the inventory was conducted—by company management alone or with the assistance of an outside C.P.A. (Certified Public Accountant) firm. Closing inventory cost figures (based on average cost; based on current replacement cost; and the resulting total inventory valuation based on the lower of average or current replacement cost) should also be recorded and retained.

INVENTORY RECONCILIATION

The physical inventory count and resulting dollar valuation must include all items which reflect as merchandise either intended for sale or that which is on hand to become a part of such merchandise—if title is still held. Inventory reconciliation is therefore necessary in some areas. Merchandise picked from stock but not yet

---

[1]Raymond A. Hoffman, C.P.A., and Henry Gunders, C.P.A., *Inventories–Control,Costing, and Effect Upon Income and Taxes* (The Ronald Press Company, New York, 1970), pp. 145-165; 382-423. Copyright © 1970 by The Ronald Press Company. Copyright © 1962 by The Ronald Press Company.

delivered, merchandise delivered but not yet invoiced, work-in-process material, items on display, special consignment merchandise, warranty returns, and applicable purchases—in transit, will each provide a reconciliation exercise.

Data from the reconciliation exercises will be used to arrive at an adjusted book value. A comparison must be made to the current month ending adjusted ledger balance. Any differences must be recorded as net loss or net gain. A support listing should show beginning inventory quantities, corrections, and adjustments and the ending inventory quantity balances.

INVENTORY AUDIT NEEDS

Audits taken during a physical inventory satisfy that all items are being counted, that all items are being counted uniformly, and that an accurate count is being taken.

Control Audits

Other audits, between physical inventories, will present a good picture on how physical parts control is working out. Audit results will determine the accuracy of record keeping and will help decide if and when a complete physical inventory is necessary. A complete inventory audit can be taken in much less time than a complete physical inventory. Although actual counts are not made, zero balance corrections can be obtained, missing merchandise can be located and stocking errors can be corrected. Complete inventory audits are not always necessary. Random sample audits will ordinarily be adequate, and must be used where manual inventory control is exercised or where storage locations are not assigned.

Discrepancy Audits

Unexpected stock variances, resulting in stock-out situations, signal the need for an inventory audit to determine if a discrepancy is valid. Most companies will average between 1% to 3% variance in total inventory. Some companies wil! naturally fall below or above this average, and will differ greatly depending upon whether quantity or dollars are used as the basis for figuring the discrepancy variance %. A leading fast food distributor experiences only a ½% *dollar* variance yearly, while a job shop printer encounters a minimum 5% *quantity* variance yearly. Regardless of record keeping, discrepancies always seem to happen. Inventory audits will apply reasoning to their presence and help keep them at a low level.

The annual discrepancy rate of a company can, however, be used to good advantage. Audit guidelines, for physical inventory taking, can be based on this rate. For instance, only those items with a count variance greater than the discrepancy rate would be recounted, while within this range the inventory count would be acceptable.

Discrepancy Audit Findings. Lack of recording sales, accidentally placing merchandise in wrong storage areas, recording receipts quantity without checking actual count before stocking, picking more quantity than asked or billed for, failure to prepare needed paperwork, and pilferage—all contribute to inventory discrepancies. Only a physical inventory, taken with proper audit control, can certify counts and recommend needed corrections in paperwork, procedures or personnel.

16

Forms and Records:
An Asset or a Liability?

This chapter provides techniques for cutting costs in forms usage, filing and control. A form's matrix solution is presented for organizing forms usage to achieve work simplification. A simplified form's numbering system is developed to permit additional control. Nine guidelines are given which, if considered and allowed for, will bring about good forms design. Properly used, forms and records can solidify meaning in a job duty, can simplify the work involved, and can truly be considered "working paper." Improperly used, they must be considered ordinary "paperwork," a probable work waste, especially in regard to a general rule of thumb that additional expense of up to 20 times the original cost of a form can be spent preparing, handling and filing it.

Filing without a filing guide can up the cost of forms storage and retrieval. A lack of this procedure will cause duplicate copies to be filed in the originator and/or user files (as a necessary evil), as general experience associated with locating or retrieving information from a central file has (historically) been too time consuming or impossible.

Proper storage of forms and records can greatly assist inventory management in servicing customers, classifying inventory information, preparing audits, or many other vital information needs. Haphazard filing and storage of order processing, or inventory support information, will result in constantly expanding storage needs, and perhaps in bulging, inefficient files. Most of the frequently sought information might get located in bottom storage drawers while the inactive information is cluttering up the best storage space.

PROVIDING A CONVENIENCE FACTOR

Forms and records are usually a good work supplement because they are organized for getting work accomplished faster. Much of the printed heading information would have to be rewritten many times during the day (with maybe some information forgotten), if forms were not used. They provide a definite convenience to the people using them. Often, though, this convenience factor is misunderstood or misused. When this occurs, we may find several forms in use where only one is needed.

This happens frequently where a principal form lacks some relevant or necessary information. Another form is simply created to provide for missing data.

UNDERGOING A SHOCK TREATMENT

A "shock treatment" review should be made of all documents (source, work forms, records and listings). This review would even include 3" x 5" cards and all other single-copy work forms used as documents. The steps taken in this review are:

1. Obtain a copy of each document used to support the inventory management functions. Prepare a form matrix with form names across the top, and employee names down one side. See Exhibit 16-1 for sample matrix. In this sample, all formal and informal documents used to support inventory activities, with their respective document numbers, frame the top of the matrix. Information regarding type of document, person who receives each document and total manhours allocated to each form's use is added to this matrix from the evaluation sheets used in the shock treatment review. The manhour information helps to set individual form review priority.

2. All individuals involved in inventory activities are to be given, and asked to prepare, evaluation sheets for each document they handle; with a document copy attached to each completed evaluation sheet. (This will insure that no form, paper processing operation, or routing step is overlooked. This should also flush out all the employee-developed informal documents—which also are to be added to the form matrix. Refer to Exhibit 16-2 for the evaluation sheet format.)

3. Review each individual's evaluation sheets separately, with the following type of questions in mind: Are all the forms required? Can any be eliminated from use? Does more than one form contain the same information? Can the common information be combined onto one single form? Are other individuals using forms which contain the same needed information? Can their form be replaced?

4. Assign a document "type" code to each evaluation sheet:

A—a document originated by the individual preparing the evaluation sheet (a source document) to be used for non-EDP purposes.

B—a document originated by the individual preparing the evaluation sheet (a source document) to be used for EDP purposes.

C—a non-EDP reference document, *not* originated by the individual preparing the evalution sheet. Does not require action.

D—an EDP reference document, *not* originated by the individual preparing the evaluation sheet. Does not require action.

E—a non-EDP action document, *not* originated by the individual preparing the evaluation sheet. Requires a specific action to be taken.

F—an EDP action document, not originated by the individual preparing the evaluation sheet. Requires a specific action to be taken.

5. Add the type code (A,B,C,D,E or F) to the form matrix, by the individual's name, under the correct form name for which an evaluation sheet was prepared.

6. Match, staple and place each group of identical documents together in a file folder. Total the manhours involved in inventory activities for each separate document, and add the total manhours to the form matrix following the last employee's name, and under the proper form name. (Leave the evaluation sheets with the documents.)

7. Place the folders in descending sequence (front to back), based on total manhours involved per form.

EXHIBIT 16-1: A Form "Matrix"

Document and Number (columns):
- D150-0014 — Open Order Transactions
- D150-0013 — Pick Tag Listing
- F150-0011 — Suggested Order Worksheet
- D160-0010 — Manufacturing Where Used
- D200-00009 — Stock Status Microfiche
- E160-00008 — Unmatched Manufacturing P/N
- A103-00007 — Catalog Change Notices
- B101-00004 — Manual Order Form

Name of Employee	D150-0014	D150-0013	F150-0011	D160-0010	D200-00009	E160-00008	A103-00007	B101-00004
ABLE, KEVIN	D		F		D			B
BAKER, MAX	D		D		D	E	A	B
FOX, PONDO				D	D	E	A	B
GEORGE, LLOYD				D	D	C	C	
HOWARD, RON					D			
JEFFERIES, RALPH	D	D		D	D			
JOHNSON, PAUL	D	D	D	D	D			D
JONES, LEROY	D		F		D			B
KELP, DON					D			
SMITH, FRANK	D		F		D			B
TOTAL MANHOURS	15.0	1.8	123.0	3.0	33.3	30.0	5.0	112.0

EMPLOYEE NAME _____ DEPT. _____ JOB TITLE _____

FORM NUMBER _____ FORM TITLE _____

FREQUENCY AND QUANTITY OF USE: DAILY ____ WEEKLY ____ MONTHLY ____ YEARLY ____

WHAT DO YOU DO WITH FORM: _____
_____
_____

HOW MUCH TIME IS SPENT PROCESSING FORM? _____ IS FORM NECESSARY? _____

----------Stop here. Attach completed copy of form. Turn in to supervision.------------

TYPE FORM: NON-EDP ____ REFERENCE DOCUMENT ____ SOURCE CREATED ____ FORM SETS ____ SNAP-OUT ____ NCR SET ____

            EDP ____ ACTION DOCUMENT ____ NON-SOURCE ____ TAB PAPER ____ DITTO ____ OCR SET ____

WHERE PRINTED? _____ FORM COST ____

FORM SIZE -- NUMBER OF COPIES	DEPT: (A)	DEPT: (B)	DEPT: (C)	DEPT: (D)	DEPT: (E)	DEPT: (F)	DEPT: (G)	DEPT: (H)	DEPT: (I)	DEPT: (J)
COPIES 1										
2										
3										
4										
5										
6										

EXHIBIT 16-2:   Form Evaluation Sheet

8. Perform a system's review on each form, using the form matrix information and the accumulated evaluation sheets. (Each form's study analysis will take considerable time, so it is important to start with the form requiring the most attention—hence the ABC type analysis approach on total manhours.)

PERFORMING WORK SIMPLIFICATION

The system's review on each form's use and flow through the inventory areas should be undertaken with work simplification in mind. Can the work flow be changed so that a document is no longer needed? If not, can the document be redesigned to make work more efficient? Does its size create a problem? Does it need to be color coded? Is the form's use fully understood?

PROVIDING ORIENTATION AND TRAINING

The form matrix contains the names of all personnel involved in handling each different form. Hold an informal meeting with involved people and go over the results of a specific form's review. Get consensus approval on where the form's use can be eliminated, suggested changes in the form's flow, and on redesign of the form. Explain form processing problems encountered. Iron out difficulties. Make sure everyone understands the purpose of the form and processing expenses involved.

DEVELOPING "ACTION" PROCEDURES

Prepare new procedures to cover a document's use as soon as each review has been completed. The procedures should be definitive in nature and lead each person (using them) through the necessary steps in handling the document. The procedure should explain what action steps are required, how they should be accomplished, and in what sequence. The "playscript" procedures-writing method should be considered.[1] Each individual can easily find his starting and stopping places, and is given directions a step at a time. All related action is there, so he can review the complete forms flow—and be knowledgeable of the whole picture.

MONITORING PERFORMANCE

Is the new form procedure fully understood? Is it easily followed? Is there any reluctance to follow the procedure? Have *new* flow changes adversely affected the inventory operation? Has a noticeable drop in forms processing time occurred? Have any bottlenecks developed? Have any informal deviations in procedures flow or forms been suggested or adopted?

Information feedback is needed to detemine if a procedure is being implemented successfully. Verification should be obtained that informal procedures are not being substituted. A formal change request should be submitted when it is felt a procedural deviation is required. An objective review of the change request should be made and, with the use of the form matrix, all people involved should attend a meeting to accept or deny the request. The meeting is justified because a change in one operating area might have hidden significance in some other area. Also, it provides a form of management participation which helps stop the use of unapproved informal ideas.

---

[1] Leslie H. Matthies, *The Playscript Procedure: A New Tool of Administration,* (© Copyright 1961. Office Publications, Inc., Publisher).

CONTROLLING NEW FORMS ADDITIONS

A control over new form design will help prevent the origination of informal documents. Several reasons exist why control should be established:

1. Most informal documents are created to serve one-time situations. Form cost is completely ignored. Documents are normally not necessary. The resulting use is expensive in time and cost.
2. A current form might already exist that would do the job.
3. Good form design and format concepts will not be overlooked if the form is really needed, and a current form can't be used.

The Control Logbook

The form matrix developed in the shock treatment review provides the ingredients of a logbook for forms control. The logbook organization is arbitrary, but should permit easy reference to specific purpose forms. The type code can be used in organizing the logbook. Six different sections would be established—one for each type code. When a form is requested, its description should match one of the type codes. A quick look in the logbook section under the corresponding type code will show all existing forms meeting that requirement. Additional information can be obtained from the form matrix, and from the evaluation sheets.

Document Numbering System

The type code should be a part of the document number if it is used in organizing the logbook. Only the controllable type codes (A,B,D and F) would be used in assigning a document number, however, as the other documents (type codes C and E) will have been designed in another department, division, etc., and will already have a document number.

The document numbering system should reflect the type of document, the department originating the document, and a unique number to provide its identity, i.e.:

```
A 2 4 1 – 0 0 0 0 1
'     '         '
'     '         '
'     '         '
'     '         ' Unique Form Number
'     '         _____
'     '
'     ' Department (number) Originating Form
'     _____
'
' Type Code to Describe Document
_____
```

An Index Is Recommended

Each section of the logbook could have its own unique document numbers; however, it is recommended that all forms be assigned a unique number which is in sequence with all other documents. An index to the logbook would contain several pages of unused sequential numbers for this purpose.

Tie Form Information Together

When assigning a document number:

1. Record the document type code, the department number (of the person who will be originating the document), and the proposed document title onto the index page beside the next unused sequential number. See Exhibit 16-3.

> In this example, a new form has been requested for relocating mis-stocked parts. Variance adjustments will be required on computer balances for both part numbers—the one it was stocked as, and the one it should be stocked as. Action is required by EDP. This causes a type B code. The warehouse will be originating the form, so its department number, 103, will be used. The next unused unique number is 00015. The form description is entered as "Restock Parts." Since this is a new form, no previous form will be superseded. The proposed form's new number will be B103-00015.

TYPE CODE	DEPT.	UNIQUE NUMBER	FORM DESCRIPTION	SUPERSEDES:
D	150	00013	Pick Tag Listing	
D	150	00014	Open Order Transactions	D150-00012
B	103	00015	Restock Parts	
		00016		
		00017		
		00018		
		00019		
		00020		
		00021		

EXHIBIT 16-3:   **Document Number Index Example**

2. Transfer the information just recorded (with the assigned unique number), into the type section of the logbook, to update that section. See Exhibit 16-4.

> This exhibit shows a control logbook section for "B" type codes. The purpose for these sections is to place all similar types of forms together, for quick analysis of a specific form need. Is there a form already available which can do the job? Can a current form be revised to do two jobs?

3. Assign responsibility to develop, proceduralize and implement the document.

4. Upon document implementation, add the form's type section information and manhour requirements to the form matrix. This updates the form matrix and collects all pertinent control data together for future form review.

FORM PART NUMBER	FORM DESCRIPTION	SUPERSEDES:
B101-00001	Part Number Record Form	
B101-00002	Open Order Changes and Cancellations	
B102-00003	Price Additions and Deletions	
B101-00004	Manual Order Form	
B103-00015	Restock Parts	

EXHIBIT 16-4:   **Control Logbook Section for "B" Type Codes**

Form Number Change-over

If the logbook is set up after the shock treatment review, document numbers will have to be added or revised on all forms affected. The numbers can be added to all existing documents when the next printing demand occurs. On EDP output listings, the document number should be added when the next change is made to the program creating the listings, or immediate changes should be made on all such listings if programming time is available. (A cross-reference form number listing will have to be established for later revision of new form numbers, if numbers are not changed immediately.)

A new document number should be assigned each time a revision is needed. Users should be notified, so that obsolete documents can be collected and destroyed when new forms are placed in use.

GUIDELINES TO GOOD FORMS DESIGN

A new form must satisfactorily provide a needed control, be simple and inexpensive to use, be easily identifiable, and must survive the test of time. To meet these criteria, the following categories must be considered when designing a new form:

1. *Purpose.* Will the form be used within departments, divisions, with vendors or cutomers? Will it be a reference document, or does it require specific action to occur? Will it be hand-typed, handwritten or computer printed? Is optical character recognition a requirement?
2. *Format.* Familiarity breeds accuracy. Compatible formats among related supplementary forms can be an asset.
3. *Filing.* Standard form size (8½" x 11") is desirable for uniformity in filing. A good paper strength is suggested where repeated handling will exist.

4. *Presentability.* The form should be clean and functional in appearance. A good corporate image should be presented.

5. *Readability.* The form should be easy to read, with emphasis on key data (i.e., use of italics, bold type, border design, shadow effects, etc.).

6. *Spacing.* Adequate space should be allowed for handwritten information. Continuous-form documents must acknowledge computer spacing restrictions of printer, and marginal machine spacing needs.

7. *Data Entry Use.* Data captured should correspond with keypunch card (or program) format, and not skip around all over the form. Use of "ballot boxes" to record data, instead of writing information, will speed form's processing and increase data capture accuracy.

8. *Mailing and Distribution.* The form should be system oriented to use window envelopes. Form copy numbers, and copy routing flow information, must be spelled out. Providing color (code) copies for recognition purposes might cost more than using all-white copies, but is good trade-off for control.

9. *Identity.* Company identity should be shown—and it affords good public relations benefits. Form identity is necessary for usage control and auditing inventory movements.

Case in point: A holding company (for customer and industrial products, aerospace and marine systems and business machines) reviews forms and records at the time additional reprints are requested. Review has resulted in work simplification and containment in the growth of the company's form volume. All forms are supported with written procedures. Procedures are continually monitored, as employees are restricted from procedure deviations without first obtaining formal approval. One individual has been delegated the company's forms design responsibility. Form numbers are assigned, with the form number identifying the type of document and the department originating (or responsible for) the document. A forms logbook is kept for control of forms. (Computer equipment is used in finished goods inventory management, and output forms are numbered similarly to non-EDP documents. The use of computer display terminals and computer output microfilm has, however, reduced output paper form volume.) This company reviews and incorporates all the suggested criteria (outlined in this chapter) for good forms design.

IMPLEMENTING FILING AND STORAGE POLICY AND PROCEDURES

The majority of filed documents are seldom referenced. It's that old "ABC" classic, again, that can prove only a few of the filed documents make up most of the retrieval volume. Actually, according to Jesse L. Clark and Gloria Wilkes, Paperwork Systems, Newton, Massachusetts,[2] 85% of the records filed will never be referred to again, and 87% of the current references made are to documents less than two years old. They also claimed that an incorrectly filed document costs the average company 17 times the cost to file it correctly!

This kind of statistics urges having only active documents in the central office files, supported with a simple and accurate file procedure. A Midwest parts distributor considers only the last six months as "active" in his central office files, with the rest "wrapped up, identified and stored" in the warehouse. References made on stored documents older than six months have been so few that the extra space gained, and

---

[2]"Better Record Keeping from Objectives to Working Manual," Administrative Management (May, 1973), Volume XXXIV, Number 5, pp. 20-21.

lack of congestion in files, has been a terrific trade-off. (The last five years have proven it.)

What to File?

Everything can't (or shouldn't) be filed within a central filing system, unless your file area is extensive and time and expense are of no concern. Departmental files, often ignored as creating a filing problem, must be objectively looked at and standardized. Not only do copies get filed by a report's originator, but, in the majority of cases, each person receiving such reports will also tend to develop files. The need to communicate solicits the need for more copy information to more people—copies that are ending up in more files. Therefore, "what to file" becomes important. Develop company standards for recognizing which forms and records are considered vital for legal or reference filing purposes. Support the need for a general records manual (containing uniform filing rules, protection capability, equipment purchases and audit reviews) to be developed and enforced as an operating manual for all departments, where a company central records file is not in use.

How to File It?

Equipment research efforts, cost studies and logic play a big part here. Manual storage methods (themselves prolific) must be compared with the many mechanical or electrical storage methods available. Hard copy paper filing must be compared with computer storage and terminal display, COM (Computer Output Microfilm), or microfilm storage concepts. An active and inactive document classification system must be set up. Document volume, retrieval frequencies, speed needed in retrieving and cost are important considerations in selecting storage equipment. Once equipment is selected, file storage location assignment and sequencing methods are needed for control. A file guide technique (part of the records manual) is helpful here, and can guarantee bigger returns on equipment and people investment.

How Long to File It?

Storage longevity should be determined at the time a document is filed, and stamped with review and removal dates—to place in inactive files, in permanent files, or to destroy. A definite method and schedule are required (also a part of the record manual), to insure that documents are reviewed and acted on accordingly. Classify and identify company documents for storage need. Outline retention dates. Show both active time span and overall retention limits. State review procedures and frequency. Detail future filing action on inactive documents, giving filing flow from active to inactive files, active to permanent, inactive to permanent, or when destroy action is allowed.

INTRODUCING RECYCLED PAPER

The concern for ecology is generating negative sanctions to strip the waste of reusable paper pulp fibers. Governmental pressure is being applied to shift more paper use to recycled paper. Recycled paper is not as clean looking as new paper, but is acceptable and can be used in many office areas, such as for interoffice memos, note or "thought" pads, program planning and other reports, or multiple copy use as second or back copies of form sets, etc. The answer may be not for a completely 100% recycled paper for all document uses, but for varying mixtures of virgin and reusable paper pulp fibers. The costs are currently higher for recycled paper, and might be the incentive needed for controlling the increased use of paper.

THE ADVANTAGES OF PAPERLESS SYSTEMS

Many companies already are substituting paperless systems to combat the almost uncontrollable use and growing expense of paper. Computer display terminals offer immediate retrieval information where on-line systems are present. (Hard copies can be printed from such display units.) COM, either as continuous roll film or as microfiche, is providing good document protection and economical storage vehicles—replacing most of the need for paper output. (Microfilm readers also have the optional capabilities of creating hard copy documents.) Paperless systems are gaining in use, and should be given considerable attention as a form or record storage concept. Paperless systems offer:

1. Good document protection.
2. Faster record document creation speed.
3. Space savings benefit.
4. Faster document information retrieval capability.
5. Less cost involved in mailing.
6. Teleprocessing capability through facsimile repro methods.
7. And, if "paperless" scares you, hard copy documents can be obtained if desired.

17

Systems Contracting: The Way to Handle Inventory Supplies

Supplies perform a vital function in inventory management. They are an expense which has to be budgeted, with their future use projected—much as if they were any other inventory item. Inventory operations can be severely handicapped because supplies, mostly taken for granted, aren't available when they are needed.

In this chapter, the full-product-line vendor is shown as an important aspect in the logistics of inventory supplies. Systems contracting is highlighted as an effective vendor means to provide supplies support for the inventory functions for the least cost. Implementation steps are listed. Report information requirements are outlined. Simplified paperwork flow is emphasized. Systems contracting benefits are given.

CATEGORIZING INVENTORY SUPPLIES

Inventory supplies ordering and maintenance can be simplified and made less expensive if they are separated into the functional categories of office supplies, EDP and special forms supplies, and warehouse and shipping supplies—to consolidate like-vendor commodities together. This restricts the number of outside vendors required, and urges the selection of full-line reputable vendors who offer a corresponding service—notably that of systems contracting.

Contract Guarantees

Systems contracting is simply assigning a single vendor full contract responsibility (and sometimes full control) over a related group of company commodities. The amount of control assigned to a vendor would be subject to individual company policy. The vendor selected for the systems contract should guarantee (for this responsibility, control *and business*):

1. Immediate availability and/or firm delivery time limits on orders.
2. Elimination or reduction of company supplies investment.
3. A simplified paperwork system.
4. Lower overall operating costs for the company.

Contract Benefits

Record keeping, expediting and pricing can all be accomplished and controlled by the vendor (under systems contracting)—big benefits by themselves. Yet other company benefits will accrue in the form of reduction of receiving inspection, delayed shipments (or lost goods), elimination of storeroom need, less obsolescence and reduced paperwork.

CONTROLLING THE EDP AND SPECIAL FORMS INVENTORY

The seemingly endless mass of computer output listings, forms, cards, letters and other related items has given impetus to increased values of forms and computer supplies inventory—even with the growing acquisition of paperless systems such as microfilm, microfiche or CRT terminal units.

Form obsolescence is great where systems innovations are promoted. Changing a system's output requires a different number of copies or different formats. Where special continuous form sets are used, such obsolescence costs can be quite expensive. The EDP and special form inventory should be placed under tighter budget control. The most rewarding result is that a form of systems contracting can be implemented that will really pay off. And, control is administered by the vendor—not by the company—with the service (and many benefits) normally free.

A Five-Step Approach

A five-step program can usually initiate systems contracting on EDP and special form inventories:

1. Organize or establish an adequate storage area for the EDP and special form supplies, with easily found (coordinate) location assignments made and item identifications assigned for each item placed in the storage area.
2. Provide a selected vendor with necessary information such as individual samples of all supply items, properly identified and described by employee need and use flow, current monthly usage rates, and present inventory quantities.
3. Receive and review an inventory management report generated by the business forms vendor which is prepared from the company-furnished information.
4. Establish a minimum balance (per item) and a maximum overall supplies inventory value (based on dollars or monthly usage).
5. Prepare, approve and issue a blanket purchase order form covering responsibility of vendor, guarantees offered to the company, and results to be achieved.

Exhibit 17-1 shows simplified paperwork flow in a systems contract for EDP and special forms supplies. A vendor is selected, and a blanket purchase order is created to cover a specified contract time limit. The PO lists all special non-EDP form sets, and all EDP supplies (continuous forms and ditto masters, cards, paper, tapes, and related items), by identification number and description. Contract prices are given for each item, and made flexible by an appropriate price escalation clause. The supplies inventory level (in either dollars or months supply) which is to be maintained by the vendor is also stated on the PO. A termination clause permits immediate termination of the contract, if desired by the company.

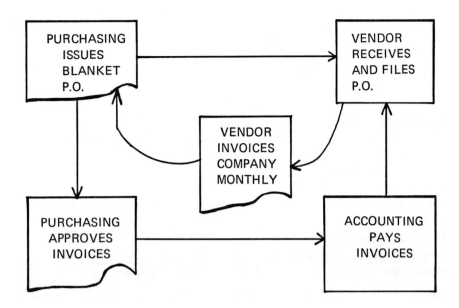

EXHIBIT 17-1: A Simplified "Paperwork" Flow

Contract Results

The first action resulting from the systems contract, and jointly taken by the company and vendor, would probably be simplification and reduction of inventory supply items. The business form vendor is especially helpful in reducing company forms because of previous industry experience in the review, analysis and combining of common information needs into fewer action forms, and in the redesign of any new forms developed.

The remaining EDP and special form supply items, after this joint effort, are then assigned to the vendor for inventory control. This control would vary by company, but can include full authorization to *"provide such EDP and special forms supplies in the volume usage required (by the company) to sustain continuous and uninterrupted machine and/or forms use; while maintaining a forms inventory dollar level below a maximum value agreed upon; without increases occurring in annual obsolescence loss or in unit form's cost; and to provide continuous inventory control over such supplies with supporting monthly status reports given to the company."*

Sound like a lot of authority for a vendor to have? It is! But remember, you never really delegate *responsibility*—just authority. Periodic company audits on the EDP and special forms supplies, for movement in and out and current inventory values, can keep things in proper perspective. The vendor, who assumes the role of sole salesman for these items, can reduce company costs through larger volume buying and still obtain an increase in overall business revenue. As a general result, the vendor will do a better overall job than that normally accomplished by company personnel.

The Inventory Status Report. The inventory status report created and maintained by the vendor can be a manually prepared or computer printed report. Usually a computer prepared report is provided. This report's format will vary by vendor, but most probably will include the following information [adapt to company needs]:

1. An EDP and special form name.
2. A physical description such as size, number of plies, color coding or other important characteristices.
3. Usage information for current month, year to date and average per month.
4. Receipts information for current month and year to date.
5. On-hand inventory status for total item quantity (in 1000's), with additional information on number of cartons and quantity per carton.
6. Storage location where item is located.
7. On-order quantities (in 1000's).
8. Minimum quantity level requirements in months and the number of months inventory quantity on hand.
9. Unit cost dollars (per 1000).
10. Total item costs for the current month and year to date.
11. Current inventory value per item and total overall inventory level.

(The report should be routed to the purchasing, accounting and EDP departments. The information given in numbers 9-11 is separated from the other information on the form by perforation, and is normally torn off the report copy routed to the EDP department.)

Benefits. A systems contract on EDP and special forms inventory items can provide many benefits. Those benefits accrued by a Midwest parts distributor involved.:

1. Direct savings through group buying of forms to get lower (per 1000) prices; elimination of rush emergency orders; forms redesign—which standardized forms and eliminated costly specifications; elimination of some forms; and prevention of company out-of-stock conditions.
2. Consistent quality and service from one vendor.
3. Time savings for company personnel by eliminating the checking of prices, issuing of requisitions or physical inventory taking.
4. Full-product-line offering by vendor, without pushing a particular type product.

EXTENDING THE SYSTEMS CONTRACT TO OTHER INVENTORY SUPPLIES

Office supplies, and warehouse and shipping supplies, can also be placed under a form of systems contracting, although more control over purchases is required due to the increased number of people and departments being involved, due to more than a single storage area often being required, or because of the high annual dollar amounts spent.

Case in point. A manufacturer of electronic measuring instruments has had systems contracting in use for two years. The company contracts office supplies, EDP and special forms, and warehouse and shipping supplies. Their vendor guarantees all the factors discussed here. 98% of the purchased supplies are promised deliverable within three days, with backorders delivered in a maximum of five days. At least 4,000 square feet of storeroom space was vacated of supplies and placed in other company use. Expediting was eliminated completely. Record-keeping expenses were reduced by 10%. Supply prices still remain competitive, with the company's overall annual supply cost reduced by more than $20,000. This company is satisfied with their venture in systems contracting, and plans to expand it into still other company supply areas.

Contract Differences

System contracts pertaining to office or warehouse and shipping supplies do not normally permit the selected vendor to automatically replenish company supplies without first receiving a company requisition. Physical inventory taking is kept under company control, and inventory status reports are not required (or received) from the vendor. However, the vendor should be required to offer guarantees: in availability and/or deliveries, in stated reductions of company inventory values, and in reduction of overall company operating costs.

A Single Vendor Is Big Advantage

Buying from a single source (with full-product-line capability) permits a standardization of items being purchased which results in volume discount. Consistent service and product support are achieved. Less purchasing time and effort are needed. The company's supply inventory value will be equal to the exact employee operating needs to cover the delivery time cycle as guaranteed by the vendor.

Paperwork System Is Key to Benefits

A blanket purchase order agreement can be created for a stated time period to cover the items which will be procurable from the selected vendor. (Items are usually referenced in the purchase order by the vendor's catalog—published by the vendor specifically for the company.) This blanket purchase order permits the designing of a new purchase order requisition form which will, upon purchasing approval, allow the form to flow to the vendor as a purchase order—saving valuable time and effort in the purchasing department. The POR form designed can actually become a combination purchase order requisition—purchase order—vendor packing sheet—company receiving report, all in one form.

Exhibit 17-2 illustrates "paperwork" flow in a systems contract for office supplies, or warehouse and shipping supplies, with minor changes to suit company policy. The originating department creates a specialized six-part POR form which provides the necessary system control. The multi-purpose POR form suggested here contains an originator's file copy (#6); a purchasing department file copy (#5); two vendor packing sheet-receivers copies (which are used as receiving reports when material is received), for the requesting department (#4) and the purchasing department (#3); a vendor's invoice copy (#2) and a vendor file copy (#1). Pricing is added by the vendor to copies #1 and #2 only—after shipment is made.

Delivery Cycles Established

The selected local vendor should commit to a firm delivery cycle (i.e., all orders picked up on Monday of each week would be delivered by Friday of the same week). A guarantee should be set on product availability (i.e., a fill rate percent should be established and maintained by the vendor, with a stipulation that the low percent of items not available would be available in the next delivery cycle). Vendor stock-outs should be permitted cancelled, if reorders are guaranteed to be delivered within the next delivery cycle. This allows the special purpose form to be uninterrupted in its multi-purpose use, by lining off back-ordered items.

Results Are Beneficial

Reliable vendor service, with product availability and delivery cycles being dependable, will help prevent employee hoarding of supplies, and will effectively reduce the overall accumulative company supplies inventory investment. The normal supplies inventory kept by the company (at the time the systems contract is awarded) could be sold to the selected vendor (for later company buy-back) to eliminate the company's current "on purpose" supplies inventory. The new combination POR form will reduce purchasing costs in preparing the purchase order and in receiving merchandise, as each POR shipment can be forwarded unopened to the person requesting the items. Record keeping, expediting and pricing information become the vendor's responsibilities, and offer bigger company savings—with periodic company audits insuring that competitive prices are maintained, and that excess purchases are not being made.

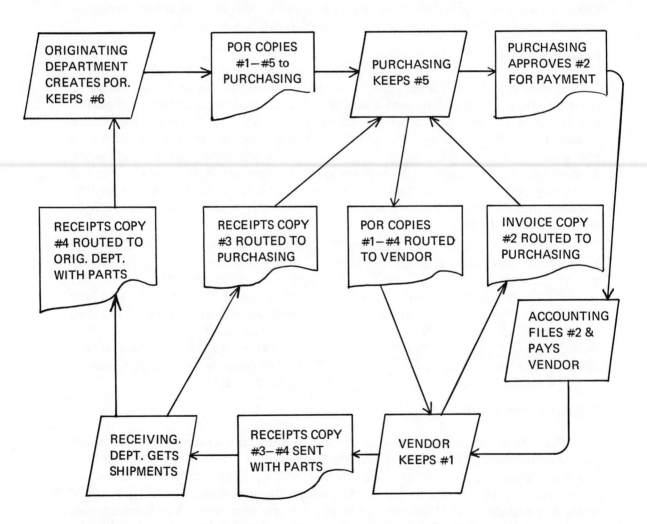

EXHIBIT 17-2:   "Paperwork" Flow Showing Minor Changes to Suit Company Policy

18

Security in Materials Control: A Seven-Point Program That Works

When we consider that theft today accounts for up to 20% of the general consumer prices, it becomes apparent that control on shoplifting and employee theft needs to be strengthened. Many of today's business failures could be prevented by the development and maintenance of good inventory security. The necessary ingredients for development and maintenance of a good inventory security program are contained in this chapter. Together, they form an effective security environment—proven in practice, measurable in success, preventive in nature, and capable of continuous improvement.

SECURITY NEEDS VARY

The *physical size* of a business is important in determining security, as a one-room business covering less than 600 square feet can be protected more easily than a multi-room, multi-plant business covering many acres of space.

The *products* carried in inventory dictate sophistication of security needs. For example, our museums carrying priceless inventories of art objects demand heavier security precautions and larger security staffs than, say, a bakery.

The *industry* involved plays an important part in security needs. To look at just two—wholesale and retail distribution—the people contact alone creates a completely different environment for protection needs. One is primarily concerned with known employees, while the other is concerned with unknown customers.

The security *approach* can vary, even for the same industry, where identical businesses market the same product. Contrast the security approach taken by two competitive adding machine/calculator dealers against the theft of mini-calculators. One relies on an extensive and thorough in-depth character check on all new employees. The other dealer developed and implemented a paperwork procedure that requires exact movement reports and accountability for each machine until after sold.

239

JUDGE WITH FACTS

The merits of someone else's system should not be judged with one which has just been implemented—without knowing the "before and after" facts. The effectiveness of any security method is determined by measuring previous and present inventory loss levels in the same environment. But there is no reason why a security system that works for one company couldn't work for another. The important fact is that with 75% of current business losses estimated as being caused by employee and customer dishonesty, some system for inventory security is needed. Determine the losses that can be attributed to theft. Select and try a preventive security system. Then, recheck your losses periodically to determine the security benefits.

IMPLEMENTING A SOUND SECURITY PROGRAM

A security system should be a preventive system which discovers potential loss problems and prevents them before they happen. The following steps provide the means for such a system:

1. Build or rearrange inventory facilities with security in mind.
2. Install adequate physical controls.
3. Select and maintain an adequate security staff or service.
4. Establish and publish a policy concerning company security.
5. Develop security-conscious employees.
6. Install electronic surveillance or closed circuit TV equipment where control is necessary and cannot otherwise be achieved.
7. Review the inventory security system periodically, for effectiveness, and keep improving it.

A Midwest manufacturer of camping and recreational products used outside professional help in establishing a sound security system. All the steps listed here were implemented except for electronic surveillance—or closed circuit TV equipment. (Concentration is now being directed towards preventive measures, however, since all the original security program's objectives have not yet been accomplished.) Although not completely implemented, the system is already contributing benefits. Within the last three-year period, this system effectively reduced overall inventory expenses, and has made possible a 30% annual reduction in previously recorded inventory losses.

Build or Rearrange for Security

The building or building complex used for inventory and supplies should be designed to restrict people movement in, or out, without being seen. The perimeter of the buildings should be fenced—where manufacturing or distribution facilities are concerned. In retail establishments fencing is awkward, or impossible, and entry must be kept simple and easy. Here, the entries can be one way, "in" only, with exits controlled through checking counters. The intent is to create an awareness that a company is security conscious.

External Safeguards. Employee parking should be located outside a fenced area, or some distance away from the actual inventory and supplies area. Employee entrances and exits should be limited, and placed to allow all openings in view from one central point. A good outside lighting system should be implemented for both employee and company protection.

Internal Safeguards. Business functions which require outside vendor contact or visitors should be situated away from any storage areas. Restroom facilities provided for visitors should not allow entry or exit to the inventory. Restrictive signs should be placed in easy view for visitors to see where they are not allowed to go.

Emergency exit doors should be provided which can be opened only from the inside, with door alarms attached to prevent ordinary usage.

The areas used for receiving and shipping functions should be separated, with all docks remaining outside of actual inventory areas.

Unauthorized or restricted areas (for experimental labs, money vaults, confidential files, etc.), should be located where easy protection and control are allowed.

Communications. A central location should be considered for control of the company's communication system. Security personnel can help supervise such equipment as telephone switchboards, telex, teletype, public address systems, etc., if their equipment is also included at the same general location. Some security personnel are normally always on duty where a security program is established and maintained. An equipment arrangement like this would require less security personnel for its maintenance and operation after working hours, and would eliminate the need for any duplication of other company personnel.[1]

Storage Factors. Compare cube storage use against square footage when rearranging the inventory areas. Current trends towards warehouse automation, or use of automated equipment, is bringing about special palletized or rack storage which is encouraging a high-rise storage concept. Rearrangement to high-rise storage is resulting in better security against theft and less damage to material because of less material handling.

INSTALL ADEQUATE PHYSICAL CONTROLS

All merchandise and supplies which must be inventoried should be stored in a lockable area. A solid wall or fence should physically surround the inventory, with access openings that can be locked. All outside exits within this area should be kept locked and contain alarm systems to prevent use except under supervised conditions.

All inventory areas should have reading light capability. This will help curb the temptation of theft, as well as prevent erroneous picking or stocking of material.

Entry-Exit Controls

One-way turnstiles and wide view convex mirrors, with full-time visual security supervision and/or monitoring devices, might be considered for entry and exit use where voluminous people-traffic occurs. Otherwise gates and doors should be used and kept locked. The variety of locks and locking methods available today will still permit easy entry for authorized personnel without a noticeable drop in efficiency.

One modern theft-monitoring device consists of identification tags, for clothing and other articles, which are used with hidden electronic or magnetic door scanners. The tags must be removed at a check-out counter, or the merchandise will set off an

---

[1]Richard J. Healy, *Design for Security* (John Wiley & Sons, Inc., New York. London. Sydney, © 1968 by John Wiley & Sons, Inc.), p.111.

alarm when carried out of a store. A special tool is required by the check-out clerk to deactivate or remove such tags.

Specialized Equipment Control

Equipment use can be restricted or controlled through the use of encoded cards and a "comparator" machine unit. One such unit, the "IDENTIMAT,"[1] manufactured by Identimation Marketing Company of New Jersey, checks encoded information on a plastic card with hand geometry of an actual hand placed face down on the "comparator" unit. Electronic data processing equipment, for example, can be made inoperable if there are nonmatching characteristics between the hand and the encoded information on the card. Even if a perfect match exists, if the person is not authorized to use the equipment encoded information will still prevent such action from happening.

After-Hours Control

The use of door or window detectors, which trip an alarm when an electric or magnetic field is broken, give further protection when on-site supervision is not available. (Such detectors can be directed to turn on lights or equipment, start electronic surveillance equipment, movie cameras, sirens, etc.). Heat sensing, and motion, sound, and micro-wave detection devices are also available for after business hours use.

Manual Inspection Control

Periodic area inspection by security personnel is necessary, with or without other physical controls, to make sure facilities are properly locked as they should be, and that physical controls in use are functioning. A four-story factory in New York suffered a near $1 million loss because sprinkler valves were inadvertently shut off.[2] Periodic area inspection could have caught this type of carelessness that does occasionally happen.

Material Movement Control

A material movement flow procedure and paperwork system is necessary for control of inventory receipts, withdrawals, scrap disposition and audits. This system performs a physical control which authorizes and supports the movement and accountability of property, and, to a large extent, is a determining factor as to the sophistification of other internal physical control requirements. Samples of suggested forms usage can be found in related chapters in this book.

SECURITY STAFF OR SERVICE REQUIREMENTS

Security personnel needs will depend on the extent of facility coverage desired and the types of physical controls to be used. Continually higher labor costs each year have made electronic equipment and electro-mechanical devices the nucleus of today's security systems—with personnel considered a necessary, but supplemental, feature.

---

[2]Healy, *Design for Security*, p.215.

The following questions form a checklist for determining the security staff needs:

— For what type of products (or services) is the program to be designed?

— What kinds of protection are needed? (Fire? Theft? Sabotage? Vandalism?)

— What size area, or building complex, will need protecting? (Consider the complexity of coverage caused by different floor levels and separation of space between buildings.)

— Will a skeleton force be used for a general area, such as on the perimeter? Or will a concentration of manpower be needed for specific areas, such as entries, exits and unauthorized locations?

— Is the security coverage concerned only with off hours, or for a full 24 hours each day?

— What kind and quantity of people traffic will need controlling? (Customers? Employees? Visitors?)

— How well is the present facility protected?

— What physical controls are already in use?

— What other physical controls are suitable for use?

— What budget limits have been assigned? (Consider lease-purchase agreements as well as buying outright. Will a service contract be more economical than staffing with company personnel? If budgets won't allow the total system implemented now, get some professional counseling for establishing a security program plan that can be implemented in phases, within budget—one that will permit minimum coverage for protection needs now, and expansion in the future to the maximum protection needs designed, with the least overall costs and best coverage possible.)

Security protection companies normally will offer free consulting advice on peculiar security needs. Trade magazines list new products available for security use, and the vendor's name and address for obtaining free literature or information. Other businesses, local police and government agencies are good sources for additional security protection information and guidance.

COMPANY SECURITY POLICY

Policy and procedural information concerning the company's security program must be published, distributed and understood by all employees. The ideal place for this information is in the employee orientation booklet, as some of this information is required by new employees in order for them to start work.

The company's view on employee permissiveness, normal work restriction information and general security policy and penalties, although all a part of the security program, should be illustrated in this booklet separately for best emphasis.

A Stand on Employee Permissiveness

The trend towards individual permissiveness, which started in the 1960's, correlates highly with the increase in employee/customer theft. Most people would quickly inform company supervision when someone is seen outright stealing a truckload of office supplies, yet would think nothing of taking a few things themselves, "as needed." A father, complaining to a school principal that his boy's pencils were always being stolen, said it all: "It's not the cost of the pencils. I can get all the pencils my boy needs from work. But, it's the principle of the thing." Yippee leader Abbie Hoffman, in *Steal This Book*,[3] condones and illustrates this type of permissiveness in today's thinking.

---

[3]Abbie Hoffman, *Steal This Book* (Grove Press, 53 East 11th Street, New York, New York, 10003, 1971).

Some companies approve a certain degree of permissiveness by allowing employees to take for their own needs, as a fringe benefit. A large manufacturer of lubricating greases permits employees to take what they need for personal consumption. They must not take namebrand containers, and they must obtain prior authorized paperwork to leave with the security guard, before taking any products home. So, a company may want to allow *some* permissiveness, but the employee must know how far he can go. Emphasize company disapproval over total employee permissiveness, and discuss the "principle of the thing" with employees in the orientation booklet.

Normal Work Restrictions

Employees should know how to identify reserved or restricted parking areas, and should know not to use such parking. Restricted parking, aside from showing status, permits security officers to know which key people are on the company premises in time of need. All other cars found parked in restricted areas should be investigated and removed.

Intentional in-out clocking of another employee's timecard is normally grounds for dismissal. Employees should notify supervision if timecards are missing or have been used.

If the use of restricted or unauthorized areas is necessary, color coded or priority travel badges will permit selected personnel unlimited travel. Where this is impractical, list the locations of any restricted areas, relate the reason for use and explain consequences for employees found in such areas without prior authorization.

Visitors are not normally permitted in inventory facilities during operating hours unless required by company business. Scheduled office or warehouse tours (maybe just on off-hours) will simplify a visitor program and will offer good control.

Restrictions over company telephone use might seem to control productivity more than security, but security also covers fraudulent company expenses. Emergency calls to employees should be permitted, even though outside local calls are restricted to coffee break or lunch periods. Where in-plant extensions are used, telephones can be fixed, if desired, so they can be used in-plant only. Long distance calls should not be allowed except for company business. The telephone company will intercede (if requested) on all direct distance calls made from all company telephones, to require a proper company credit card or special number, and to prevent any calls if the number is not given.

Employee-Signed Security Statement

All new employees should be informed of the company policy on security. A statement should be signed by each employee agreeing to this policy before being hired. This statement should announce that:

> . . . the concealment of or actual theft of any company property (supplies, finished goods or proprietary information), or any willful destruction to company property made voluntarily will result in immediate dismissal; and, at company discretion, will be followed by the filing of criminal charges against the employee . . . .

Further restrictions made on proprietary information should be contained in a copyright-patent agreement which the employee should also be required to sign.

Emergency Procedures

Fire prevention information should include the placement of hydrants and hoses, and contain a general explanation on any sprinkler system installed.

Disaster control information should describe emergency exit routes from work locations or direction to shelter in cases of fires, floods or tornados. Emergency operating procedures should be listed.

DEVELOP SECURITY-CONSCIOUS EMPLOYEES

Communicate with employees about what's happening. Explain the losses or inventory discrepancies which are being reported. Impress employees with the amount of company sales dollars that are needed to offset the current inventory loss figures. For example, $750,000 in sales is required to offset a $15,000 loss—if a company is operating on a 2% net profit basis. (Figure the sales dollars needed to fit your projected net profit picture.) It's surprising how security conscious your employees can be—if an idea is communicated in the right way.

Several methods are available for communicating with employees. To bring about security consciousness, try:

Posters. Illustrate the effect of property loss dollars on higher prices or lower wages. Use cartoon figures to prove a point. Moving posters catch the eye better. Catchy phrases improve message retention.

An Award Program. Develop a suggestion box program for ideas concerning reduction of property damage or loss. Have a traveling "security ideas" award, with a monthly write-up in the company paper on the current recipient and the winning idea expressed. Or offer monetary awards based on a confirmed reduction of company loss. Many retail stores offer cash bonuses where employees catch a customer in the act of stealing.

Advertising Campaigns. Select public relations information from an award program for external company publicity. Develop a program to orient the public against shoplifting and larceny. Let them know they are paying for theft. Solicit other businesses to cooperate in the program. Philadelphia-area retailers started such a program: STEM, Inc. ("Shoplifters Take Everybody's Money"), to combat shoplifting. A 12-man association committee of top level executives was organized, backed up by an advisory board consisting of two Senators, a Governor, the local Mayor and a host of other political, civic and religious leaders. An ad campaign was prepared, as a public service and without any compensation, by Spiro & Associates—a local ad agency in Philadelphia. First year results of the original five stores that started with STEM confirmed a near 20% reduction in store pilferage rates. This program concept has spread to more than eight states now, with several other states having used either parts of the campaign or having expressed interest in it.[4]

Use soft drink cups in company vending machines that contain slogans against theft or property damage. Such slogans can also be superimposed on timecards, postage meter stamps and interoffice memo forms. Use the bulletin board to post information showing new companies going bankrupt due to business losses, or to show specific proven property losses and effects on employee productivity.

Unannounced Security Checks. If all other methods of communication fail to do the job, implement an unannounced "search and seize" inspection plan on employees at

---

[4]"Philadelphia's Way of Stopping the Shoplifter" (*Business Week*—Copyright © 1972 McGraw-Hill, Inc., 330 West 42nd Street, New York, N.Y.), May 6, 1972.

quitting time. This is a harsh method to use and creates employee indignation, but it is an effective tool in communicating the security idea to employees.

Follow up with immediate reprimands to uphold company policy where actual theft is uncovered—but the main theme of communication with employees should be to picture the need for prevention and not punishment.

INSTALLATION OF SURVEILLANCE EQUIPMENT

Motion picture cameras, with or without time-phase photography, and video tape recorders, integrated into a closed circuit television installation, are two good methods of on-site surveillance. The movie camera does not allow "real time" viewing—as with video tape—because the film must be developed at a later time to determine if any forced entries have been made. Recorded video tape can record what a security guard might miss—when temporarily having to leave a console viewing area—but the tape can be replayed immediately upon returning, to see what was missed. It then can be filed, or erased and reused after viewing.

Closed circuit television is a good substitute for some of the security manpower requirements. One security guard can monitor many store security points at the same time, and with proper communications and remote controls can thwart a criminal in the act of stealing or illegal entry.

> The misuse of modern techniques and devices can result in adverse psychological reactions within the facility. For example, a great deal of critical comment from congressional investigations, as well as other sources, has resulted in recent years from the use of clandestine listening devices. It is also possible to use closed circuit television to observe individuals without their knowledge.... As a result, an information program ... should be considered an essential element in any security plan so that there will be no lack of understanding or a potential adverse psychological result, which would actually defeat the use of modern techniques and equipment.

> Signs, bulletins, stories in the company house organ, and other usual means of transmitting information can be utilized to inform the individual involved. In this way, any implication that a "big brother" type of project has been instigated which may infringe on individual rights to privacy will be eliminated.[5]

SECURITY REVIEW AND IMPROVEMENT

A security system is designed to be preventive in nature. It therefore is difficult to measure what might be stolen—but isn't, because of the security system implemented. But, two things can and should be measured periodically:

1. The dollar trend on thefts taking place.
2. Security system expenses.

The system might be considered a success, by some, if it led to a stablization of dollar losses due to theft. However, the right system should produce an overall reduction in such losses, or more system improvement might be warranted. There must be a measurable improvement in protection. Make sure physical controls are being monitored properly; that all system malfunctions are explained. Plan and initiate a program of deliberate theft attempts to keep security personnel alert and watchful and equipment monitored all the time.

---

[5]Healy, *Design for Security*, p.p. 277, 278.

Keep tabs on security expenses. A well-planned system should result in a minimum security expense. A new system, replacing an older manpower system, should result in an overall reduction of security expense; but don't overlook trade-offs. A measurable improvement in theft losses might well offset any proposed reduction in security expense.

A security protection system is a preventive system, with needs varying as to industry, the size of a business within an industry, the products carried in an inventory or the type of approach taken. An overabundance of security controls (mechanical, electrical, electromagnetic and electronic) exist today, which can outperform and are generally less expensive than man, even though man can never be completely replaced. Because man must implement and monitor the security system, misuse of modern techniques and devices must be guarded against to prevent any violation of civil rights. An information program must alert employees to the security system implemented, and must be documented with company policy statements, with genuine company efforts to develop security-conscious employees. The value of a security system is measured by and is commensurate to the reduction of theft losses which result. Consequently, the system must be constantly reviewed and improved upon to maximize its value.

19

An Earnings Improvement Program Promotes Optimum Inventory Operations

An earnings improvement program doesn't just happen—it must be planned. This chapter illustrates how to accomplish the planning and implementation for such a program: from goal setting, organization and authority assignments, to motivation, communications and recognition awards. More, this chapter will show you how to ask the right questions that should be continually raised as to why there is little or no investment return on certain operations, or on communication or equipment usage. A crutch is no longer a needed investment for a person with a broken leg, *after* the broken leg has healed, and the decision to stop using it is easy to determine. In business, operational "crutches" are not always thrown away when their need is eliminated. An earnings improvement program is a good tool for auditing total inventory operations—for determining where "crutches" are being used, and when to stop using them.

ENACT PROGRAM GOALS

Specific program goals should be developed prior to introduction of an earnings improvement program. These goals should be expressed in two ways:

1. Expense reduction and/or productivity increase goals.
2. Return on investment goals.

Prepare an ABC analysis on the current operating expense budget. (See Chapter 3 for details.) Areas with largest dollar costs are the best potential for cost reduction and for setting goals. Code each expense item as fixed or variable. Only variable expense reduction should be considered true savings. When manpower savings equal a full man within a given department, a corresponding actual reduction of labor should be made—if the suggested savings were really true savings, and providing additional workloads have not occurred.

See Exhibit 19-1 for an ABC analysis of an operating expense budget, which allows emphasis to be placed where the most good will occur. This information can be used in developing program goals.

EXPENSE ITEM		VARIABLE OR FIXED COST	ANNUAL BUDGET DOLLARS	% OF TOTAL	ACCM. %
Labor:			$ 95,133	51.2%	51.2%
Warehouse	($34,914)	V			
Office	($23,403)	F			
Warehouse	($19,122)	F			
Office	($17,694)	V			
EDP Charges		F-V	$ 28,800	15.5%	66.7%
Miscellaneous Overhead		F	$ 25,084	13.5%	80.2%
Shipping and Shop Supplies		V	$ 10,219	5.5%	85.7%
Transportation (freight)		V	$ 7,246	3.9%	89.6%
Communications		V	$ 5,946	3.2%	92.8%
Miscellaneous Overhead		V	$ 4,274	2.3%	95.1%
Publications		V	$ 2,601	1.4%	96.5%
Postage		V	$ 1,858	1.0%	97.5%
Purchased Repairs & Maintenance		V	$ 1,672	.9%	98.4%
Office Supplies		V	$ 1,164	.6%	99.0%
Utilities		F	$ 1,066	.6%	99.6%
Copying Equipment		V	$ 743	.4%	100.0%
Total Fixed Costs:		F	$ 97,475		52.5%
Total Variable Costs:		V	$ 88,331		47.5%
Total Expense Budget		F-V	$185,806		100.0%

EXHIBIT 19-1: An "ABC" Analysis of an Operating Expense Budget

ASSIGN PROGRAM COORDINATION

Don't stifle employees' enthusiasm by having them provide justification or dollar savings for ideas offered. Assign a program coordinator to:

— receive all earnings improvement suggestions.
— log and keep records on all earnings improvement suggestions.
— determine the validity of each suggestion, its expense reduction capability in dollars and cents savings, and implementation time-phasing.
— provide program continuity.
— determine monthly individual awards.
— determine monthly departmental awards.
— conduct a yearly awards drawing.
— periodically audit approved and implemented suggestions.

START WITH A POSITIVE ATTITUDE

Understanding, attention and support are required by both company management and employees, if a successful earnings improvement program is desired. The program should be developed as a joint management/employee activity. Management must not use this program simply as a means of coercing employees to increase performance rates. If the employees feel the program is one-way, and just another means to up production rate or performance, a negative attitude will quickly develop which could jeopardize the entire program. A positive attitude must therefore be developed among each member of the company.

The purpose of the program must be simple and clear. Associate the results of inflation, and reduction in contributed profits, to the current level of employment. Convince everyone that the program is to benefit employees as much as management. Then convince employees that their benefits will be of greater importance. Simplification and standardization of work duties, coupled with the concept of "working smarter instead of harder," can allow the employees to increase output without increasing effort; to increase safety and reduce fatigue while reducing overall expenses. Provide positive motivation for program participation. A special money award could be offered as part of an employee recognition plan.

GET ATTENTION

A program's success can be helped by advance publicity preceding the program announcement. Use advance information to build up suspense in all employees. Select a motto or a theme to support the program, and post it on company bulletin boards in the cafeteria, by the guard house, by the coffee machines, etc., and place it in the company's "house organ." Start a cartoon series to print in the last few consecutive issues of the company's publication prior to announcement time, to arouse curiosity without giving the program away. When the cartoon series is started in the house organ, select the announcement date and print it on the front cover—in about a one-inch-square size. Increase the size of the date on each following issue, until on the given announcement date the date completely takes over the cover page.

ANNOUNCE THE PROGRAM

When the announcement date arrives, have the earnings improvement program information printed in the company's publication. The story should contain all important features of the program, such as:

1. The program's purpose, goals and positive approach to success.
2. Program duration.
3. Program rules.
4. The name, department number and phone extension of the assigned program coordinator. (Also, you might print his picture.)
5. The method developed for calculating the value of an earnings improvement suggestion.
6. The method for employee recognition and awards.

Program Rules

The program rules should be kept simple. Items covered by policy or procedure should be restricted from entry. Such items would include inventory reduction suggestions, which are already the duty of inventory control personnel; suggestions on merchandising programs to stimulate sales, which are duties of the sales manager or merchandising manager; and suggestions on general price increases, which are controlled by the accounting department. However, should someone suggest a merchandising program, for instance, which is an original concept and which could offer good sales success, it could be allowed to qualify. Program rules should qualify *other* entries by definition, such as:

1. A specific action is suggested.
2. A dollar value can be assigned.
3. The suggestion, after rating, is found to either improve profits or reduce expenses.
4. Improvement results can be measured.
5. Reoccurring savings are possible.

EARNINGS

IMPROVEMENT

SUGGESTION

_____
(Participant's Name)

_____
(Dept.)   (Phone)   (Entry Date)

Prepared By—Employee

Suggestion:

Prepared By—Supervisor

Where is work performed: DEPT._____   By whom?

Check Frequency: DAILY   WEEKLY   MONTHLY   YEARLY

Estimated Manhours saved:

Material Savings: Material Cost:

Supervisor's Signature:

STOP HERE	ANNUAL MANHOUR SAVINGS	DIRECT LABOR		INDIRECT LABOR		MATERIAL SAVINGS DOLLARS	TOTAL SAVINGS DOLLARS	STOP HERE
		RATE	EXTENSION	RATE	EXTENSION			

Date of Origin   Implementation Date   Completion Date

MONTH ___ DAY ___ YEAR ___ MONTH ___ DAY ___ YEAR ___ MONTH ___ DAY ___ YEAR ___

_____
(Entry #)

_____
(Approved—Program Coordinator)

EXHIBIT 19-2:   Suggestion Form

Submitting the Suggestions

All suggestions are to be entered on pre-printed program forms which require write-in information, name, phone extension and/or department number of participant. (See Exhibit 19-2 for a sample form. All earnings improvement suggestions would be entered on a form similiar to this. The signature of the entrant's supervisor is necessary before the form is acceptable. Suggestion boxes would be placed in convenient areas for each department's use. Program forms and pencils would be placed on top of the suggestion box for easy participation. The program coordinator would pick up completed forms daily. A quick look on each form at the pick-up point would allow him to obtain missing or omitted information before leaving a department's area.

RECORDING THE SUGGESTIONS

The program coordinator will establish a log book for recording each suggestion received. The log sheet would contain areas to record the participant's name, department, phone extension, date of entry, type of suggestion, the true savings potential and whether the suggestion is rated valid or not. The information entered in the log would be given the log's next unused entry number. This entry number would be written on the actual entry form whose information was logged.

Refer to Exhibit 19-3 for sample log form. This logbook form is used to record all earnings improvement suggestions. Each separate suggestion has its appropriate data added against the next unused sequential number. This sequential number is then handwritten onto the corresponding suggestion form, for control purposes.

PROVIDING PROGRAM CONTINUITY

A suggestion may be assigned to an assistant for determining its validity, depending on the volume of suggestions received and the type and complexity of the suggestions received. In all cases, the approval or disapproval of suggestions will be made by the program coordinator himself. In approving or disapproving a suggestion, it is necessary to first determine that the entry is not a duplication of a previous suggestion. The second step is to determine if it qualifies, by definition, according to the program rules. Financial data is verified by accounting. An implementation date and completion date would be assigned after the entry is approved.

PROGRAM CONTINUITY

Just as the program needed advance publicity, it needs continuing publicity to keep attention, interest and employee support. A monthly report should be printed in the company's employee publication. This report should accomplish three things:

1. Statistically show the volume and dollar value of suggestions received for the current month and year to date. Separate suggestions into those received, those approved and those implemented—by department (or operating function). Departments (or functions) would be listed in descending sequence by dollar value approved on a year-to-date standing.
2. List all departments (or functions) in tabulated form. Show annual goals established, for each department, and year-to-date performance in the earnings improvement program.
3. Recognize the individual and the department (or function), and the corresponding approved suggestions, which produced the highest current month's dollar value.

EARNINGS IMPROVEMENT SUGGESTION LOGBOOK

For Month of _____

Entry	Employee Name	Dept.	Phone	Date	Type of Entry	True $ Savings	Valid?
0000001							
0000002							
0000003							
0000004							
0000005							
0000006							
0000015							
0000016							
0000017							
0000018							
0000019							
0000020							
0000021							
0000022							
0000023							
0000024							

EXHIBIT 19-3:   **Logbook Form**

DETERMINE MONTHLY INDIVIDUAL AWARDS

Dollar value categories can be set up to permit more interest in the program. Such dollar value categories might be assigned as:

$ 1–$ 499 Annual Savings (Individual $ 5.00 Award)
$ 500–$1,499 Annual Savings (Individual $10.00 Award)

$1,500–$4,999 Annual Savings (Individual $25.00 Award)
$5,000–$ UP Annual Savings (Individual $50.00 Award)

Instead of recognition for the four awards (as shown above), a single monthly award of $75.00 as prize could be offered, or a plaque could be given each of the four winners, with a monetary award made to the top entry only. Many prize selections can be made.

CREATE DEPARTMENTAL AWARDS

The dollar values for approved suggestions will be accumulated by department (or function) each month to determine which department has the highest cumulative dollar value savings and will win the departmental award. A roving earnings improvement plaque, each month, would be presented to the department maintaining the highest cumulative dollar savings amount. A special publicity entry would be made in the company's employee publication to picture the presentation, and to show the previous departmental winner relinquishing the award. Where the award is retained by the same department, tell how many months the award has been won in succession by the current month's winner, and the total times won year to date. The department's total dollar suggestions that have been approved year to date can also be given.

ADD THE ANNUAL AWARDS DRAWING

All approved suggestions would be eligible for the annual awards drawing contest. Each suggestion approval will result in the participant receiving a drawing ticket labeled as to which dollar category the suggestion pertains to. The participant would be required to deposit these tickets in the drawing boxes located in the guardhouse prior to the annual drawing. Award prizes would be selected on the basis of the dollar value categories assigned. A weight factor could be used to determine dollar awards for each category (with total dollars awarded limited to a set percentage of the total "true" annualized dollar savings accumulated). Or arbitrary prizes can be selected as shown below:

TRUE ANNUALIZED SAVINGS	MULTIPLE PRIZE AWARDS		SINGLE PRIZE AWARDS	
$ 1–$ 499	1-1st	$ 50 Each	1-1st	$ 125 Each
	2-2nd	$ 25 Each	1-2nd	$ 65 Each
	3-3rd	$ 10 Each	1-3rd	$ 25 Each
$ 500–$1,499	1-1st	$ 125 Each	1-1st	$ 250 Each
	2-2nd	$ 75 Each	1-2nd	$ 125 Each
	3-3rd	$ 50 Each	1-3rd	$ 50 Each
$1,500–$4,999	1-1st	$ 350 Each	1-1st	$ 750 Each
	2-2nd	$ 250 Each	1-2nd	$ 375 Each
	3-3rd	$ 150 Each	1-3rd	$ 150 Each
$5,000–$ UP	1-1st	$1,250 Each	1-1st	$2,500 Each
	2-2nd	$ 750 Each	1-2nd	$1,250 Each
	3-3rd	$ 500 Each	1-3rd	$ 500 Each

Drawing Restrictions

Certain restrictions should be made on the awards drawing. If less than four entries are approved within a given dollar category, the single prize awards will be selected. Perhaps you might want participants to be present in order to win and claim a prize; otherwise prize winners would be redrawn. Top management people should be made exempt from winning any prizes.

Exhibit 19-4 shows a typical drawing ticket.

```
Name   _____

Dept.  _____ Entry  _____

        DOLLAR VALUE CATEGORY:

$      1 - $   499 _____  $   500 - $1,499 _____

$1,500 - $4,999 _____     $5,000 - $  UP  _____
```

EXHIBIT 19-4:   Drawing Ticket

SELECTING POTENTIAL EARNINGS IMPROVEMENT ITEMS

There are many areas where inventory costs can be reduced. The potential is great. By using the five-question approach on value analysis, as developed by Lawrence D. Miles in his book *Techniques of Value Analysis and Engineering* (see Chapter 10), many earnings improvement suggestions can be obtained. The following hints should activate responses in other specific areas not covered, such as packaging expense, warehouse supplies, parts handling and/or order handling procedures:

1. *Labor* is one of the biggest reoccurring expenses everyone has, and is a logical first place to look for expense reduction. Can work operations be made more simple, or accomplished in a standard method to reduce labor charges? Can a reorganization into a results-oriented operation reduce manpower requirements through eliminating duplicated effort or supervision requirements? Can union agreement be obtained to permit one man to do two different jobs, where the second man is really unnecessary (in terms of real work load)?

2. *EDP* expenses forever seem to climb higher. It was once judged more economical to process computer-printed listings on standard 4-, 5- or 6-part paper form to prevent having to change paper several times a day to vary the number of desired copies within a given job stream. However, it now is practical and feasible to computer-code each output listing requirement; to let the printer unit reprint originals until the exact number of copies is obtained.

Special computer forms (such as those used for packing sheets or invoices) can be expensive where sales volumes are high, and several shipments are made on a given customer's order. Many wholesalers are reducing such forms' usage in half, by single spacing lines instead of normal double spacing. Alternating colors on the form prevents reading (in error) from one line to another line.

Some firms are combining invoices so that several shipments (packing sheets) can be billed together. Other companies simply reduce an unwanted copy of a special form set, and reap big benefits—especially in paper handling and filing operations.

COM microfiche has replaced large monthly stock status listings (and other massive listings) for big savings—particularly where outside EDP service is purchased.

3. *Freight* charges might be reduced by a company self-insuring its parcel post shipments, instead of buying insurance. Insurance costs are replaced by the cost of merchandise lost or damaged in transit.

4. *Communications* can always be improved. Schooling on how to use a telephone, how to prepare TWX, TELEX or cables, when to use night letter rates; etc., can help reduce expenses—if such schooling has previously been ignored.

WATS (telephone) lines have offset toll call charges for many companies where the telephone is a depended-upon, vital business instrument.

Discretion on the use of multi-extensions on a single telephone can reduce operating expenses. For instance, suppose an office had four telephones with each of the telephones having the same four station numbers (extensions), and a common dial line connecting them. The monthly charges would be:

Common dial line	$8.00/month	$8.00
Special charge for multi-buttons	$3.90/month	$14.60
Individual station charge	$2.55/month	$10.20
Total monthly charge		$32.80

By changing to four telephones, each with a private station:

Common dial line (not required)		
Special charge for multi-buttons (not required)		
Individual station charge	$2.55/month	$10.20
Total monthly charge		$10.20

This example shows a net savings of $22.60 per month, and does not include any time savings in direct answering of telephones.

5. *Administrations* offers earnings improvement through the functions of training, job outlines, job descriptions, procedures, job appraisals and performance monitoring. Training should condition employees to perform work in a manner utilizing simple, direct work methods. Job outlines and descriptions offer a printed guide to work duties, and supplement the training program. Procedures document the best method of performing work duties.

Job appraisals stimulate work success. The management-by-objectives principle in job appraisals allows the individual employees to set their own goals and to self-monitor work to correct for ambitious goals by doing work more efficiently.

Performance monitoring measures operating efficiency and consistency in work, and provides an earnings improvement catalyst. It can pinpoint poor productivity and bottlenecks. A follow-up systems study should find those suggestions needed to regain efficiency.

The biggest single factor, in administration, that will assist earnings improvement is control over procedural change. The electronic computer has taught us how to handle deviations, and even encouraged us to use them in complex and sophisticated ways. However, when manual deviations are added to the work environment, unplanned by management and therefore not properly controlled, inefficiency can (and generally does) result. It might take months to associate the ramifications that might occur in other work areas to these informal deviations. Bad decisions can be made by supervision where work procedures have been changed unknowingly without supervision support. Procedures should be questioned, but followed until formal change is approved. Contrary to old belief, rules are *not* made to be broken. This has the probability of creating work chaos.

6. *Capital equipment* analysis can help. The fast speeds of low-priced electronic desk calculators make it almost a sin to have employees using older rotary mechanical calculators, where a large volume of multiplication and/or division problems must be completed.

Mobile hanging files for tab paper listings would do much for the familiar problem of wide folded-up computer listings which are either bulging out folders, cluttering desks or filling storage bins. (Better organization can be had, less effort would be required to use them, and work areas could be used more effectively.)

Functional office equipment offers office mobility, can increase office efficiency, and should not be overlooked.

DEFINE "OPEN" AREAS

Ideas may be solicited, by employees, from other companies or outside vendors. A different perspective of the company's activity will often bring about good ideas—and results. The employee may also team up with other employees within the same department, or with employees in other departments. Since the purpose of the program is to promote an optimum inventory operation, all work operations and performances are, or should be, open to critical view by any employee. Departmental lines can therefore be crossed intentionally—or indirectly, due to effects of another suggestion. Credit should be given to all individuals or departments involved in formulating a specific suggestion.

PREVENTING DANGERS IN
OPERATING EFFICIENCY

It would be a catastrophe to produce an inefficient work duty while trying to improve it. Over-zealous employees might unintentionally suggest an action in another work area which could create problems. A suggestion to do away with a needed operation might be the result of lack of job knowledge on an employee's part. Ambiguity must be discouraged, as a general suggestion to "do better work" is meaningless without defining a specific action. Friction might develop between employees because of those employees who would "build a better mousetrap." Refinement of an approved suggestion, to further reduce expenses, can occur if a suggestion is not completely reviewed before being turned in.

Disapproval action on suggestions such as these might precipitate bad feelings or misunderstandings as to the real aim of the program. Proper handling of such suggestions, whether approved or disapproved, will create a better work environment—if more knowledgeable participation is afforded each employee.

A PERMANENT PROGRAM

An earnings improvement program should not be a crash project done on a one-time basis. It should be a permanent, continuing program, and the responsibility of each employee. Most successful programs require motivation, to orient people to think constantly in terms of earnings improvement. This is why an awards incentive is recommended. In fact, the awards incentive is a good investment—especially when an "acceptable" return on their investment results.

Another means of insuring permanency is to inspire each department (or operating function) to set their own earnings improvement goals. This goal setting should be carried over from one fiscal year to the next. Only those ideas that have been approved and implemented should be credited towards the established goals. This encourages swift implementation of approved suggestions, and causes cost reduction to be realized sooner. These two factors will do more to insure permanency of the program than anything else.

20

Profits Will Last if Training Comes First

This chapter proposes a continuing company training program as an answer to the everlasting changes in technology, business growth and people. Eleven factors are stressed that, when properly satisfied, should establish a successful training program. An additional profit generator is offered in the form of a voluntary job enrichment program: six steps that can provide employees with new and creative challenges to tackle, with future work advancement becoming a self-perpetuated thing.

The wide range of existing employee personalities can cause operating problems. In order to achieve operating efficiency, a company must try to condition employee attitudes so that a common unity of purpose exists.

Technological changes can't be ignored. They bring about the need for new or additional education requirements for employees.

Plant expansions require training of new personnel normally unskilled in the work they will perform.

FORMING A TWO-WAY STREET

The company's training program can solve most of these problems, if it is correctly developed, administered and supported. Its biggest benefit is in the two-way street it forms between employees and management. Employees are made ready for knowledgeable work participation through training; specific answers are provided for job duty questions that come up; a single, uniform, acceptable method for performing work is prescribed; and employee attitudes are conditioned to the work environment. As a result, overall company supervision requirements can be reduced (resulting in lower costs), and increases in productivity can occur.

CREATING THE TRAINING FUNCTION

Eleven basic factors are normally satisfied in creating a company training program:

1. A profit justification must be found.
2. Training objectives are formulated.

3. Positive methods are selected and outlined for performance measurement.

4. A training budget is planned and approved.

5. Staff personnel are selected.

6. A facility or classroom is obtained.

7. The training program curriculum is planned and developed.

8. Training support equipment is rented or purchased.

9. Training courses are tested as completed.

10. Training results are measured.

11. Training result reports are prepared for management review.

Profit Justification

A training program must be supported as a profitable venture if top management acceptance and approval are to be obtained. It must clearly be shown how training can affect the profit picture, by either preventing or reducing employee accidents, increasing equipment life, reducing or eliminating inventory damage or obsolescence, increasing employee productivity, reducing operating costs, or a mixture of these items—or all of them. (I.e., a simple investigation into increasing outgoing freight expense might suggest that the employee's use of larger carton sizes than necessary is the cause. A training course designed to illustrate a method for determining standard size cartons (for use with similar type shipments), might save many times the cost of the individual training course designed.)

Of course, profit justification must concern itself with total inventory management. This would include the organization structure, all of the operations being performed, and responsibilities for existing personnel. A large amount of systems analysis and planning work is needed to accomplish this profit justification. This effort won't be lost, however, as it is also necessary knowledge—essential to developing the training programs.

Case in point: A large eastern paper mill considers employee training as a profit generator. The company has had an active employee training program for more than 15 years. The company's training objectives are being met—with continual increases occurring in productivity. New employee orientation consists of hand-out booklets on company policy and work information, walking introduction tours through the facility, and use of reference material, work shop and/or programmed instruction courses. Training devices (used) include employee performance reviews, the use of position descriptions and periodic job rotations, lectures, seminars, trips and active participation in professional societies. The company believes in an employee's job enrichment program and places heavy emphasis on employee consideration. The training timetable is established around the employee's off-hours; training classes are held in a location convenient to work areas; and career counseling is offered and given all employees.

Objectives Defined

The profit justification premises the objective of the training function. This objective is solely to create a profitable result. Objectives can be stated very simply—as increasing employee productivity and reducing operating costs. However, the specific desired results can be listed, such as "effectively reducing shipping costs through standardization of carton size used," or "increasing customer service through increased employee productivity by reducing the order processing time elements." Objectives should be listed in sequence of their importance.

Measurements Established

Measurement methods will be established to compare actual work performance (as a result of new training methods) against the training objectives. In many cases, existing methods of work measurement may be utilized to confirm training results. Such measurements might include a monitoring of shipping expenses, elasped out-the-door time on customer orders, picking performance, etc. Where *new* performance measurements are to be used, a "before" rate of performance must be established so that valid training results can be proven. Existing measurements should be listed for each objective. Anticipated results can be forecasted and shown, if desired.

Budget Consideration

An operating budget will be required for the training function, and should list all expenses necessary to perform those training activities which will achieve the training objectives. The budget should particularly include adequate training personnel; facility space for conducting company and customer training activities; proposed equipment rentals and/or purchases; and special expenses for staff personnel to attend training seminars, trade shows, other company events, professional meetings, etc., to keep up with technical advancements in both equipment and teaching methods.

The People Investment

Staff personnel should be selected for their ability to learn and to teach others to learn. A "real" investment is in these people—with a return on this investment expected from the people they teach.

Each training specialist must familiarize himself with company history and with the organizational structure and operational plans of the company, and personally relate to each of the job functions he teaches. A thorough knowledge of how to perform each job is necessary, as he must also know if a job can be performed better—if done differently. He must know the job well enough to satisfactorily perform it himself; then he must present this knowledge in such a way that it creates interest, and imparts enough factual information that another person (unfamiliar to the job duty before training), could do the job. The training specialist must prepare employees for practical job application, and allow them application participation, measuring the capability of each employee as to the knowledge he illustrates.

> Teaching is helping individual to learn. It is not just the presenting of information. The instructor teaches *people*, not subjects. In the final analysis, the test of how successful one's teaching has been is how well the student has learned.[1]

The Training Facility (Room)

Centrally located corporate education, or training, centers are becoming a company status symbol. Where a complete training facility is not feasible, or isn't in

---

[1] Charles C. Denova, *Establishing a Training Function* (Copyright © 1971 by Educational Technology Publications, Inc., Englewood Cliffs, New Jersey 07632), p. 73.

long range plans, a single multi-purpose audio-visual room can do a good job, with proper planning.

Lightweight sliding walls can achieve separate special purpose rooms, each with its own lighting and sound control. In this manner, each segment of the multi-room can be used independently of the others, or they can all be used as one room. (This gives the capability of having small conference rooms, larger workshops or classrooms, or a single auditorium as the need arises.) Built into this multi-purpose room would be rear projection screens, with some covering (sliding) corkboards or chalkboards; video screens; storage areas; a library; and a control lectern. The multi-purpose room should be planned for employee comfort during training (conducive to the learning process), with balanced lighting, temperature and sound control. Distractions, either physical or noise-wise such as wires, floodlights, projection equipment, etc., should be kept to a minimum.

Planning and Development of the Training Program

... The most essential step in the development of a successful training program or even a single course is the establishment of detailed and accurate training needs. Many training needs are not obvious without a searching analysis.[2]

The analysis referred to by Denova is a "three-prong analysis" into the areas of organization, operations and man. This analysis should cover present and future company plans for organization, new programs, program expansion, and manpower staffing. A personal skills inventory should be taken on all personnel. A results-oriented operating concept should be compared to the present organization structure for more efficient grouping of management. Review and analysis of company organization charts, and short or long range management plans, will be required. Job description review and job analysis work will be needed. In effect: a consulting approach in depth. Job demands must be identified, digested and interrelated to the total company's operation. Company growth potential and direction are to be correlated with the need for training assistance.

The training specialists, then, must plan and outline the curriculum, the courses contained in the curriculum, presentation methods, employee participation, and the training evaluation.

The Curriculum. The approved budget, assisted by the training objectives, will guide planning of the curriculum outline—for obvious reasons. This curriculum should include courses designed for:

— employee orientation
— increasing technical proficiency
— conditioning attitudes
— development of management skills.

The Course. Each instruction course should be interesting, educational, allow the employee some form of active participation, and be fullfilling to the individual being instructed. The actual giving of these instruction courses should condition personnel to their work environment; provide an information link with other work functions; offer information to allow new personnel to do a task (or group of tasks) without further

---

[2]Denova, *Establishing a Training Function,* p. 51.

assistance; arm present personnel with new methods or technological information to improve the task (or group of tasks) now being performed; but primarily should promote and bring about job enrichment and growth potential to the individual—with profitable benefits to the company.

Presentation Methods. The training specialists will each have his own technique for helping someone learn. These techniques will vary by the number of existing instructors. However, the technique is dependent largely upon the training device selected for use. Some training device approaches follow:

1. Orientation training devices might include silent or sound films on company history; hand-out booklets on company policy and work information; walking "introduction" tours through the new facility; use of video tape closed-circuit television for "mass" introduction of key personnel to multi-plant people; a personal discussion period with new employee on job description and where the employee "fits in"; coffee, and introduction to co-workers; use of reference material, work shop or programmed instruction course on specific work duty; a pre-planned work schedule developed; and a one-week or two-week follow-up interview.

2. Training devices for increasing technical proficiency, management skill, and/or conditioning attitudes, might continue with performance reviews or appraisals; personal skills inventory taking; coaching; special work assignments; use of position descriptions and job rotation; job objective training courses; "assistant to" assignments; management meetings (as chairman or sit-in for the supervisor); lectures; and use of employee newsletters. External devices could extend training capability by including manufacturer's conducted "vendor" schooling; manufacturer's programmed instruction courses; university correspondence courses; seminars; trips; and professional association membership and participation.

The planning and development of the complete training program, limited only by the conceptual and analytical ability of the training staff—based on objectives and budget allocations—will include most or all of the above training devices, and perhaps much more. The methods established for course presentation will be restricted only by the equipment and facility space available for training's use.

Refer to Exhibit 20-1 for *training techniques utilized by small and medium-size companies.* These results were compiled through questionnaires returned from randomly selected businesses. A continuing training program was offered by nearly 60% of the businesses participating in this survey. Of particular interest is why only 33.3% of the companies used a company policy and procedures manual in their training program, when three out of four companies had such a manual available for use.

COMPANY TRAINING TECHNIQUE	COMPANY PARTICIPATION
On-the-job training	100.0%
Staff briefings	83.3%
Seminars offered by vendors	75.0%
Sales briefings	58.3%
Trade magazines	50.0%
Trade show	50.0%
In-house training	50.0%
Seminars offered by educational institutions	50.0%
Technical magazines	41.6%
Company policy and procedures manuals	33.3%

EXHIBIT 20-1:   Training Techniques Utilized by Small and Medium-Size Companies

Employee Participation. The instructor must allow each employee the opportunity for active participation. A person must identify with something in order to be a part of it.

Flip charts and slide presentations often have examples which the instructor explains to the employees. A pause at the correct time will bring forth answers. If none follow, then the instructor must generate these answers by asking pointed questions. Where programmed instruction courses are used, the employee is an integral part of the instruction and *must* participate. Vestibule or work-shop training provides a simulated working condition. Actual work duties are performed, as if in a true work relationship, and here again the employee *must* participate.

If the instruction course is a lecture, film slide, strip-flim or movie film presentation, oral or written tests can be given to measure employee participation. Later, on-the-job evaluation is monitored, and is generally used to determine course effectiveness—and employee participation.

Evaluation of Training Results. The evaluation of training courses is generally made by the training instructors. This can be accomplished by employee testing before the instruction course is given, "personal opinion" testing by the instructor during the course presentation, and formal testing after completion of the course. However, the true results will be found in actual employee performance—after the course is completed. Analysis of future employee performance, by management, will objectively show effects of training on the individual, and also a rating on the instructor giving the course. (Instructor rating should be a consensus from all course participants, however, and not a rating based on one failure—or unhelped individual—even though such results are important.)

Equipment Selection

Happily, for the training people, we live in an age of gadgetry and electronics. Movies, slide presentations, or strip-films can be shown without a projector in sight—on movie screens camouflaged by sliding corkboards or chalkboards, or hidden by walls which disappear or appear from out of nowhere. We have magnetic tape that talks and even produces pictures with the aid of electronic machines; and we have robot instructors, called teaching machines. These, and more paraphernalia, truly make it simpler for advancing the training function; but at the same time, they complicate decisions on equipment selection.

Equipment needs should be correlated to the curriculum developed, and planned just as carefully. The equipment must fit a useful need, perform a profitable function, and do it economically—to justify its purchase. It must lend itself to the long range training plans. Cost (both unit and operating); practicality (whether specific or general in use); reliability (ease of use, continued use span and expected life); usability (handling characteristics, fixed or portable); compatibility (interchangeability with other vendor equipment)—all are determining factors in selection of equipment. The budget will act as an overriding deterrent to counteract wholesale buying.

Testing the Training Course

A training course must fullfill the purpose for which it was intended. Therefore, each training course must be field tested prior to being adopted for the training curriculum. Select two or three employees (or some university students with comparable backgrounds) for whom the course is intended. The classroom chosen for the test should be identical to actual planned conditions. A pre-course test should be given. The course should be presented as planned and outlined. All questions should be recorded, with areas in the presentation noted, where subject matter appears to be lacking or is ambiguous.

Measuring Training Results

A final test should be conducted after completion of the course, to measure subject matter retention. Separate interviews should be conducted with each employee (taking the course) to obtain pertinent information for improving the subject matter of presentation method. It should be explained in the interview that this was a planned test. Results of all interviews should be compared, with complaints or comments noted. A follow-up should be accomplished on actual work measurement of employees to see if work is being performed more productively. Any noticeable change in an employee's attitude or work behavior (after taking the course) should be communicated to the training specialist by the employee's supervisor.

Management Reporting on Test Results

A critique of the test results, and course modifications made, should be submitted in report form to management. The report should answer questions similar to:

—Was the training objective met?
— Did the employee learn anything?
—Are there noticeable reductions occurring in employee grievances, absenteeism or sick leave?
— Has productivity improved?
— Are employees producing higher quality or larger quantity output?

The instructor's personal recommendations on the course's future should also be a part of the report.

Case in point: A company producing beer and malt liquor considers their training program a successful venture for the more than ten years it has been active. A measurable productivity increase has been noticed throughout this continuing time period. Orientation training, motivational training, training in technical proficiency, training in management skills and a job enrichment program—are all offered by this company to their employees. All of the 11 basic factors (listed here as inherent in a successful training program) are satisfied by this company.

Case in point: A large New York bank, with an active training program for almost six years, also satisfies all of the 11 basic factors necessary to creating a successful training function. Their training objectives are being met. Employee grievances, absenteeism and sick leave, all have been reduced since the training program has been established. Productivity has improved, and a good sign that employees are learning what is expected is shown in the nearly 7% reduction in errors last year—and is directly attributable to the training program by the company.

APPLYING TRAINING TO INVENTORY MANAGEMENT

Orientation and learning of new job skills are necessary when new employees are hired. But what about training needs brought about by new management concepts, technological changes, employee advancements, turnover and environmental problems?

New concepts must be learned, even by old employees, and training is still the tool for this learning. The ideas considered here, for inventory management, are to fullfill these needs in advance and to be prepared when a change is required.

A Voluntary Job Enrichment Program

A principal component of both learning and work productivity is *motivation*. A voluntary job enrichment program is a good training method that will allow motivation to occur. The desire by employees to know how individual efforts affect a total operation, to want to learn for higher job advancements, and to tackle work challenges that tax their creativeness are all offered in a voluntary job enrichment program. The program also permits an accurate skills appraisal to be completed on each employee taking the courses.

The job enrichment program would consist of six basic steps:

1. *Build up program awareness.* Furnish employees with a questionnaire concerning a voluntary job enrichment program. Let *them* decide the need for such a program; what functions they desire to know most; what time they would like training classes to be held; and how long training classes should be. Use the questionnaire as a starting point for an employee skills appraisal, where currently not developed, to indicate job interests and personal desire for advancement.

Exhibit 20-2 presents steps in developing a skills inventory. Useful notes: The personnel department is best suited to assume responsibility for the development and maintenance of a skills inventory. Company use of EDP resources can create a ready file of employee skills, so open positions can be processed (by the personnel department) against this ready file to select all existing personnel possessing the critical skills required. Departmental promotion charts can then be checked to qualify potential candidates. (The promotion chart data can also be on an EDP ready file to reduce clerical operations, if confidentiality is preserved.)

DEVELOPING A SKILLS INVENTORY

1. Prepare an itemized checklist of all skills used within the company.
2. Place three columns on the checklist beside each descriptive skill. (One column will be used to indicate skills currently being used by the employee; one for skills possessed by the employee but not being used; and one for non-practiced skills that the employee has interest in.)
3. Give each employee a copy of the skills checklist, with instructions on how to mark. Ask for written comments for each item marked in the second column (skills possessed but not currently being used), to support the level of experience or education possessed by the person. Have the employee enter date of last use of these skills, give department number (or operating section name), and date and sign form.
4. Place form in employee's master record file. (Place on an EDP master file prior to filing in employee's folder, if EDP resources are used.)
5. Review periodically, and update each employee's skills inventory to a current factual condition.

EXHIBIT 20-2: Steps in Developing a Skills Inventory

2. *Plan and develop learning courses.* Start the training program with development of courses most popular to employees. (These training programs might already be available, but might need to be rewritten.) Then extend the curriculum planning to other courses. Courses should be planned for all the principal duties of inventory management—both for the warehouse and office functions, including training itself.

3. *Establish the training timetable.* Prepare a training schedule for when training courses will be held, and list the locations where training will take place. Stick as close to employee-suggested time periods as possible. Select a training spot close to the employee work areas. Since this program concerns off-hours voluntary participation, make the time and place as convenient as possible for the employee. Make it easy to participate.

4. *Conduct training classes.* Select a training location with comfortable surroundings and a relaxed atmosphere. Start each class with a pre-course essay exam to discover the employee's current knowledge and what he expects to learn. Provide an informal, highly participative presentation of each subject. Note and record employee's subject interest, and add to skills appraisal data. Keep the subject language and learning concepts of each course commensurate with the educational and experience background of employees taking the course. Test each class after completion of course with an essay type test. Obtain employee's course information retention, his opinion of the course's subject matter, and suggestions for future presentation improvements. The test results would also be added to the employee skills appraisal data.

5. *Create an employee promotion chart.* Review skills data and conclude the potential of each employee, his interests, his job promotion capability, the training felt necessary to assist the promotion, and replacement name for all promotable employees.

In Exhibit 20-3 we see a sample departmental promotion chart. This form is prepared and maintained by each departmental manager, with the assistance of his staff supervision. A periodical update is required on this chart. A logical update time would be when merit review or employee appraisals are made. Properly used, this chart can benefit both the employee and the company. This data can be kept on an EDP ready file, if EDP resources are used, and if confidentiality is preserved.

6. *Counsel employees on career field.* Prepare each employee for advancement and select a replacement for him. Point out strong job interests or good proficiency results (from tests), and indicate career direction that an employee should take. Alert employee to experience or educational needs to strengthen his work background for career field development. Record traits, attitude and employee reactions towards counseling, and add to the skills appraisal data.

The dollar return expected (from the training investment) results from what the employees learn and how they apply what they learn. If they learn well, and apply what they learn well, productivity increases will result in higher company profits. If they learn well and apply poorly, or learn poorly and apply it well, then an adverse effect would result. The idea is to give the employees training in what they want. They will learn better, retain it longer, and benefit the company more.

A Safety Program

A job can be done in one of three ways: the way it's being done, the right way, and the wrong way. When it includes safety, it could be disastrous. A special safety course should be established to illustrate the correct method of maintaining safety habits in inventory storage areas, and to achieve uniformity and awareness in safety applications among the various job functions. This course would not explain safety differently than in the individual job courses given, but would be general in nature and apply to all personnel alike.

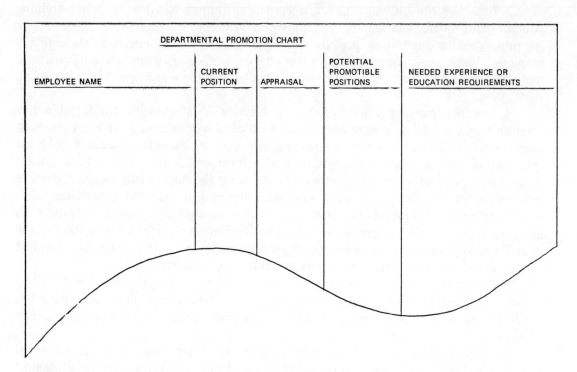

EXHIBIT 20-3:   A Sample Departmental Promotion Chart

Federal Legislation Makes Safety Mandatory

OSHA (Occupational Safety and Health Act) legislation has contributed an industry standardization for safety, in application and in method, and covers all industrial items which affect the safety or health of people. Federal citations for violations of OSHA are resulting in company fines that are quite expensive. Assessment is on a daily basis from the date of citation until violation is taken care of. OSHA rules should be integrated into a company's safety program—if this has not already been done—or should be considered as a special safety program by themselves.

Support a Training Program

Training must be a continuing thing, not a hit or miss proposition or a function to be abolished when company profits shrink. Training can offer a trade-off to profit shrinkage with a good earnings improvement training course, or by providing existing trained *promotable* employees to counteract personnel turnover problems.

Management thinking is changing to recognize the true importance of the training function, as witnessed by the many corporate training (or education) centers seen sprouting up and becoming more popular. This trend is helping to add *permanence* to the training function.

Index